RUNNING
ON
EMPTY

RUNNING ON EMPTY

ANDY BLACKFORD

SPORTS
BOOKS

Published by SportsBooks Ltd

Copyright: Andy Blackford © 2007
First published February 2007

SportsBooks Limited
PO Box 422
Cheltenham
GL50 2YN
United Kingdom
Tel: 01242 256755
Fax: 01242 254694
e-mail   randall@sportsbooks.ltd.uk
Website www.sportsbooks.ltd.uk

Cover art by Dave Smith

A CIP catalogue record for this book is available from
the British Library.

ISBN 9781899807 48 2

Printed by Creative Print and Design, Wales

My special thanks to:

Paul Hart for getting me running in the first place.
Nick Troop, erstwhile publisher of *Runner's World*, for his support and good humour over the years.
Roger Manton and all the other members of Numbskulls AC (i.e. Rob Wright).
Roger Weatherby, Simon Eadie, Brent Jones, Alan Gold, Matthew Hudson, Peter Fordham, Rory Coleman (sounds like a folk song) and the whole regiment of friends who have made running such good fun.
James Pryor at HHB for sound advice.
Randall Northam for enjoying the book, as well as publishing it.

CONTENTS

INTRODUCTION

RUNNING IS awful. It hurts, it's exhausting, it's hugely time-consuming and ultimately it's pointless. At best, it gets you from A to A by the most primitive, least energy-efficient means available.

Being *about to* run is unsettling. It hangs over you like a cloud. You can't eat, you can't drink, you can't really do anything — because at the back of your mind, you know you've got to go running. Until you do, you're effectively paralysed.

But *having run* is marvellous. The feeling is matched only by the one you get when you stop trying to gouge your own eyes out with a red-hot spatula. The bath is deep, the beer is cold and all is well with the world.

As a runner, I am and have always been a profoundly talentless amateur. I'm only thankful I'm not a professional. I can't think of anything worse.

The elite athlete, like its biological antithesis the sloth, spends most of its life asleep. Its few waking hours are devoted entirely to training.

B'noko Banumboki, the fabled Kenyan marathon man, slept continuously except when competing. He was conveyed to races in a specially-constructed mobile hammock and was only roused by his coach at the start line.

Even for second division professionals, it's the track, then the gym, then a carton of some unspeakable complex carbohydrate drink with the smell and consistency of estuary mud, then back to the gym and home to bed via the track.

Not surprisingly, top runners are crucifyingly dull. If the highlight of your day is shaving three hundredths of a second off your 10k time, you're hardly going to be the toast of café society.

My motivation is very different. I have always been a champion of the Balanced Lifestyle. By which I mean, if you're determined to plunge yourself into self-destructive behaviour with an abandon that would have scared Caligula, then you'd better balance it out with something vaguely restorative.

Otherwise you're likely to end up drowning in a slurry pit of your own lipids, with your internal organs resembling the contents of the Out tray at a transplant clinic.

Besides, who was it said, *running is sightseeing for the man in a hurry*? I know — it was me and I was right.

Thanks to *Runner's World* — and the magazine's... unusual editor, Steven Seaton — I've been to places nothing could otherwise have induced me to visit: the Greenland ice cap, the Amazon rainforest, the Sahara desert and that disgusting little path that runs beside the River Dollis from East Finchley to the Neasden reservoir.

This humble volume is my attempt to capture some of the high points, and a great many more of the low points, of a running career that spanned more than two decades. One which was effectively terminated last year when I underwent the resurfacing of my right hip.

The book is a chaotic jumble of my *Finish Line* (originally *Late Starter*) columns for *RW*, accounts of races and general diary jottings. Where possible, I had intended to attach dates to the pieces — but quite honestly, looking back, it's all a bit of a blur.

Andy Blackford, Litlington, November 2006

THE FALLEN ARCHERS
– AN EVERYDAY TALE OF
CROSS-COUNTRY FOLK

I LOVE the wild places. The remote wildernesses of the Earth where the primordial silence is broken only by the howl of 737s over Stansted and the death rattle of endangered species as they drown in tidal waves of agricultural pesticide.

That's why I moved from the North London *cul de sac* (where fox clubs frolicked in the garden, owls kept me awake and I saw my only kingfisher) to South Cambridgeshire, the Family Size Weetabix pack of England.

It was a huge shock to my system. I've seen *Springwatch* as often as the next man, but nothing could have prepared me for the spectacle I witnessed from Royston Heath, as the seemingly limitless herds of Mondeo and Fiesta swept majestically eastwards along the A505 to their breeding grounds near Duxford.

Beckons the mysterious East (Anglia)

YESTERDAY WAS a monumentally significant one.

I tottered out of our house in Hampstead with the traditional Sunday morning hangover and Oscar the dog, and swayed blearily down the hill to meet the usual suspects — Highgate's equivalent of the Chelsea Pensioners.

And then it suddenly dawned on me that next Sunday would be the first for twenty years when I wouldn't tread the well-worn path past the blackened remains of the stolen moped — wouldn't trip lightly across the little wooden bridge over the stinking ribbon of slime that was once the River Dollis — wouldn't wind my way between the pits on the Heath Extension, where once was mined the sand that soaked up the spit on the floors of Victorian boozers.

So much romance, so much history.

The boys were kind. They pretended to listen while I defended my decision to move to the country. They even waited for the dog while he sexually assaulted a Golden Retriever in the long grass — a weekly occurrence throughout my long association with the Geriatric Wing of the Harriers.

It was a bright, spring morning. We hobbled past the café at Kenwood House where Oscar had once terrorised the customers in a sort of North London middle-class re-make of *The Hound Of The Baskervilles*.

Under great and ancient oaks on landscaped lawns, children were gaily braining one another with softball bats.

The old tramp who dosses in the shed behind the house was hawking noisily into the bushes. I was overwhelmed by a deep sense of order and tradition.

And yet a part of me tingled in anticipation of the great adventure on which I was about to embark. There on the misty horizon of my dreams, beckoned Royston.

What serpentine byways awaited me out there in the uncharted wilderness of South Cambridgeshire?

In which I encounter the Daily Llama

SO WE'VE finally moved, then. I am now officially Country Folk.

The best thing about our new house (besides the 500-year-old saw marks on the beam that bisects our bedroom at shin height — a charming 'feature' which may lose some of its shine as the months go by) is that there's more than enough room to swing a cat.

Which is just as well, since we don't have a cat. As you may know, we have an enormous dog and, to his consternation, there's even room to swing *him*.

Steve, Alf, Pat or Pauline at *The Whore and Abbot* already enquire, 'Pint of cider, Andy?' as I stagger into the Snug at 6:50, still shaking from the lunatic race up the A1 on the Ducati.

Life in Litlington is like an endless edition of *The Archers*. Nothing wrong in that. I remember doing the Highgate Harriers' long Sunday run, ooh, twenty years ago, with a grief counsellor who cared for the relatives of those dying of AIDS.

As we reached the final three-mile stretch, I was completely shagged out. But he dug in and accelerated remorselessly.

'Sorry, Hun,' he panted. 'Got to get back in time for the Omnibus Edition...'

Anyway, I'm sitting here in the 15th-century study where, centuries ago, they tortured witches and mixed up potions for the Natters and the Bloody Flux, and the sun is setting benignly over an ancient, bucolic landscape, as old as the (in this case entirely imaginary) hills.

I'm listening to Ralph Vaughan Williams' *Pastoral Symphony*: it seems so much more appropriate here than my perennial London favourite, *Knickers Off, You Dozy Bitch (The Very Worst of The Unpleasants)*.

The running is brilliant. I was pessimistic, I have to say — this is East Anglia, after all, the Wheat Bowl of England where the arable land is worth more per square inch than Jordan's breasts.

You'd expect the public footpaths to have been annexed decades ago by cynical, greedy landowners. Not a bit of it. The paths are so evident as to be almost compulsory. They're signposted and traced annually with weed-killer across the arable land.

Our house lies about two hundred metres from the Icknield Way — an ancient drovers' track that runs westwards from Hunstanton on the Norfolk coast until it joins up with the equally-venerable Ridgeway.

It's a broad, straight, chalk swathe across the landscape, lined with hawthorn and sloe — a Neolithic motorway, now as quiet as the graves of the Iron Age engineers who conceived it.

Apparently it's the oldest road in northern Europe. As northern Europe's oldest runner, that resonates well with me.

Every day I explore a new route. Yesterday's led me through eerie, silent cornfields until I arrived at a fence with a stile. Now aged nine, Oscar (allegedly the World's Fittest Dog) still can't do stiles. It's pathetic, but I have to lift him, whimpering, over anything higher than a female Basset Hound.

There was something weird about the field. It was all too perfect — the rural equivalent of Pleasantville. There was a palpable tension, a too-green artificiality, a peculiar absence of birdsong.

Then the llamas attacked. Four of the bastards, one white, three brown, bearing down fast out of the sun. Their eyes were bright with a preternatural incandescence — they coughed, they spat, they bit — they were just generally horrid. We fled.

I'm prepared to tolerate lots of new nature stuff, so long as it's neat and properly packaged, like John Craven's *Country File*. But getting savaged every morning by the Peruvian cousins of the camel in a Cambridgeshire meadow is simply not bloody on.

More rural ramblings later — unless I get genetically modified and turned into slurry.

In which I discover the true meaning of 'running club'

Q: What's the difference between a weasel and a stoat?

A: One's weasily recognisable, the other's stoatally different.

It might be my all-time favourite joke, but I still couldn't tell you which brand of vicious little rodent it was that I caught murdering a rat on my morning run today. We'll assume it was a weasel.

The rat was of the rural variety — sleek, brown and inoffensive. As I approached, the weasel legged it into the undergrowth leaving its maimed victim jerking convulsively on the footpath.

I quickly despatched the rat with a blow of a stone to the

skull, then nudged the corpse into the hedgerow so the dog wouldn't get it.

Only then did I notice the little, frozen knot of runners staring at me in horror. They hadn't seen the weasel — just me, braining a rat with a rock then brutally booting it into the hedge.

I considered trying to explain, then settled for a weird, psychopathic leer and ran on. It wouldn't do them any harm to regard me as some latter-day Pied Piper, pledged to exterminate the rat population of Royston.

Now you might think that since my move from North London to a Cambridgeshire village, I'd be kicking wildlife out of the way every time I leave the house. In fact, nothing could be further from the truth.

The countryside down our way is a huge, sterile, agricultural factory in which all forms of bird and animal life are regarded as a costly distraction. They are discouraged violently with a whole arsenal of weaponry, from shotguns to broad-spectrum pesticides.

Supporters of hunting will often protest that they very rarely kill foxes. This is because foxes, notoriously wily, noticed long ago that it was unusual to be chased by hounds down Hampstead High Street.

And that if you hung around outside a KFC in the early hours, you got chicken that had already been caught for you. And cooked, for that matter.

In London, we saw a fox a night. Since we moved to Litlington, I haven't seen a single one.

Then there's the birds. Nowadays, I skip along meandering brooks, their crystal waters tinkling over pebbles, wafting fronds of weed between stems of iris and bullrush.

In London, I ran beside the Dollis, a stinking, polluted health hazard abandoned, apparently, as a bad job by the National Rivers Authority.

And where did I see the kingfisher? London. A flash of vivid, Chinese-silk blue, darting above a sluggish, anoxic cocktail of effluents.

That's because the Dollis still has flies. Whereas, around here, anything with six legs and wings is annually nuked by huge, tractor-towed tankers of insecticide.

In Hampstead Suburb, owl noise was a real problem. Our nights were so disturbed by their abominable screeching and hooting that our Neighbourhood Owl Action committee pressed the local council for a cull.

After two years in this, the bucolic landscape of Constable and Rupert Brooke, the hours of darkness have been quite devoid of shrieks. I've seen an owl though, once, while out running. It was slumped on a fence post in broad daylight looking severely depressed. It may have been contemplating suicide.

I put it down to the absence of trees. The farmers have cut them down, except for a handful of scrubby copses, that are preserved as pheasant shooting galleries and so are more dangerous for bird, man or dog than Passchendaele in 1915.

So while clubbing a weasel-ravaged rat to death might not seem like your idea of fun, to me it was a glorious affirmation that I really do live in the countryside. And not in an open plan grain silo.

In which I miss the rich biodiversity of London NW11

IT'S SPRING in Litlington.

I can tell because I've discarded one layer of polypropylene and swapped the Greenland Arctic-certified gloves for the Kevlar and Gore-Tex gauntlets with the pouches for the paraffin hand-warmers, as endorsed by Orkney trawlermen.

It's hard to imagine that last August I would jog virtually naked though these fields at 6am, to the consternation of the village's more tweedy Labrador exercisers.

On the other hand, I now have to run at a 45 degree angle to avoid being flattened by the continual tempest that sweeps in from the west, unobstructed for a hundred miles by anything more robust than a blackthorn hedge.

Talking of hedges, the ones around our place are valiantly trying to recover from the mauling they received during the winter.

Laying a hedge is a dying rural craft. It involves half-severing the stems of shrubs and trees, bending them groundwards and weaving them together. Initially, it's labour intensive — the vegetable equivalent of drystone walling — but then the results were lovely to behold and lasted for hundreds of years.

Nowadays, you just clamp a giant clipper on the back of your tractor and rip the hedge to shreds, leaving a trail of torn branches and paths strewn with thorns to puncture your dog's feet.

Oh, God. I'm turning into Victor Meldrew.

Other seasonal indicators: it's impossible to run along The Stret (quaint local dialect for the Roman road at the end of our garden) without tripping over baby rabbits. There are literally hundreds of them. Rabbits must breed like, well...

Then there is the sudden explosion of lark activity. You can't run a step without alarming swarms of the little bastards. They bolt up vertically from the fields, twittering in terror. Why? My theory is, they've never got over the Tudors. They assume that every human is propelled by a psychopathic need to rip out their tongues and set them in aspic.

Skylarks are supposed to be a threatened species. This I can understand (hysterical little retards). But I can reassure the RSPB that they've all moved to Litlington where they're doing very well indeed.

The dog Oscar, in stubborn denial of his advancing years, has a serious case of Rising Sap.

In one sense, he's quite fussy. He's only turned on by golden hair. In another sense, he's less discerning — he doesn't give a monkey's whether it's blonde or blond.

I set off at a decent pace with the Middle Group. We toil up the hill from the clubhouse. I glance over my shoulder and the wretched creature has vanished. Wearily, after just five minutes in the company of my fellow Royston Runners, I excuse myself and jog back down the hill bawling the dog's name until I'm hoarse.

And there he is, back at the club, dry-humping some geriatric castrato Retriever who simply doesn't have the energy to repel him.

The look you get from the victim's owner makes you feel as if *you're* the pervert: 'What kind of man *is* it that has the kind of dog that would do *that* to dear old George?'

Come back winter. All is forgiven.

Ring-necked doves. Nature's morons

WHEN I lived in London, I would once in a while abandon my Ducati in a reluctant acceptance of my slightly unstable state and take a cab home.

Peering blearily through the misted windows as we crossed the threshold of midnight on Regent's Park's Outer Circle, I would make out the ghostly forms of runners, jogging the worn slabs of the capital's legendary treadmill.

In five years or so, they'll have worn right through the pavement and gouged a five-foot trench around the Park. Then you'll just be able to see their heads, bobbing along at kerb height.

Even in my inebriated state I couldn't suppress a thrill of wonderment: what in God's name did these sad bastards think they were doing? Didn't they have a partner to go home to? Or somebody else's partner, at least?

Hadn't they been out for a proper lunch, consisting of two bottles of a jolly decent red and preceded by a pint and a half of Addlestone's so appropriately-named cider?

Hadn't they returned home to be confronted by an eight-year-old child with enormous eyes demanding a *Rupert Bear* story and a game of *Enchanted Forest?*

Didn't they understand that once the daughter was safely consigned to the Princess Bed, it was *University Challenge* followed immediately by *Never Mind The Buzzcocks?*

Clearly not. Otherwise they would recognise, like any runner of sound mind, that the evening is not for running. The morning is for running. And running very early in the morning is best of all.

Of course, I can say that now and with a certain smugness, because it's four o'clock in the afternoon. I wasn't quite so smug at six this morning when I dragged myself from my bed and tried to plug in the kettle without opening my eyes.

Actually, I'd been awake since five. Next time anyone tells you that one of the great boons of country life is the silence, refer them directly to me.

My London home was in a narrow triangle of land between the A1 and the North Circular Road, and I slept like the dead.

But Litlington is plagued by pretty, moronic doves who begin cooing endlessly and tunelessly at dawn. To my mind, doves are the single most convincing argument for relaxing the gun laws. They make a soft and insidious racket that is utterly impossible to sleep through. I'm surprised someone doesn't record them for use in fire alarms. If birdsong is really a language, then doves must bore one another to tears.

Getting ready to go running in our household requires a complex series of feints and deceptions designed to keep the dog in ignorance until the last possible moment. Otherwise he becomes seized with a maniacal excitement that makes him prance around the house like a Lipizzaner stallion.

Nevertheless, it's hard to maintain the illusion of non-running for more than a couple of minutes — if I strap on my sports watch instead of my regular one, he knows. White socks, also, are an instant giveaway for Oscar.

When we leave the house he is so consumed with wild, explosive joy that he is barely able to effect any forward motion. His muscles are locked in a stricture of ecstasy so intense that he can only stand and vibrate.

When we finally get going, though, all the painstaking dissimulation and the effort of getting up pale into insignificance. We turn out of Malting Lane into South Street and within thirty seconds we're skipping along a narrow path between swaying oceans of wheat.

The sun is low, the sky is a wash of blue, a cool breeze brushes my face and arms. The dog charges about as if he's just been released from a twenty-year spell of solitary confinement. Occasionally he'll startle a lark and it will ascend while twittering a competent rendition of Vaughan Williams' *The Lark Ascending*.

Diamonds of dew gleam on the ripening ears of wheat. Young rabbits scamper in panic at our approach. There is no other soul, human or canine, to be seen. It's as if we'd been invited to a private viewing of the Creation.

It takes a while for the legs to wake up, but after twenty minutes (once upon a time it was ten) I begin to pick up a little pace and push experimentally up the long hill from Home Farm. I pass the spot where I found the dead mole last week.

I have to wait for Oscar who is chasing chickens in the farmyard — a trait that in these parts is probably corrected with two barrels of a twelve-bore.

The only sound is the drone of bumble bees and the sigh of the warm south wind in the crops.

Then it's home for a leisurely shower and a cup of tea while the dog retires, panting, beneath the farmhouse table in the kitchen.

I feel as if I'm positively glowing with fitness. And my mental state is steady and alert, quite devoid of the homicidal urges I used to feel in the city, when getting up was something you did five minutes before joining battle with the other dregs of humanity on the Northern Line.

All this being said, it's now early June. Whether I'll feel quite so poetically-inclined at six on a January morning when it's pitch black outside and the only sound is of the sleet flaying the frostbitten flesh off my face, is open to speculation.

I may have to net a couple of doves and keep them in a cage above the bed.

Not that the climatic conditions will worry Oscar. He would

quite happily have gone running during the fire-bombing of Dresden.

Still, whatever the weather, there'll still remain one of the great incentives to run early: that by 8am it's all over for the day, and you can get hammered at lunchtime with a clear conscience. That's worth a lot.

Convinced? See you at Dead Mole Bend at 6:30 tomorrow. Be there, or be asleep.

Notes from the Rolling Road

YOU'RE PROBABLY aware of the fierce debate over the funding of science in our institutions of higher learning.

The Pragmatists insist that the taxpayer should only be expected to finance socially valuable projects like, say, improving the design of depleted uranium tank shells.

The Purists, on the other hand, say we should be funding research into the sexual preferences of woodlice, or why so few people think clowns are funny.

I'm firmly in the Pure camp, because today's Pure is tomorrow's Practical. For instance, if we knew what woodlice found sexually disgusting we could introduce it into their genetic fingerprint and condemn the pointless little fuckers to the evolutionary dustbin.

The same with clowns.

What am I trying to say? Just this. That at first sight, the next section is pure whimsy — a sump into which have trickled all the random reflections and inconsequential musings that didn't fit anywhere else.

But who can tell when such meanderings might spark a radical new approach to our sport? Remember, architectural masterpieces are built on landfill sites.

[*Is that really true?* — Ed]

[*Who cares?* — AB]

In which I glimpse the elusive Knock-Parrot

IF I should let drop that I've just run twenty miles to the gym and back, just to idle away a dull morning, I can count on one of two responses from my audience.

'Run? I can't even run for the bus, me!'

Surely, I reply, that depends on who's on the bus? For instance, if it happened to be the scantily-clad members of Atomic Kitten, producing fifty-pound notes from the lacy margins of their lingerie, then you could rely on most of the blokes I know to break 3:30 for the mile in their haste to board the bus.

Then there's, 'I tried running once, but it was so bloody boring.'

'What?' I exclaim. 'Did you run on a treadmill in a darkened room, then?' For running, it seems to me, is just living while moving your legs.

Take this morning's modest effort. It was nothing special — only my customary six-mile canter about the Heath. And yet no more than ten feet from my front door, I was brought face-to-face with Nature, red in tooth and claw. For a large, bronze-coloured beetle was struggling to stay afloat in a pool of rainwater, contained within the folds of a punctured football.

And perched triumphantly upon its back was a fat, brown and cream striped spider.

I stopped my watch at 2:07 secs and bent the better to observe the unfolding of this minuscule drama. Was I witnessing a mugging by a psychopathic arachnid? Or was the beetle merely trying to supplement a meagre income by offering ferry rides across the lake to rich spiders?

Anyway, I helped beetle and passenger to dry land and experienced the glow of satisfaction enjoyed by us Buddhists when we manage to accumulate a spot of merit through good karma.

Moments later, I was jogging along beside the lovely River Dollis — as dismal a rivulet of suppurating, rat-infested filth as you'll find anywhere in the effluent South-East.

What is it drives Modern Youth to hurl shopping trolleys into streams? In my day, we contented ourselves with tossing pennies into fountains and making wishes. Perhaps it's the same principle, but tonally adjusted to suit the times: you chuck the trolley into the water and wish that every sodding bastard would fuck off and die of Weil's Disease.

Mind you, I've never actually witnessed an instance of trolley hurling. Perhaps Youth isn't involved after all. Perhaps the trolleys, reduced to bleak despair by their meaningless, mechanical existence in our supermarkets, make a bolt for freedom at closing time — then faced with recapture by the brutal, brown-uniformed guards, choose glorious self-extinction over slavery and subjugation.

Off the Dollis Green (hah!) Way and into Little Wood. As usual, no sign of the elephant. A local resident of incalculable antiquity once told me that during the early years of the last century, a showman had offered elephant rides on Hampstead Heath, and that the poor beast had been over-wintered in this diminutive scrap of ancient woodland by the side of the A1.

Nowadays, there are hardly any huge, exotic beasts at all in Little Wood. But you might be lucky enough to spot any of our three native species of woodpecker. One summer, a particularly fine specimen was strutting his stuff on our lawn. I woke our young daughter — it was early morning — and pointed out the bird to her.

Next day at 5am our curtains were ripped wide and I awoke to see her peering sleepily into the garden. 'What on earth are you doing?' I grumbled semi-consciously. 'Lookin',' she replied, 'for the Knock-Parrot.'

So here I am, only four minutes into my run and I've already explored entomology and etymology, history, sociology and ornithology.

I mean, exactly how interesting do you want?

Cough up, you bastards. It's charity time

THERE'S ONLY one thing worse than running a marathon, and that's prising the money out of those who swore to sponsor you.

I used to ask, politely, once — twice — five times. I would nod and smile indulgently as they went through the ritual turning-out of empty pockets, the pointless poking around in purses.

I used to shrug and make up the money with a cheque drawn on my own account.

Not any more. Now, I just pull a knife and herd them to the nearest cashpoint. Or kidnap their bewildered old mothers and stick them in a hole in the ground with no food or plumbing until their tight-fisted offspring cough up.

This seems perfectly reasonable to me. After all, I've gone through the mental stress of under-training for a big race. I've alienated my friends and family, neglected my work, placed intolerable strains on the NHS with an endless catalogue of petty injuries, then dragged my bloated cadaver along a 26-mile corridor of grinning, chanting morons.

Meanwhile, out there on some litter-strewn English riverbank, the last surviving family of water voles squats shivering, waiting for the Blackford marathon money to save them from an ignominious extinction.

And what happens? You don't pay up, so the dosh never arrives. The golden mirage of the Vole Sanctuary recedes into the domain of wishful thinking. Quietly, unremarked by the busy world that rushes by just feet away, the tiny creatures expire in a foamy soup of industrial pollutants, plastic bottles and rusty bike frames.

The destruction of a species is not gradual. It happens in an instant. One moment, there's a Venezuelan Pig Bat flitting happily across the surface of the planet. The next, there isn't. That particular sort of bat has flut its last flit.

Now if your much-vaunted charitable donation had arrived even five minutes earlier, catastrophe might have been averted. The Society For The Preservation Of Pig Bats would not have been £5 short of its monthly rent bill and thus would not have been forced into liquidation. The proposed WWF Pig Bat Expedition might then have set out as planned, and that last surviving Pig Bat snatched from the one-way trapdoor to evolutionary oblivion.

(Of course, in the absence of a second Pig Bat of the opposite sex, such a rescue would only have delayed the inevitable. But you get my drift.)

And that's just your bat and vole charities. Let's apply the same logic to the Save Venice Fund.

I hobble round to your place, blisters still bleeding from the Baffin Island Brain Dead 100 Mile Stage Race, to collect the sponsorship money you solemnly promised me. But you have only £1.49p, which happens to be the price of a can of Tennant's Super Lager. You hesitate, but only for an instant. Could you possibly pop round with the money tomorrow morning?

Next day, you arrive with your fiver. But I brush you away. You're too late, mate. The freak collision of a cold front from the Urals with the decaying remnants of a Saharan dust storm produced overnight a cyclone of such terrifying intensity as to generate 60-foot waves in the Lagoon. These crashed through the fragile canal system, destroying at a stroke Civilisation's most divinely-inspired artistic and architectural masterpieces.

Venice is just a memory now. Along with the Venezuelan Pig Bat and the Vole.

That's three V's in a row. Perhaps extinction occurs in strict alphabetical order. Perhaps tomorrow it'll be wombats, wurzels and Worcester.

Or Whizz-Kidz, the charity that gets disabled kids moving, and for which I once ran the New York Marathon.

To avoid this eventuality, please make your cheques out to Whizz-Kidz and send them to me *right away*, c/o *Runner's World*.

Ta.

In which I'm Sleepy, Grumpy and Sneezy

MY FRIEND Hudson won't meet me for at least two weeks after I've run a big race. 'I don't like you,' he candidly admits. 'You go all weird.'

He's right. For a day or two after the end of an ultra-marathon, I'm a demi-god. I'm privately astonished I'm still alive — that my muscles have only shrunk to the diameter of waxed dental floss, that I've lost just the three toenails, permanently wrecked a hip and both knees and thrashed my blood to the colour and consistency of blackberry jam.

I wear my medal on the Tube. I harangue colleagues, family and occasionally the homeless with step-by-step accounts of my heroic achievements. And then suddenly I slip into a slough of dark despond.

It was the same when I was a musician. Immediately after a recording session I'd swagger around under the illusion I was Jimi Hendrix's vastly more talented brother. Then, after three days, I'd listen to what I'd played and realise that I was, in fact, John Prescott's stone-deaf chiropodist.

After a race, I'm not a glass-half-full person. I'm a completely-drained-Waterford-crystal-goblet-knocked-off-the-table-onto-the-stone-patio person. I think it's the endorphins. During these taxing events, my body pumps me so full of pain-numbing, positivity hormones that the comedown is inevitable.

I spend six days in an elevated state in which the emotions become wildly exaggerated. I ricochet from desperation to elation in an ever-shrinking cycle. I'm apt to embrace my fellow runners with the fierce, protective love of a female cougar for her cubs, then seconds later I have to be restrained from setting about them with an axe.

One minute, the natural beauty of my surroundings swells my heart with poetic inspiration. The next, I'm flailing in a blind rage at the nettles that have just assaulted me and hurling clods at the pheasant that reduced me to jelly when it crashed out of the thicket across my path.

At the end of this, an experience of almost hallucinogenic intensity, it's no wonder that the world seems dull and flat and bleached of meaning. You've been playing dice with the gods and breathing pure oxygen. Now you have to pay your council tax and get the MOT for your M-reg Astra.

Then there's plain old exhaustion. All I'm good for after an ultra-marathon is sleeping, eating, then sleeping again. The only way I can find time to work, or even to acknowledge the presence of my wife and daughter, is to eat in my sleep — a grizzly business that I am still some way from mastering.

They say the beneficial effects of a long run last for about a month. You could really capitalise on that — use it as a springboard to undreamed-of heights of fitness.

However, for at least six weeks after a long race, the sight of a pair of trainers immediately conjures up the smell of four-day-old shorts mingled with the taste of soggy power bars and lukewarm water. So instead of running, I slouch around town, eating chips, catching colds and growing steadily more pallid, slack and disconsolate.

The sight of runners in the street fills me with an ugly mixture of arrogance and self-loathing: 'What do *they* know, with their pathetic five-mile jogs? But at least they're out there, the smug, self-satisfied bastards, while I'm swilling down this tripe-and-lard sandwich with a pint of sweet sherry.'

The only way out of this black hole is to start training again. It requires a gargantuan effort — like raising the dead or liking Will Self.

But once you've turned the supertanker and you're back on course, the dark clouds miraculously disperse and lo! you're a runner again: neurotic, obsessed, utterly shagged out and, of course, perfectly contented.

In which I try to stop trying to stop time

I'VE JUST completed the Jordan Desert Cup. I ran 120 miles in 48 hours. The experience has left me with a profound sense of awe: it's simply astonishing what the human body can't do.

It can't get up at 8am on a cold, wet Sunday to join the Highgate Harriers' morning run.

It can't resist lounging in the pub at lunchtime when it promised Barry it would go to the gym with him.

It can't walk past the Agra Tandoori House at 11.15pm.

It can't bear to shed two stones of its unsightly flab, when this would only mean occasionally declining the third pint of Guinness and the dry roasted peanuts after work.

In fact, for the most part, it's a weak and lily-livered waste of space. How I ever managed to drag it from Wadi Rum to Petra with a seven-kilo pack on its spineless back is a mystery to compare with the Immaculate Conception.

The BUPA ads tell us, *You're Amazing*. Bollocks. It's precisely that sort of mealy-mouthed, sycophantic bullshit that gives the human body ideas above its station. The truth is, the human body is bone idle. It's a back-sliding waster. For thousands of years, it pretended it couldn't run 26 miles and 385 yards. 'Oh! Oh! Stop! The pain, the pain!' And we believed it.

And then we woke up one April morning in the early 1980s and said, 'Sorry, mate, you're going to do this, like it or not.' Result: 20 years on, any arthritic octogenarian in a hippopotamus suit can run the course backwards.

If we listened to our bodies, we'd all end up like the Royle Family. Only given a sufficient degree of brutality or a rich enough incentive will the body grudgingly do what you ask of it.

This is my theory, anyway, developed in Jordan. And I plan to prove it on May 26th, when I will run 145 miles from Birmingham to London along the Grand Union Canal. If I stop for more than 40 minutes at one time, I will be deemed to have left the race.

As any ordinary, well-adjusted person will tell you, this is an impossible feat. But I predict that in twenty years' time, Michael Winner and Brian Sewell will jog gaily across the finish line as a pantomime horse.

What evidence can I produce in support of this admittedly radical hypothesis? Only that at the end of any race, be it the Sri Chinmoy Two Mile or the Himalayan 100 Mile, I will swear that I couldn't run another step. But that feeling is no more intense after 100 miles than it is after two. So why should it be any worse after 145? Or 200, or 500?

Given water, decent shoes, enough blister dressings to wrap

a mummy and an infinite supply of power bars, man could run to the moon.

And once the first human body has been bullied and cajoled across the 250,000 miles to our planet's satellite, it will only be a matter of time before David Bedford is appointed Race Director and the event is oversubscribed by a factor of five.

There remains only the technical question of how one trains for these hyper-mega-ultra events. After all, to prepare for a marathon, you need to put in a handful of 20-mile training runs. So should I bash off three or four 100-milers to limber up for the Canal Race?

No, thankfully. I've found that the most effective training for long-distance events is to talk about them a lot. It's simply not feasible to run the required number of miles, but you can log up many valuable hours of bragging in bars and writing in *Runner's World*.

Thus, over the course of weeks and months, you can convince your body that what you're demanding of it is not as inherently stupid as it first sounded.

Watch this space.

Would I prefer to run through an ice tunnel or a war zone? Let me think...

BY SOME subtle and mysterious process, I have become confirmed as *RW*'s Resident Loony.

As I grow older (which I seem to be doing at a geometrically accelerating rate) Seaton is sending me on ever more taxing assignments. This can only end in catastrophe.

In 2007 — projecting forwards on a graph plotted on the basis of my last six years' experiences — I shall be forced to run non-stop from Virginia Water, Surrey to Goma Nurgsk, Kamchatka in a moose suit.

My next hurdle, I'm told, is to be a three-day race in Sweden staged so far above the Arctic Circle that electricity flows backwards. It will take place in June when the sun is constantly above the horizon. And so, to avoid even the remotest risk of pleasure, a substantial portion of the race is to be run underground.

I agreed to this lunacy because the only alternative was the Kabul Shit 100.

Now I've dived with Bull Sharks in the Bahamas, I've ridden psychotic horses over mountain passes in Morocco that made my testicles retreat so far into my body cavity that it took a crack team of lap dancers to coax them out. I've run in Israel and across the Jordan Desert, skipping gaily through minefields and dodging between the husks of burned-out tanks.

But the Kabul is something else. The mandatory equipment list includes a SAM missile launcher, fake beards of varying lengths and styles, and a cyanide pill.

It was only a matter of time before some bright spark organised an adventure race in a war zone. It was the logical conclusion of a trend that has rapidly gathered momentum in recent years. I blame the French and their Saharan stage race, the Marathon des Sables. This was the first event in which the organisers demanded to see your venom pump at the start line. A far cry indeed from the Cabbage Patch 10.

The MDS is a delicate balancing act: ensuring that the race is a hideous ordeal for the participants, while stopping short of actually killing them.

I ran it in its eleventh year, when temperatures soared into the mid-30s. Every vestige of shade was removed by the Bedouin as the rim of the sun first crept over the dunes. Heavily-armed guards prevented us from running until 10.30am, by which time my shoes had melted and fused to my feet and my power bars had spontaneously combusted.

Within minutes of the start, distraught Italians were staggering about the dunes, engaged in what the uninitiated might have taken to be a projectile vomiting contest. Many had to be rescued by camel, since the terrain did not allow access by four-wheel drive or helicopter.

That night, the foot clinic resembled a field hospital in *MASH*. The screams of the injured reverberated eerily around the wadi.

And yet today, a mere six years later, the MDS is dismissed as a girlie's stroll by the hard men of adventure running. After all, nobody dies, or falls down an ice crevasse, or becomes the host of fatal brain parasites, or is forced to eat his own extremities just to survive. You're given fresh water every ten miles and you get to sleep at night. Why, it's almost like being at home, except you don't have to go to work.

Proper races are non-stop, like the Trans 333. If you don't lose two stones during the event and suffer irreversible damage to your joints and tendons, it's not worth entering.

And of course, Seaton and *RW* must shoulder much of the blame for this dizzying descent into running madness.

Perhaps if you were to write and complain, he'd send me to run something quaint and old-fashioned like the Stevenage 5.

In which I visit the dark side of the moon

WHEN I get tired, I get ratty. And the more tired I become, the rattier I am. Eventually, I become so tired, I turn homicidal. During the Marathon des Sables, it was only the absence of a suitable blunt instrument that saved the life of the race organizer and his entire supporting cast of arrogant, shrugging, Gallic oafs.

If Geordie Dave and I had run into the Singing Nun during our descent from the mountains to Petra, I would have garroted her with her own rosary, just for being so bloody cheerful.

97% of the world's stones are in Jordan. I'm surprised they don't export them to Iraq for throwing at Americans. At least then they wouldn't be strewn all over the track for me to turn my ankle and stub my toes on in the half-light of dawn when I'm incredibly tired and ratty and I've run out of batteries for my head torch.

I swore loudly and without interruption from the checkpoint that had blown off the cliff edge in the freezing gale five minutes before we reached it, to the near-vertical hillside on which one of our party had just broken his arm.

Every long race has its moments of despair, just as it has its times of wild optimism and unreasoned exhilaration. As the body struggles to find enough energy to fuel the muscles, strange things happen to the brain.

Mood swings become increasingly frequent: one moment you're rejoicing because there are only fifty miles to go. The next, you're plunged into the bleakest depression because fifty miles might as well be fifty light years, and this terrible discomfort and this crushing weariness will clearly never, ever end.

Geordie Dave and I fired up our tiny solid fuel stove. Its sooty flame flickered impotently in the wind. In an hour or two the rocks would be cracking under the onslaught of the desert sun. But now the freezing gale that had plagued us throughout our night on the mountain was cutting us to the quick.

My hands were so numb that I splashed far too much water onto the freeze-dried risotto. It melted to a thin, tasteless gruel and we ended up burning our lips as we tried to drink it from the saucepan.

Still, the hot food restored our spirits a little and we packed up and hobbled off into the dawn on bruised and bleeding feet.

Three hours later we were rewarded for the indignities of the previous two days. As the sun rose over the desert rim, its rosy fingers unpacked the astonishing, serpentine canyons of Petra — a 4,000-year-old city carved with breathtaking artistry from the mountains and one of the wonders of the ancient world.

The path suddenly realised that what it really, really wanted to be was a vertical drop. David and I plummeted over the edge, and half tumbled, half scrambled down a horrible, vertiginous face of loose rocks and rotten shale.

We were lucky not to break our necks. Several of our fellows ended up with severe cuts and bruises — particularly those who had attempted the descent in darkness. (That would teach them to be so bloody keen).

Petra, just like Geordie Dave and myself, is one of the ancient wonders of the world. We spent far too much time gazing at the impossibly ornate temples, carved into the red sandstone of the canyon side.

Then we realised that if we were to achieve a decent time, we would have to put on a bit of a spurt. We charged along the kilo-metre-long canyon like a brace of bulls through Pamplona and hurled ourselves across the finish line. Dazzled by the majesty of our own heroism, we looked around for the bevy of beautiful girls would festoon us with medals and shower us with rose petals.

We didn't get so much as swig of lukewarm water.

I'd like to describe the feeling of sheer relief that overwhelmed us as we collapsed onto picnic chairs in the sunshine with a litre of cold water, no pack to carry and nowhere to run. But I can't. My powers of language simply aren't up to the task.

Those who don't run adventure races generally ask me three questions: How do you train for an event that is at least five times longer than a marathon? Why do you do it? And are you in psychotherapy?

First, the training. The truth is, there isn't really any special regime for endurance events — that is, if one is trying to hang on to a job and hold a family together.

In my experience, the best preparation is to talk loudly in pubs about your next lunatic project. In this way you can begin to convince yourself that the Transcontinental 500-miler is a reality to which you're irreversibly committed. And more importantly, by boasting about it in public, you make it virtually impossible to withdraw should sanity ever try to reassert itself.

Of course, a certain amount of running is also a good idea (although not entirely necessary, as I proved when I broke three ribs in an incident involving Stella Artois and a motorcycle, just six weeks before the 150-mile Marathon des Sables).

I try to run for fifty or sixty miles a week for the three months before a big race. I don't care about speed — it's simply the amount of time you spend on your feet that counts.

Only last Sunday I set off in the dark to run along the Grand Union Canal. It was like travelling to a parallel universe in which the Victorians had been annihilated by a neutron bomb and their industrial infrastructure left to moulder quietly beneath a rising tide of ivy, nettles and buddleia.

As I wove through grimy, abandoned foundries and crumbling breweries, I was astonished to find myself crossing London's North Circular Road on a cast-iron aqueduct. Old fishermen dozed away the morning while a torrent of traffic roared beneath them.

In run-down Alperton I almost collided with a heron, flying at head height from one reed bed to the next.

A pair of swans skimmed along the canal at Greenford. In Southall, out by the airport, the amplified call of the muezzin called the faithful to prayer.

After thirty-five miles, I popped up from the deserted backwaters of Osterley Park into the 21st-century maelstrom of the A4. The time machine had landed.

You see, even on a training run that never strays beyond ten miles of Big Ben, distance running has a strange romance of its own. And even if it doesn't lead you into the uncharted dunes of the Sahara, somehow it will always show you the dark side of the moon.

Which goes some way towards answering the 'why' question. It's sightseeing for the man in a hurry. You could cross the Moroccan desert in a Landcruiser and you'd gain some impression of its scale and grandeur. But it's only when you have to run across it, without the luxury of suspension and air conditioning, that you can truly comprehend the enormity of the landscape.

It was the 56-mile day of the Marathon des Sables. My friend Roger and I had battled up a suffocating canyon between cliffs of jet-black basalt. The temperature must have been in the high thirties. The valley was clogged with sand and it was a case of three steps forward, two steps back. When we emerged at the head, it was to behold a vista so incredible that it stopped us in our tracks.

A dried-up lake stretched away to the horizon. In the far

distance sparkled the snow-clad peaks of the High Atlas. We could make out a knoll, standing proud of the plain in the middle distance. This must be our next checkpoint, we decided — perhaps a mile away.

Then we saw a thin straggle of dots on the desert floor, winding their way towards the knoll. And we realised that these ants were runners — and that the checkpoint must be at least eight miles from where we stood.

That meant that the banks of the lake bed — towering cliffs, at the feet of which tornadoes whirled — must be twenty miles apart. And that the mountains were at least a hundred miles away.

We were simultaneously elated and dismayed by this realisation. But mostly elated. The desert was vast, pure and uncompromisingly beautiful and we had earned our right to be there.

It's true: there is no gain without pain. When I return from the Himalayas or the Jordan Desert, I am bigger than when I set out.

And as for Question Three, believe me — I would be far more likely to require psychotherapy were I to spend the rest of my days behind a desk in an office in darkest London.

Fun run. The consummate contradiction in terms

RUN. FUN. Rarely does the transposition of a single letter wreak such a profound alteration upon the meaning of language.

Fun is going out to lunch in Covent Garden and waking at dawn in the Hotel Antoinette, Mexborough. (This happened to me recently. Mrs Blackford is eagerly awaiting the result of the official enquiry.)

Run, on the other hand, is shivering in a scrum of flatulent middle-aged men smeared with horse liniment, only to waddle stiff-limbed between drab suburban villas with no expectation beyond the carving of another notch upon the downward curve of your diminishing physical ability.

Run is being overtaken by pantomime goats while fat, unshaven men with beer deride your knees.

Run is cramp and Vaseline and plastic cups of lukewarm bilge water that tastes of Dettox.

Fun is reducing Seaton's nerves to the consistency of electrified spaghetti by starting last month's column *next* month at 5am with a hangover as big and bleak as a Central Asian republic and a faulty internet connection.

Run is the momentary moment of elation as you cross the line, followed by the onset of that depressive psychosis that stems from sugar depletion and lactic acid poisoning.

Fun is setting your mobile phone alarm to go off on the Tube, then conducting a conversation with an imaginary caller so that everyone thinks you can receive calls 100 feet below ground.

Run is trying to persuade ten Frenchmen that they're in the wrong tent when you've just hobbled 56 miles across the Sahara and you know that the only alternative is to sleep outside on a dune in a sandstorm of biblical ferocity.

Run is trying to distinguish the mud from the dog shit in freezing fog on Hampstead Heath when, through an administrative error, you've been selected for the club's Met League cross-country team.

Fun. Run. It's almost inconceivable that the two words originated in the same solar system. They are the etymological equivalents of matter and anti-matter. What, then, makes us go running? Name another voluntary activity during which your only desire is that it should end? (All right, apart from going to a James Blunt concert.)

It forces me to reflect on our deepest psychological drivers. For instance, the American constitution insists that we all pursue happiness — as if happiness were the unquestionable aspiration of every human being. Well, let me tell you, I've tried happiness and it's not all it's cracked up to be. I soon found myself yearning for a bit of honest anguish and self-loathing, and returned thankfully to my proper state of grim pessimism and general, all-pervading anxiety. Because I'm really only happy when I'm not.

That's why I'm a runner. Why would I sit at home before a blazing fire, savouring a good Burgundy with the one I love when I could be rupturing my Achilles tendon in a frozen ditch somewhere?

Basically, we modern humans have a minimum discomfort requirement. If we had to spend all day ploughing the hundred acre behind a team of oxen, we wouldn't dream of joining Royston Runners. Our sport has grown in popularity at almost exactly the same rate as central heating. The more comfortable we become, the more we need something to make us inconsolably miserable.

Only then can we know life for what it truly is. Not only is the glass half-empty, it's got a crack in it and the contents are leaking out all over the new carpet.

Running shows us the Human Condition like it is first thing in the morning after the dinner party, before it's had time to put its make-up on.

Furthermore, it's a lot cheaper than a James Blunt concert.

In which I buy twice my body weight in useless equipment

AH! SICILY! Land of Sicils!

It was to her hot and rocky shores that I betook myself last month to run off the pale flab of an endless English winter.

I stayed on the coast at a family hotel — that is, a hotel owned by the Family. But it was my consuming desire to drive up into the remotest highlands of the interior and run.

I thirsted for freedom. I treasured this picture, a mental home video of myself, powering effortlessly across high mountain passes, eyes bright with the sheer here and now of it, muscles taut as hawsers beneath a skin nut-brown and oiled, breath short and hard, every sense humming with the raw electricity of living.

Just me, my shorts and shoes and the towering majesty of creation.

Morning flooded the landscape with the ancient, golden light that once fell on Ulysses. I donned my trusty off-roaders and a pair of hurdling shorts, snatched up the car keys and with spirits soaring, left my room.

The ancient golden light blinded me. I almost walked off the balcony. How would I cope on the dizzy precipices of the interior? I popped back to my room and snatched up my sunglasses.

As I crossed the courtyard, the sun struck me smartly across the shoulders. I could feel its rays picking between the thinning strands of hair in search of virgin scalp — and it wasn't yet 7am. Perhaps a hat would be prudent. And a light T-shirt, to protect my upper arms.

I picked up a tube of sun block, too, for good measure.

Within a few minutes of leaving the coastal strip, with its cool, Mediterranean breeze, I began to feel the full, oppressive weight of the Sicilian summer. Even with all four windows open, I was sweating profusely. Glancing up at the arid hills, I concluded that to rely on the presence of potable spring water would be folly.

The keeper of the little grocery shop in Scillata resembled a sun-dried tomato. Wordlessly, he handed me a two-litre bottle of *aqua minerale*. Then his wizened old face cracked in a toothless grin. He pumped his arms to represent running and raised an eyebrow quizzically. I nodded. He shuffled into the back of the shop and returned with a large-scale map of the Madonie National Park — the mountainous nature reserve in which I had set my mental home video.

He was right, of course: to set out into that baking wilderness without a map would have been madness.

He grinned once more and handed me a whistle. Right again. Stupid to venture out alone with no means of raising the alarm.

I paid him and turned to leave, but he motioned me to wait. He returned with a pair of thick socks. I'd intended to run barefoot, but perhaps I'd been naïve. There were gravel tracks out there, and thistles and vipers.

When I finally left the shop, I was carrying water, map, socks and whistle, plus two cheese rolls, a flare gun and compass, an Italian phrase book, a plastic statuette of the Madonna, a disposable camera and a first-aid kit with venom pump included. He'd also sold me a robust straw basket in which to carry all this essential equipment and a ball of string from which I might fashion some kind of harness.

I staggered up the dusty street under the merciless glare of the sun. My temples were pounding under the sheer weight of my load. Above me, the towering majesty of creation was contorted into stony, sneering faces and its cruel laughter rang in my ears.

Bollocks. I dumped the basket in a ditch and turned the car back towards the coast.

Gone running. Bach in a fugue minuets

WHAT ABOUT those morons who jog on the spot while they're waiting to cross the road? Surely, the whole point of running is to get from A to B as quickly as possible? There a[re no medals for getting from A to A.

[Surely this is in direct contradiction of your 'A to A' point in your introduction? – Ed.]

[So? – AB]

On the open road, a real runner will keep going through ruptured ligaments and a cardiac arrest; but if the little red man is showing at the Pelican crossing, she'll lie down on the pavement and sleep.

The other glaring sign of amateurism is Running With An iPod. Firstly, it distracts the wearer from the fundamental unpleasantness of the activity. Running is supposed to be painful. If you want a comfortable sport, take up Crown Green Bowling. But in my view, there'll be plenty of time for such saccharine, Radio 2-type pastimes later on, when you've damaged your body so irreversibly by running that a little light ornithology is all you can manage.

Secondly, for all but a handful of professionals, running

is sightseeing for The Man In A Hurry. As you amble along, you notice how someone's put a brick through the window of Threshers in the Broadway and how the doves along the beck are trying to build a nest with used contraceptives. And, aha, there goes that girl from the Highgate Harriers with the legs and the pink shorts she must have borrowed from her eight-year-old sister.

It's all part of life's rich tapestry, to which you'd be completely oblivious if you were off with the Arctic Monkeys on your MP3. The fact is, running is a jealous mistress. Never content to be an item on your multi-tasking agenda, she demands your single-minded attention.

When I was battling manfully against chronic injury I weakened and bought myself a Shuffle.

I downloaded — I believe that's the term — some music onto this almost supernaturally minuscule device, wedged the funny little bean things in my ears and hobbled off across the meadow.

I soon encountered the prime drawback to running with an iPod: namely, that musicians go to some length to imbue their compositions with *rhythms*. And that these are physically compelling to the point of being irresistible.

I sprinted up the scarp of Royston Heath to Rimsky-Korsakov's *Flight Of The Bumblebee,* and descended to *The Lark Ascending* at a snail's pace.

To the astonishment of the villagers, I waltzed through Steeple Morden to *The Blue Danube.* But things really came to a head with *Unsquare Dance* and its famous 5/4 time signature. Having just the two legs, I was forced to adopt an impossibly complex gait, eventually tripping over my feet and careering headlong into a ditch.

In the middle of a field near the clubhouse a young woman stood motionless on one leg as if frozen, mid-stride. It turns out she was listening to John Cage's controversial *4'33" of Silence.*

Alarmingly, the effects of iPod running can be even more dramatic. For it's not just the rhythm of the music that determines the runner's behaviour, but the mood. After the club's last Sunday run, the A&E Department of our local hospital was overflowing with runners. Three had been resuscitated on the river bank after trying to run to *Crazy Frog*, and another had slashed his wrists just two tracks into *The Best Of Morrissey*.

As for me, you won't catch me running with an iPod again. My generation is used to making its own amusement.

So now, if you'll excuse me, I'm off for a jog in the woods with the tuba.

Anally retentive? What, old devil-may-care me?

NON-RUNNERS HAVE always accused us of obsessive behaviour. It's one of the ways in which they excuse their own indolence. Most of us will drop dead with burst hearts, they warn us, just like Jim Fixx did. And those who don't will be condemned to a twilight world of mental illness.

In fact, nothing could be further from the truth. I have been running for twenty years, and there is nothing even remotely obsessive about my enjoyment of the sport.

Take this morning, for instance. My alarm went off, as always, at 5:29am. Actually, I should say, 'as always *between April and October*'. From November to March I set the alarm for 5:27, because my winter kit takes two minutes longer to put on than my summer kit.

My stretching exercises are synchronised precisely to the news headlines on the World Service (it seems there was a minor earth tremor last night in Tierra del Fuego), allowing me to leave the house at 5:48 on the dot.

As I trot down Brookland Rise, I sing the chorus of *Younger Girl* by the Lovin' Spoonful (1967). That's unless it's raining. If it's raining, I'll hum the first movement of the Elgar Cello Concerto instead.

There is nothing strange or obsessive about this. It's perfectly rational. The only time I sang *Younger Girl* in the rain was on June

3rd, 1995. I slipped and grazed my knee and, as a result, I lost two minutes. I have never managed to recoup that lost time.

When I arrived back at the house, it was two minutes later than usual. I was two minutes late for work, and thus two minutes late home in the evening. I went to bed two minutes late, and woke up two minutes late.

This is why my alarm is now set for 5:29 in summer. It used to be set for 5:27 (5:25 in winter), but alas, those days are long gone.

My workmates will ask me how often I run. Every day, I will promptly reply — but in fact, this is not entirely true. On the second Wednesday of each month, I will run twice — once at 5:48 as usual, then again at 6:35pm, when I will execute one lap of the Heath Extension in an anticlockwise direction.

This is because on the evening of Wednesday, March 9th, 1989, I happened to pass Gabriella Evangelista as she jogged a clockwise circuit of the Extension. (She may not have been called Gabriella Evangelista — this is my private name for her — but she was easily the most physically attractive human being I have ever met. I said to her, 'hello', and I will never forget her reply. 'Hello', she said.)

My workmates are not runners. They are unexceptional, lumpen creatures, who drift through life with no purpose or direction, and no sense of their own divinity. When they taunt me about my running, I rarely give them the satisfaction of a response. But occasionally I will round on them and explain: not only does running slow the process of decay and dissolution that is the affliction of most mortals, but in my case, it has actually reversed it, so that I am *actually growing younger by the day*.

This sometimes invokes some queer looks.

What happens if you miss a day, they want to know. My face will cloud over: for every day I don't run, I reply, I age *three* days. Maybe four.

I can feel the blood slow down in my veins. My muscles lose their tone, my mind its clarity and focus. As my cells start to die, their detritus builds up in my pancreas, making me morose and explosive.

After two days of not running, I must fight to suppress the urge to snap the aerials off parked cars.

After four days, I will retire to my bedroom and with the curtains drawn, polish my collection of Korean assassins' knives until I can see my face in their coldly wicked blades.

'Don't you want to know what happens after *five* days?' I ask. But by now, I am usually alone.

What-ho, Seaton!
My perfect race weekend

'SEATON! SEATON! Dash it all, where are you, man?'

My butler, the erstwhile editor of *Runner's World,* insinuates himself soundlessly into my penthouse suite at the Hotel Quatre Saisons, Davos.

'With your pardon, sir, I was just applying the thorn-resistant wax to the laces of your racing shoes.'

'Surely you did that last night?'

'Yes, sir. But in my experience, one can't be over-meticulous in these matters.'

'Which vest am I wearing in the morning?'

'I have laid out three, sir, but I expect your preference to be for the grey, lightweight Gucci.'

'And the safety pins?'

'The 18 carat gold *Mappin & Webb*s would serve tolerably, sir.'

'Hmm. Thank you, Seaton. When are the masseuses expected?'

'The Thai girls at any moment now, sir. The Inuit are booked for the morning, after your hot tub.'

I have always found ten kilometres to be an unpleasantly exhausting distance: and so, for me, the Swiss 9900 Metres is the ideal race.

The 11am start time, too, is highly civilised. It allows time for a fellow to rise at a reasonable hour, to partake of a leisurely breakfast whilst scanning the newspapers, perhaps even to conduct some trifling business with his stockbroker before submitting to the Baffin Islanders' pre-race muscle-toning programme.

The Quatre Saisons, of course, was chosen for its proximity to the start. In fact, the race commences in the air-conditioned comfort of the lobby, a few steps from the penthouse elevator. The helicopter pad is only the icing on the cake — although it is undeniably agreeable to be whisked directly to one's hotel from Glorious Goodwood immediately following the last race of the day. (We always arrive in time for the traditional eve-of-race Lobster Thermidor party at the Restaurant Mirabelle — across the road from the youth hostel where the rest of the runners enjoy their congealed, lukewarm pasta.)

Naturally, I'm aware that the weekend places an unusual strain upon Seaton. He must iron and fold my socks, shave my legs, prepare my champagne and horse-liniment compress, mix my personal drinks for the race (it can be tricky, tracking down my preferred brand of absinthe when abroad), reserve a quiet place for my transcendental meditation and retain the services of a dozen attractive, well-mannered young natives, to be scattered carelessly around the furniture in the suite.

In normal circumstances, I would lend a hand. But complete rest before a race is as vital as all the training that precedes it.

I appear in the lobby precisely two minutes before the start of the race. This allows me to take my place behind the elite runners — one doesn't wish to be caught up in any unseemly displays of athletic zeal — yet sufficiently in advance of the baying herds of pantomime animals and cocktail waiters.

At this point, I am joined discreetly by my *Runner's World* double — a logical extension of the magazine's marathon pacing service. At the starting pistol, I skip lightly down the hotel steps then swerve through the crowd, tear off my number and re-enter the building through a service door at the rear.

I then follow the race on TV over a whisky sour in the comfort of my dressing room.

Seaton announces himself with a discreet cough. 'Would sir like to receive his medal in person, or would he prefer the Other Gentleman to accept it on his behalf?'

'Did I win?' I enquire.

'Sadly not, sir.'

'Then let the Double have my medal,' I declare magnanimously. 'It's the least I can do.'

'Yes, sir. As ever, sir.'

How to train yourself unfit

I'M WRITING this in the hope that it may help in some small way to hasten the progress of sports medicine. Perhaps some hapless researcher out there, trying vainly to comprehend the intricacies of the human mechanism, will glance at my scribblings. And who knows? Perhaps they will trigger in him the blinding supernova of enlightenment, and my suffering will not have been in vain.

You see, my metabolism has gone into reverse.

I first noticed it about a month ago. My training for the Jordan Desert Cup was going along nicely — I'd managed the Cape Wrath Ultra without collapsing in a pool of my own bile. I'd jogged a couple of twenties with Oscar, The World's Fittest Dog, and I can safely say I looked better than he did by the end, as we crawled up the garden path to our respective water bowls.

And then things began to go badly wrong. The more I trained, the more unfit I became. My response was to up the mileage — but this only dragged me into a vicious cycle of ever-increasing knackeredness. Soon, merely putting on my shoes was enough to exhaust me.

I weighed myself. I was the heaviest I'd ever been. I embarked upon a virtually fat-free diet. Tuna and baked potatoes, obscure leaves and roots. Soya. Pale, thin milk like blood with the red cells filtered off. Cottage bloody cheese.

Instantly, I put on weight. I began to feel like a character in a sequel to Stephen King's *Thinner. Tubbier.*

I resolved to clean up my act — to renounce once again the good old firm of Grolsch & Kronenbourg. But far from feeling cleansed and invigorated, I found myself waking to debilitating hangovers of an ever more crushing intensity.

What was happening to me?

I stalked the house, fretting away the small hours. Reluctantly, I concluded that *I had accidentally mistaken myself for my own negative*.

Somehow, I must have stepped inadvertently into a powerful magnetic field, flipping my DNA over into its mirror image.

I began some tentative experiments at the ad agency where I work. No more Mister Nice Guy, I resolved — I would be brutally rude to everyone I met. I would reduce innocent account executives to tears by addressing them exclusively via a grotesque hand puppet, and by dangling them by the ankles from my office window.

I applied the same techniques to my clients. They left the agency in droves.

My career took off immediately. I was appointed chairman of the Institute of Practitioners in Advertising and presented with a Lifetime Achievement Award by the Creative Circle.

I decided to extend the experiment: perhaps if I worked less, I might be paid more?

In my new regime, I rolled into work at 11am, read the papers, pondered which restaurant most deserved my patronage at lunchtime, summoned a company cab and disappeared with my Corporate Amex Card until 5pm.

Sure enough, my salary doubled almost immediately and was re-routed to a tax-friendly account in Liberia. I was appointed Chairman of the Creative Circle and presented with a Lifetime Achievement Award by the Institute of Practitioners in Advertising. Overnight and without explanation, my company Toyota Corolla GL was replaced by an Aston Martin.

And then it occurred to me: this was all perfectly normal in my line of work. Far from proving that I had become my own, living antithesis, it simply reinforced the time-honoured way of 'getting ahead in Advertising'. For our business is less about making friends and influencing people than stabbing your granny in the back and mortally offending everyone else.

So perhaps I wasn't contradicting every physical law after all. Perhaps it's just that I'm growing old — that my metabolism is grinding slowly to a halt, my hormones drying up, my muscles atrophying, my vitality draining away like the juice from a shagged-out battery.

So that's all right, then.

In which I stumble upon the interface between two parallel universes

IT CAME as quite a relief when I discovered that our airing cupboard was the terrestrial terminal of a space–time wormhole.

I'd always assumed that the missing running kit was just a symptom of my own forgetfulness.

In our house, items disappear then surface again, unaccountably, months later. I used to put it down to some cyclical mechanism, like a convection current. The Lanzarote Challenge T-shirt is worn, washed, placed at the bottom of the pile; then over the centuries, it rises gradually to the top where it is eventually exposed, worn, washed, *et cetera*.

Nothing strange in this, you say — a perfectly ordinary process like evaporation and precipitation, or sedimentation and erosion. And I would agree — had I not searched the pile a hundred times for the missing garment, only to have it materialise later at some arbitrary point in time.

When logic robustly refuses a mundane explanation, one has two choices. One can adopt the Hippy Position, smile superciliously and drawl, 'Hey, man, that's really weird, but there's more, like, cool shit goes down in, uh, heaven and earth than is dreamed of in our philosophy... '

However, it's precisely this kind of mindless, slack-jawed,

dope-induced drivel that makes me want to address the New Age with a shovel to the side of its head.

This leaves the second alternative: that behind the absent shorts must lie some perfectly rational explanation that is nevertheless beyond our current scientific understanding.

One day, just like the magnet and the solar eclipse (once attributed to witchcraft), the events that baffle us today will succumb to explanations derived from patient observation and rigorous experiment.

My instincts were vindicated last Tuesday when I discovered that The Old Slaughterhouse, Beethoven Street, London N2 is in fact the interface between two parallel universes.

I was searching in the airing cupboard for my Brendan Foster Jumbo Money Belt when into my outstretched hands dropped a running vest. Imagine my amazement when I identified it as my precious Highgate Hairy-Ears Veterans 10k shirt, bequeathed to me on his deathbed eleven years earlier by poor old 'Stinky' Stan Honeyball.

Perhaps it had become caught on a ledge, high in the upper recesses of the cupboard. I stuck my head inside and found myself peering, not into dusty crannies of wood and old plaster, but into the blazing glory of a stellar constellation.

My face was fanned by the solar winds as the vast congregation of stars wheeled majestically overhead. My small knowledge of astronomy told me this was no familiar neighbouring system, but some strange galaxy from the primordial backwaters of time.

Then a dark shape momentarily obscured the tail of the cosmic spiral — and then another, and another. And as my eyes became accustomed to the darkness, I was able to decipher a legend on one of the dark objects:

Man vs Horse Mountain Marathon, Llanwrytd Wells, 1991. Sponsored by William Hill.

My eyes brimmed with tears. I hadn't seen that shirt for years. It was followed rapidly by a pair of lime-green shorts, the backside emblazoned with the words:

Numbskulls AC. We're Running Backwards For Christmas.

My dear old club shorts, dating back to when Roger Mental Manton and I ran from Westminster to Blackheath on London Marathon day. With a happy sigh, I recalled how we were almost lynched by the frenzied mob in Wapping.

And as I watched, entranced, literally dozens of my favourite shirts, shorts and socks sailed gracefully by. I had thought them lost but lo! here they were, captives of the gravitational field of an alien sun. Now and then, I deduced, they must slip through a black hole and return, temporarily, to our airing cupboard — only to be sucked once again through the crack between the dimensions to this distant star system.

You could have knocked me over with a feather.

THE GOOD LIFE

THERE'S AN old Buddhist fable about a layman and an ancient monk. The layman is excited by the little he knows about Buddhism and he manages to collar the monk as he walks abroad in the monastery gardens.

'Monk,' says the layman, 'Please tell me how I can achieve Enlightenment.'

The monk replies, 'Let's have some lunch.' And he hands the layman an orange. After their meal, the layman presses the monk. 'Now will you tell me how I can find Enlightenment?'

'I'll tell you how to eat an orange,' replies the monk.

The layman is indignant. 'What do you mean? Any fool can eat an orange.'

The monk shakes his head. 'I was watching you. You detached a segment of your orange and put it in your mouth. But the moment it was in your mouth, you were busy detaching the next segment. So you never actually ate the orange at all.'

'All right, all right,' snaps the layman. 'So you've told me how to eat an orange. Now will you teach me the secret of Enlightenment?'

'I just did,' says the monk.

Now you're probably asking, what's all this got to do with running? Is Blackford the monk? Or is he supposed to be the layman? Or the orange?

Actually, I included the parable because it made me realise that I shouldn't waste my life on anticipation of the future, or regrets about the past. The secret of a happy life is to live in the Moment. And running is the ideal expression of this philosophy — in fact, it's a metaphor for life itself.

Yearn for the end of a race and it will never arrive. Beat yourself up about your past performances and you will achieve nothing except a mental stress fracture.

But live each moment of 'the race' for itself, fully and intensely, and you will be truly alive. You will eat your orange and savour it too.

Anyway, after years of applying this philosophy to my running, I discovered its fundamental flaw: namely, that every moment of a run can be plotted on a downward curve between acute discomfort and unmitigated agony, with apprehension, self-doubt, raw terror and abject despair thrown in for good measure.

It is only imagining the finish line that stops you ripping off your number and hobbling back to the start.

In running as in life, I concluded, the fantasy is far better than the reality.

So I renounced Buddhism, gave up oranges and now devote myself to avoiding the moment like I would Green Monkey Fever.

Meet the new, squeaky clean me

IT'S NOW six weeks since I gave up everything that makes life worth living. Tea, coffee, meat — and, of course, alcohol.

On forty-two mornings, I have brushed my teeth without the comforting sensation that I am about to vomit.

I have risen in good time to take Oscar for a constitutional scamper on the Heath. Skipping lightly through the dawn mist, I have bid astonished rabbits a cheery 'good day!' and smiled benignly upon Brownie, the homicidal Doberman cross whose sole ambition for six years has been to chew my leg off at the knee.

I have been so sickeningly alert on my way to work that I have only twice boarded the Bank train instead of the Charing Cross.

When asked by my colleagues what I did last night, I can actually remember.

I work in an industry where, on a good day, people stab each other in the front. And yet in the office I am calm, relaxed and reasonable, optimistic, helpful and industrious.

At home, it's the same story. After three years of living like a specimen in a jar, I have finally put up curtain rails in the living room. And when I was engulfed in the inevitable avalanche of rotten plaster, did I throw the rocking chair through the French windows? Absolutely not. I merely smiled.

Indeed, Mrs Blackford has compared me to Jack Nicholson in *One Flew Over The Cuckoo's Nest* — after the lobotomy.

The ship of my abstinence is steered by two helmsmen: a running coach who looks like Buddha, and a Buddhist who looks like Rigsby in *Rising Damp*.

My coach is Frank Stein, of whom his wife once remarked, 'Who?' He lives in the East End but rarely escapes the gravitational draw of the West. He is part of Soho, almost architecturally. Indeed, *The Coach & Horses* was named in his honour.

He managed 2:19 in the London Marathon before his knee packed up. From that day on, he has applied himself to self-abuse with the same, unerring dedication that he once applied to athletics.

I am Frank Stein's monster. When the subject turns to running, the jolly *bonhomie* evaporates and his brow is furrowed with steely determination.

His watchword is consistency — the precise weekly distance is unimportant. If I choose to make it forty miles, then forty miles I must make. Even if it means making up the missing thirty-nine in one go, right through Saturday night.

If I don't, he will fracture my ribs with that scientific precision for which Leytonstone is so justly famous.

Here's a funny thing, though: you'd expect, given my blameless new lifestyle and my nutritious, toxin-free diet, that I'd be running like a fiend. But I'm not. I don't seem to be any fitter today than when I ran the South Downs 10 with a Camelbak of Bacardi. For one thing, my legs hurt. Maybe it's because I'm running for the first time in twenty years without the benefit of anaesthetic.

Still, I'm enjoying running badly more than I used to enjoy running well — although this won't help me crack the sub-three marathon to which I've foolishly committed myself.

Perhaps that's where Siddartha The Buddhist comes in.

If you don't spend your evenings in bars, boring young women with inaccurate renditions of sketches from *The Fast Show*, how do you fill the hours? You do a meditation course, of course.

Every Monday, I sit cross-legged for three hours on a rug in Covent Garden and try, for just one second, to live in the present.

From the outside, we meditators must look very mystical and other-worldly, if not completely barking. Actually, behind that mask of transcendental bliss, we're fighting off trivial, intrusive thoughts like flies: should I have Demerara sugar with my bananas tonight? How do you spell *anaglyptic*? Scarborough is nicer in winter.

Then, for a moment, we manage to concentrate on what we're supposed to — our breathing, usually — and bingo, we've switched our attention to how clever we are. It's all very frustrating — like trying to rub your belly and pat your head at the same time.

However, I'm assured that by Lesson 6, I'll be a better, more self-knowing and fulfilled individual. The only thing that worries me is whether I'll feel compelled to act on my self-discovery. Suppose I decide I have to give away my shirts to the poor and sit under a tree in a loincloth? Will I be allowed to ride unfeasibly fast motorbikes on my day off? Do Bodhisattvas *have* days off?

Om.

When the going gets tough, the tough go drinking

HOW AM I doing in my new, stainless lifestyle?

I'm constantly and entirely sober. No harmless creatures have laid down their life to feed me (apart from the fish who don't count because they smell and have no sense of humour).

Last month, my running had descended to an all-time low. While training in the Peak District, I was overtaken by a large, granite boulder. For a moment, I was deeply shocked and depressed: had I really become so old that even inanimate objects were faster than I was? Then to my immense relief I realised that the boulder was merely the harbinger of a massive rock fall, and that I was about to be crushed to death.

I escaped with my life, but what little self-esteem I still possessed was seriously eroded by the episode. After all, here was I, living a life of blameless purity — and far from enjoying a sort of athletic Indian summer, a swansong of blistering times and smashed Super Vet records, I was relying upon Oscar to drag me up high kerbs.

I was beginning to wonder whether perhaps, after all, the secret of great achievement in athletics is gross excess. Listening to some of the old pros at the Lanzarote Challenge last year, they seemed to train on a diet of Guinness and curry.

'Remember Daffyd Thomas from Pontypridd?'

'Aye. I wuz out with 'im, night before t'seventy-three European Championships. Sixteen pints, he put down, an' 'alf a pint of *crème de menthe* in the taxi. I 'ad to carry 'im upstairs to bed. Turns out it wasn't even 'is 'ouse. T'were 'is next door neighbour's. To make things worse, he were sick on their cat.'

'Aye. He ran a crackin' race next day, though. Knocked three seconds off t'Commonwealth 10,000 metres record, as I recall.'

'Four.'

Ah, says the angel on my left shoulder, but for every brilliantly-talented piss-artist in the annals of running, there are ten true heroes who attain the pinnacle of fitness by dogged discipline and ascetic self-denial.

True, smirks the devil on my right, but they're always bloody ill. You can't thrash your cardiovascular system day after day, month after month, on a diet of Quorn-flavoured multi-vitamins and expect it to stand up on the big day. There's no antibiotic like an industrial strength meat madras at the *Light Of Poona* — no vitamin to match a skinful of Barsted's Old Flyfumbler at the *Bedford's Revenge*.

The fact is, when the going gets tough, the tough go drinking.

I was vacillating between these two contradictory positions when my running unaccountably began to pick up. I found I could jog across the Heath quite happily without gasping like a foghorn or seeing the landscape though a mist of blood. I was able to wave cheerily at other runners and wish them good day without wishing they'd be struck down by mysterious, debilitating diseases.

What had happened? Perhaps it had taken my internal organs ten weeks to emerge from the swamp of festering wood alcohols and pork fat which for so long had choked my body cavities?

Anyway, whatever the reason, I'm definitely experiencing a late return to form. As soon as I've finished this piece, I shall strap myself into the sledge harness, buckle myself to the dog, swallow the morning's dose of slippery elm food, rattle off a couple of mantras at the shrine and set out to work.

As I skip through the waist-high mud on the Heath Extension, the air will resound to the rattle of the woodpecker and the mindless witterings of the song thrush, God will be in his heaven and all will be well with the world.

In which I skip gaily through the London Marathon

I DIDN'T go to the pre-London pasta party because since I Gave Up Everything, my entire life is one endless pasta party: sensible, subdued, responsible and sometimes, it must be said, a trifle pale compared to the excesses of my forty-year adolescence.

On the plus side, just like after a pasta party, I usually wake up with someone I recognise and I'm able to run the Race of Life without throwing up in a litter bin.

I can honestly say I enjoyed the Marathon. This was a first for me — I've always regarded the race as a self-imposed penance for basing my training regime on the Hibernating Newt model.

April after April I've sat on the Blackheath special, bleary of eye and rumbling of gut, filled with undigested toast and a terrible sense of foreboding: *Oh-ho, you've really done it this time, Blackie! Armageddon awaits you, just behind the Cutty Sark. Still, at least you'll get a decent view of the Millennium Dome from the air ambulance...*

This year, though, I felt positively chirpy. I rose at 5am and enjoyed an hour's meditation, appreciating the essential emptiness of everything.

Meditation, for the uninitiated, has a lot in common with marathon training. For weeks you plod along with no visible signs of improvement — then suddenly, without any special effort, you knock ten spiritual minutes off your tranquillity 10k time.

I went through one of these breakthrough phases shortly before the London. It was as if I'd been hammering on a solid wall — and then someone opened a door and I simply walked through. Now, whenever I meditated I found myself drifting in a kind of limbo, surrounded by slowly-tumbling items of mental junk. Look — there's that raft Dip and I built at Runswick Bay. And isn't that a racoon? Aren't people like oil lamps? Eucalyptus.

My instructor cautions me to ignore all this mental flotsam and get back to the serious business of observing my breath. But before I do, I'm going to take a good look around. It's altogether very jolly and relaxing — like scuba diving with plastic sharks, or space-walking in a belt of asteroids from Toys R Us.

So by the time I'd extinguished the incense, turned off the CD of the Tibetan temple bells and pinned my number to my shirt (why is it impossible to position a number centrally on a running vest?) I was in a state of benign and sunny tranquillity.

I positively sauntered to the start. My nostrils quivered at the heady scent of Deep Heat as I exchanged pleasantries with nervous young fillies in Help The Aged T-shirts. I waved gaily at the TV cameras and danced a flamboyant tango along the 0 degrees meridian in my black bin liner.

Seldom — never — had I been so thoroughly prepared for a race. My Whizz-Kidz log book was a dense fog of tiny writing and arcane symbols representing shoe type and ambient temperature. The chronic injury to my right hip was just painful enough to remind me that I wasn't Ethiopian without significantly degrading my performance. I had taken on enough fluids to get me through the first few miles without feeling like a flatulent camel.

I hardly noticed the starting gun. Before I knew it, I was walking, then striding, then jogging (then walking again) towards the Start, over there by the two hundred foot-high flying bouncy castle on the Heath.

The race seemed far more professional, somehow, than last time I ran London. There wasn't the old Liar's Riot as four-hour runners scrambled into the three-hour section on the basis that everyone else would.

Even the *crowd* was professional: hardly any toothless old hags offered me treacle pudding in Deptford. Nor were we forced to run the gauntlet of fat drunks playing *When The Saints Go Marching In* outside East End pubs with big screen sport and Sunday roast for £4.95.

Result: I knocked 20 minutes off my New York time, came in around the 8,000th mark and jogged to the tube station.

Next year, with a bit more meditation under my belt, I should be able to win the bloody thing without even leaving the cushion on my living room floor.

In which I try to stop trying to stop time

AS A teenager, I went through a mystical phase. Reading the tortured outpourings of the mad monk-poet Gerard Manley Hopkins was like eating barbed wire and cream — I knew it wasn't good for me, but I couldn't resist it.

I wrote poetry, too — sort of 'Shelley meets Bob Dylan but they don't get along' — and smoked horrible French cigarettes. It was around this time that I came last in the school cross-country.

Then I discovered Lobsang Rampa — a Buddhist monk who revealed in a series of million-selling paperbacks the innermost secrets of Tibetan magic.

I was particularly impressed by the ability of Tibetans to run hundreds of miles at a time, flat-out. It never occurred to me to wonder why Tibet, rather than Kenya, wasn't the Mount Olympus of marathon running. Nor was I especially disappointed to learn that Lobsang was really a London cabbie to whom the Far East meant anywhere beyond Dagenham.

What stuck in my mind was this apparent connection between Buddhism and running. I was convinced that long-distance running must have a lot in common with meditation — that the hypnotic tedium of placing one foot in front of the other, then the other foot in front of the one, was the physical equivalent of chanting *om, mani, padme, hum.*

I was wrong. The whole point of Buddhism is that things change, so we'd bloody well better get used to the idea. We grow old, we die — and yet we spend our lives denying it. We expend fantastic amounts of energy trying to stop the sea of time washing away the sandcastle of circumstance.

And among the most fruitless wastes of energy is running. We do it, most of us, to hang on to our fading youth. At the end of the third 1,000-metre interval, we nervously interrogate our watches: was that as fast as the last one? At the end of the marathon, we compare our time not with the winner's but, neurotically, with our own performance in last year's race.

Running is trying to stop time. Our patron saint is Peter Pan. If we miss two days' training, we're cast into a pit of self-loathing: 'O Woe! We're on the slippery slope to slobness!'

Buddhism, on the other hand, is about reality. Life is good, it tells you — get one. Enjoy running, but enjoy it for *itself* — not because it's going to make you live forever, or because you might become a world-beating athlete at 55, or because it'll keep you two stones lighter than Fat Jack next door.

Run because you might catch another glimpse of the woodpecker on Sandy Heath, or that Chinese girl in the string vest from Muswell Hill Runners.

A Buddhist running watch only reads 'Now'.

Of course, I'm just as bad as you are. I have this mental picture of myself, based loosely on Steve Reeves in *The Giant Of Marathon* — the finely-sculpted musculature of my bronzed thighs effortlessly adapting to the terrain as I, warrior-poet-sorcerer-prince, power across the mountain fastnesses.

Then I see the photo they took of me at Mile 12 of the Kingston 16: the pallid, overweight bloke with the sweaty, thinning hair and the expression of someone who has accidentally strayed into Dracula's castle at sunset. I look so profoundly unathletic, so desperately middle-aged, so fundamentally shagged-out, so pathetically *human*.

Where's all this leading, you ask? Same as usual, I reply — nowhere. Except that in future, I'm going to run just for the sake of it, rather than as the means to some impossible end.

I will grow old, I will die. And somewhere between the two, running will give me up. And I shall sit in front of the fire and read my running diary and remember what it was like to climb out of the valley on a chalk track, breathing in the summer morning mist, breakfasting upon the scent of peat and bracken and the incandescent song of the lark.

And what a poor, sad old bastard I will be.

In which I learn to run in an entirely illusory world

> (i) Life is pain
> (ii) Life is illusion
> (iii) Therefore, pain is illusion

It's simply one of the more irritating consequences of Samsara — the imaginary world in which we're all condemned to stagger about blindfold, bumping into imaginary objects, physical and mental, thereby sustaining a host of imaginary cuts, burns and bruises.

Since I set out on the Noble Path to Enlightenment, I have explored in great depth the notion that pain does not really exist. In fact, I have read about it until my eyes hurt, and thought about it until my head ached. I have sat and meditated on the subject until my legs were racked with such excruciating cramps and my spine locked into a series of S bends so acute that it took an osteopath, two chiropractors and a hydraulic jack to straighten me out.

And while I am now satisfied that pain does not exist, I'm having a hard time convincing certain wayward elements in my non-existent body.

Take my right hamstring, for instance. It all began twenty years ago when I fell down the lighthouse on Lundy Island. I won't go into details, but it explains why Nature in her wisdom has allotted such different habitats to the cider apple tree and the cannabis plant.

My pelvic bone misread the accident as a decree of independence. It was as if my DNA Secretariat had said, 'Right-ho, Pelvis, you've been an exemplary bone, now, for twenty-five years — and as a small token of our gratitude, we're awarding you the Freedom Of The Body. From now on, you can grow wherever the fancy takes you, without the irritating formality of Planning Permission.'

My pelvis accepted this honour with enthusiasm, and set off at a brisk pace down the muscles of my right leg.

A year later, the declaration was rescinded and an orthopaedic surgeon retained to hack off the new extension with, they tell me, a mallet and chisel.

The result has been a chronic weakness of the hamstring, which becomes acute whenever I run fifty miles up vertical Swiss rock faces.

A month or so ago, it decided to remind me that I was still mortal, and I've been trying to shake it off ever since.

Until now, I've relied entirely upon Buddhist meditation techniques to sort the problem out.

First, I tried Mindfulness of Breathing while running. This is a method I filched from the Zen archers of Japan. By becoming one with the breath, the bow and the target, they are able to hit the bull with their eyes shut.

At the first twinge of discomfort, I would concentrate all my attention upon my breath, observing the life-giving Nothingness as it flowed over my sinuses, cold and pure, then osmosing through the membranous walls of the alveoli in the linings of my lungs, enriching my blood and extending the sacred life force along endless miles of capillaries to the furthest extremities of my corporeal being. It was while conducting this tricky spiritual exercise that I ran into the low branch and almost knocked myself out.

Everyone knows that head wounds bleed disproportionately to their severity, but it can be quite alarming trying to limp across four lanes of traffic on the A1, semi-conscious and blinded by gore.

I decided to try another meditation method — the Metta Bhavana. This involves fostering a mood of intense friendliness and compassion and then applying it to increasingly unlikely subjects — from your best mate through to poisonous snakes and estate agents.

Compared to the limitless power of this all-encompassing love, mere physical pain should evaporate like an early mist in the sunshine.

I was wrestling with the thorny task of generating kind feelings towards the Conservative Shadow Cabinet, when I was nearly run down by a minicab. The driver leaned out of the window and shouted, 'Mind where you're going, you stupid fucking twat!'

In the ensuing fight, I sustained a pulled shoulder ligament and a nasty cut above the right eyebrow.

So now, if you'll be good enough to pass me the ibuprofen and the absinthe, I've got a track session to run.

In which I run with ten thousand of me

I'VE JUST received the official photos of the Puma Marathon. There's a fine shot of me pulling athletically away from my gasping editor — and another, less satisfactory one of me being humiliated by a grinning Whitby Jimmy in Meadowbank Stadium.

Then, mysteriously, there are two snaps of complete strangers — and a wide shot of the entire field, like a spread from *Where's Wally?*

I suppose I should simply have slipped them into the envelope provided and returned them to the photographer. But I was possessed of a sudden surge of curiosity. Who were these people? What were their stories? What strange concatenation of circumstance had brought them together on that chill, misty morning in Dunfermline?

Since becoming a Lovely Lotus Floating Over The Lake Of Mundane Reality, I have whole eternities of time to ponder such questions. And so I decided to trace the mysterious strangers.

I won't bore you with how I failed, in the ordinary sense, to track them down. Suffice it to say that the Tibetan detective agency I hired for the task far exceeded my expectations.

Karmic Investigations (Lhasa and Haringey) Ltd is the only such outfit in the world to be run along strict Buddhist lines. Their report, delivered over a meal of okra poached in Perrier at a Bloomsbury vegetarian restaurant, was a revelation.

The unidentified subjects of the photographs, it seems, were *none other than myself* — each one the result of a different set of possible circumstances.

The first was Hector Blandish, an estate agent from Surbiton.

In a previous existence, explained the private third eye, I had been a feudal warlord in the gruesomely-named 'Red Belt' of strife-torn Surrey. I had committed a series of unspeakable atrocities against the local population of simple, uneducated stockbrokers, until my very name was execrated throughout the Home Counties.

The horrific consequences of my deeds spread out in ever-widening circles, like ripples on a lake of blood, blighting the lives of all they touched.

At one point, I was so far beyond salvation that in my next incarnation I was to be cast into a pit of foul, viperous demons to endure a thousand aeons of torment. However, at the last minute, apparently, I managed to tip the balance slightly in my favour by running a sponsored 10k for the Viperous Demon

Defence League, and my sentence was commuted to twenty years of estate agency.

I was shaken, I can tell you. But it didn't end there.

The lady in the second shot was Sister Maria Francisca of the Order of the Little Sisters of the Blessed Meddling — a dedicated band of roving, religious social workers. In yet an alternative previous life, it turns out, I had been a journalist working on a running magazine. Refusing all but the most insignificant of token payments, I had striven selflessly for the happiness of my editor with no thought for personal gain. I had run uncomplainingly across deserts and up mountains, submitting gems of ageless prose on time and to the correct length, until my health had finally collapsed.

Racked by hamstring pain, I was forced to eke out a meagre living by writing whimsical twaddle about Buddhist detective agencies and parallel lives, in the hope that my loyalty would be repaid in the form of a rise.

The gumsandal from Karmic couldn't confirm whether I ever received my earthly reward — only that upon my death, I came back as Maria the running nun.

I sat, stunned, in the *Quiche Me Quick*, my food barely touched. What about the *Where's Wally?* photo, I asked — although I already knew the answer.

'They're *all* you, pal,' replied the private dick. 'Every single one of them. Even the crow at the top left. It seems the photographer accidentally set the aperture to eternity instead of infinity.

'Would you like to know how you came back as the scuba-diving Buddhist from Middlesbrough?'

I rose and limped slowly from the restaurant.

A BONE TO PICK:
THE CANINE CHRONICLES

WHY DO we love dogs? It is a riddle wrapped in a mystery inside an enigma.

My dog ate my car.

His hysterical barking makes every journey a misery. He never comes when he's called, yet he arrives with depressing reliability when he isn't.

In the night, he stealthily insinuates his great, shaggy carcass into the middle of the bed, then gently squeezes Mrs Blackford and myself towards, and eventually off, our respective edges.

He's a shocking thief but he does guilt so brilliantly, you can't find it in your heart to scold him beyond a bit of ineffectual finger-wagging.

However, he has been my constant running buddy for twelve years, so I suppose that must be worth something.

Recently, like me, he's had a spot of bother with his hips. But whereas I was able to have mine fixed, the technology isn't yet available to dogs (or even poor people in the post-industrial North).

Still, I met a woman in a field who recommended a rare elixir that costs four times as much as the single malt whisky I bought my brother for his birthday. The effect of the elixir on the dog was roughly the same as the whisky on my brother (immediate and astonishing) so from now on, I'm going to dose the dog up with 15-year-old Macallan.

When I took him into work with me, the chairman was much taken with him. 'What a lovely coat!' he said.

'He will be,' I replied.

How to baffle dogs

EVERY ROAD is really two roads. Travelling down it is an entirely different experience from travelling up it.

Take this morning, when I ran my usual route in reverse. I don't mean I ran backwards — that would have been dangerous, because it was still dark and the fields around our village are strewn with abandoned, tetanus-infested agricultural paraphernalia from the horse-drawn age.

Having said that, you do occasionally see people running backwards. Why do they do that? I suspect they're American. It annoys me intensely — like the people who jog on the spot while they wait for the lights to change.

Anyway, today we did the Litlington–Morden Grange–Litlington circuit in the clockwise direction, instead of the usual anti.

Consequently I had to cross the ploughed field just five minutes into the run — then struggle up Dead Mole Hill in gigantic clay boots weighing half a hundredweight.

What's more, it completely baffled the dog. This isn't really surprising: your nose and mine contain around 5million olfactory sense cells. Oscar's contains 550million.

To Oscar, the rabbits were suddenly and mysteriously *before* Grange Farm, instead of after. And the ammoniacal scent of fox unaccountably preceded The Place Where The Hares Are.

His world was turned on its head and because, for all his olfactory cells, his brain contains only three Common Sense ones, he nearly had a nervous breakdown.

This was only averted by his discovery that Steve-From-The-Pub's dustbins were now at the end of the run, not the start. Next thing, he's head down in the wheelie bin marked 'Organic Matter Only'.

It took me twenty minutes to fool him into dropping the chicken carcass so that I could grab a clump of his hair thick enough that it wouldn't come away in my fist.

Dogs aren't supposed to eat chicken bones — they splinter and cause all kinds of internal damage. However, it's at moments like this that I'm tempted to find out how chickens cope with dog bones.

All the same, wouldn't it be terrific if we really could run backwards? If we could slip into a metaphysical reverse gear and cruise slowly through the flotsam of our untidy histories, adjusting and, where necessary, correcting through the miraculous binoculars of hindsight?

Imagine if it were possible to reverse all the terrible mistakes we made in the past. (*Darling, why don't we get a dog?*) Then, if we travelled backwards fast enough, we'd begin to get younger.

Which, of course, is really why most of us run forwards.

In which I am dog tired (i.e. tired of dogs)

LAST SUNDAY morning, I was creeping naked around the house. Naked, because Oscar the Belgian shepherd dog intently monitors my state of dress for any suggestion that I might be going for a run.

A sock or a marathon T-shirt is enough to send him charging about in a mad, child-waking mazurka.

He stared at me from the sorry, mud-encrusted ruin that was once our *fin de siècle* chaise longue.

As casually as I could, I buckled on my sports watch. His ears pricked up. For a moment he performed his impression of Alert Intelligent Protector of the Flock. Then, with an improbable bound, he launched himself at me and pursued me around the room like a heat-seeking missile.

But now, with a piteous yelp, he suddenly sat down on the limp rag that was once our hand-woven Moroccan carpet. This was unprecedented. Why hadn't he smashed any priceless antiques?

He held out one front paw and whimpered in a hurt, bewildered sort of way. There could only be one explanation — the World's Fittest Dog was injured.

It felt strange, leaving the house without him. For one thing, I didn't have to stop five times before the end of the road while he vented his bladder at strategically important sites.

Nor was I dragged across the dual carriageway of the A1 in pursuit of a one-eared ginger tom.

In the woods, I was spared a thirty-minute battle of wills over the decomposing corpse of a squirrel.

Nevertheless I missed him sorely. And so, it seemed, did the rest of North London's running fraternity. I was stopped on the Heath by an old boy I didn't recognise. 'I'm sorry,' he said, 'I don't know your name. But where on Earth's Oscar?'

From then on, everyone I passed wanted to know where Oscar was. At first I would stop and explain to the concerned devotee that he'd injured his paw while cavorting in the foul-smelling extended kennel that passes for our living room. But after a couple of miles I grew bored and began to experiment with alternative explanations.

'He was abducted by aliens in Neasden.'

'Kidnapped by Muswell Hill Runners. They demanded a 50p ransom but I refused on the grounds that such a sum vastly exceeds the dog's true value.'

'He's working undercover for DEFRA in the Brecon Beacons, monitoring radical elements in the sheep community.'

'He's realised that in his heart, he's really a Yorkshire terrier. He's resting up before the op.'

I have to say, by the end of the run I was peeved. Seaton has always refused to include my photograph in *Finish Line* — what we journalists call a 'picture byline'. 'Such a flawless physique as yours', he insists, 'would only depress our readers.' Consequently I've never had to endure the inconvenience of celebrity while running through North London.

So to be recognised as the owner of a bloody dog who isn't even there is just plain humiliating.

Annoyed and deflated, I limped over the threshold. Oscar was lying on his back in the hall with his legs in the air. He surveyed me through one half-closed eye. I swear he was smirking.

Around him was the usual litter of half-eaten mail. Only

one letter remained intact. The envelope bore the logo of the Himalayan 100 Mile Race. Eagerly, I tore it open.

'Dear Oscar,' it read, 'we are pleased to confirm your owner's entry...'

In which I wriggle out of the Canine 9k. Almost

'LET'S HAVE lunch,' suggested Seaton in a startling display of magnanimity. 'There's some interesting stuff going on this year and we need to sort out your diary.'

I could hardly contain my excitement — mostly because I was finally going to discover the colour of my editor's credit card.

Was I to be the first Westerner to run across the trackless wastes of the Gobi Desert? Or to wrestle giant alligators in Australia's 300 Mile Swamp Romp? Or slither down stalactites in the 10-day Malaysian Deep Cavern Challenge?

Seaton broached the second 35ml bottle of still mineral water. 'The Canine 9k is a brand new and absolutely unique event — wait, you're going to love this — *for dogs and their owners!* And best of all, it's in Surrey. So you won't need to drag yourself halfway around the world to slog through some godforsaken wilderness.'

I searched his face in case he was kidding. He wasn't. 'The Canine 9k,' I repeated slowly.

'That's it! Ha! Ha! Quite an amusing name, eh? Made me laugh, anyway. In fact it was that wacky humour that made me think of you. I thought, this one's a bit of fun — right up Blackie's street. So whaddya say, Big Man?'

'Well,' I began, staring at my plate. 'Thank you for thinking of me. I'd love to have run it. Virtually nothing I can think of would have given me greater pleasure — except perhaps being stuck in a lift for twenty-four hours with a drinks trolley and Shania Twain.

'But sadly, the dog is dead.'

It couldn't have been worse if I'd struck him in the face.

He slumped in his chair and whispered hoarsely, 'Oscar? *Dead*?'

'Yep. 'Fraid so. Very sudden.'

'I'm pole-axed. What happened?'

'Er… Embolism. He ate a squirrel without chewing and, well, sparing you the details, it gnawed its way out. You know squirrels — vicious little rodent bastards.'

'Good God. Well, I must say, I'm devastated.'

'I hadn't realised you were so fond of him.'

'Fond? No, no — I can't stand dogs. They disgust me. They lick their own genitalia, you know. No, it's just that I'd already put you down for the race. Had to pay for the bloody dog, too. And I don't suppose for a moment it's refundable.'

'I'm sorry to be the cause of such distress, Steven,' I replied stiffly. 'You suffering puts into perspective the mere loss of a much-loved and faithful friend.'

'Forget it,' he waved vaguely. Then, 'Look — you don't know anyone who could lend you a dog, do you? I mean as long as you *pretend* to like it for the photos, who's going to be any the wiser?'

There is a point where insensitivity attains almost surreal proportions, and this was it. I was searching for some appropriate response when there was a frantic rapping on the window directly behind our table.

It was Beverley, my PA. Her face was contorted with panic — and the gargantuan effort of trying to restrain Oscar. Having caught sight of me, he had his front paws up at the window and was barking like a thing demented.

Beverley mimed profound apologies and helplessness. Seaton observed the whole ghastly performance in granite silence.

Finally the dog wriggled free of his collar, barged through the swing doors and launched himself at me in a frenzy of unconfined joy.

We're running the Canine 9k.

On the lead, but not in it

I TELL you straight, that was the weirdest Sunday I've had since I slipped the leash in North Finchley and ended up stealing the falafels from the bowling alley.

It started out quite normally. I woke Him as usual by scoffing a kilo of gourmet tripe and liver pate, then wiping my gob on his face. He swore a lot as he stumbled about in the dark, trying to put on His running pants.

But then, instead of us trotting off towards the Heath, He bundled me into the car with the Mistress and the Little Ear Yanker and drove us halfway across Europe. Well, OK, halfway round the M25. But when it's eating into running time, it seems like an eternity.

Anyway, we pitched up in a car park in the middle of a wood. The LEY took me for a stroll. The ground was covered in old, cream balloons and there were lots of tissues to eat. There were gallons of foul, stinking mud, too. Things were definitely looking up.

Until the others arrived. There was this black Samoyed. I mean, can you imagine, darlings? He looked about as natural as a miniature wolfhound. And a Springer bitch who was frightened of her own shadow. Talk about neurotic. Apparently, she was so spooked on Bonfire Night, she spent the rest of November under the sofa.

Anyway, as more and more of these freaks and weirdos turned up, I began to wonder if this was a casting session for David Lynch's sequel to *Lady & The Tramp*.

Then I twigged. All the humans were wearing running stuff. This was a race — a race with humans and dogs.

We all lined up facing the same way (except the Springer space cadet) and a bloke blew a whistle and we were off.

God, what a nightmare! I mean, my idea of a run is you mooch about a bit, take a pee, snuffle in the grass, suddenly remember you're supposed to be with Him, charge after Him like a loony, then take another pee and another snuffle and so on.

But He put me on the lead and went off as if we were being chased by a pack of psychopathic Rottweilers. He dragged me past really fascinating trees, wonderfully alluring puddles and piles of rabbit shit. Nine kilometres without so much as a mooch.

I felt like telling Him: imagine how *You'd* feel if you were taken to a lap dancing club — but only for ten minutes, and on the end of a three-foot rope.

Anyway, it was all right in the end because he got lost and spent ages muttering and wandering aimlessly about.

I could tell he was embarrassed. Seaton was at the halfway mark with his camera, but we missed him completely.

The Master seemed to lose heart after that, so we completed the second lap at a more civilised pace. Between you and me, He was knackered, poor old sod.

Mind you, they still gave me a medal. They even gave one to the LEY *'for being a nice person'*! She's obviously never sat on their heads and extracted their body hairs, one by one.

On the way home, He told me we're going to run this bloody race again next January.

It's the only time I've ever been grateful that one of His years is equivalent to seven of mine.

FITNESS, FUEL AND FALLING APART

INJURY IS the spectre that stalks every professional sportsperson. Will Striker A's metatarsal knit before the crucial cup fixture? Will fly half B's unsightly pimple subside before the Cosmo photo shoot on Thursday?

And yet these are elite athletes, honed to the peak of physical perfection. How much more likely then that the barely-trained 45-year-old lard-arse weekend jogger will rupture a ligament while sneezing or turning over in bed? Your correspondent is a case in point.

My running career has been a woeful catalogue of injuries. I have fallen down lighthouses, fallen down hills, fallen from horses, fallen down stairs, fallen off motorcycles. Where I differ from your professional is that only two of my injuries were incurred through running. One, while stretching after a cross-country in Woking; the other, tripping over a dog near Highgate Ponds.

So as your virtual sports physio, my advice is i) avoid stretching and ii) give a wide berth to all dogs, especially German Shepherd–Collie crosses called Clumsy Bastard (if I heard his owner right).

Anyway, the next bit is all about how to avoid getting injured by training and eating properly. Then, when that fails, how to waste hundreds of pounds enriching the charlatans who will pour out of the woodwork and promise to fix you.

In which I go all fungal in the jungle

WE WERE wading up to our manly chests in the impenetrable brown broth that passes for water in the Guianan rainforest when Jeremy turned to me and said: 'You know — when I get home, I'm going to surrender myself to my doctor and get a complete screening. This place must be full of filthy diseases.'

Now Jeremy is a hard bastard, long-term TA soldier and all, so you have to take him seriously when he expresses even the slightest anxiety about anything.

However, it went against the grain. As far as I could see, the Amazonian rainforest came pretty close to the Garden of Eden. No nettles, no brambles, no midges, no mosquitoes. Just lofty, dignified trees and sinuous vines and cute little frogs and the odd, flesh-necrotising centipede.

Frankly, you'd endure more discomfort running through a copse in Surrey than you would in French Guiana.

But on the flight home from Cayenne Jeremy slipped me his Index Of Unspeakable Sicknesses.

I homed in immediately upon Chagas' Disease. Apparently, you get this from little creatures who live in the walls of mud huts. Now Jeremy and I stayed in lots of huts that had no walls at all. But one of them did — we called it Dengue Cottage, after a fly-borne condition that makes you bleed through your eyeballs.

Chagas' (or *trypanosomiasis*) is altogether subtler than Dengue Fever. Provided you notice the bite of the mud-wall-dwelling tick, it's treatable — although, in the ominous words of Jeremy's manual, 'there are side effects'.

The effects of ignoring the bite, however, are not so much 'side' as 'fatal'. After twenty years, all your internal organs suddenly explode and you die.

Give me *cutaneous leishmaniasis* any day. This merely eats your face away. Presumably, the *mucocutaneous* variant does the same, but from the inside.

As I read the entry on *filiariasis*, I realised with a flush of panic that my shoes felt tight. I was certain that by the time we landed at Orly, the tiny worms infesting my lymphatic system would have caused my legs and testicles to swell 'to gigantic proportions'.

It was only a question of whether the *myiasis* would get me first. The maggots had, of course, already burrowed into my skin. But how long would they take to hatch and burrow through my gastrointestinal wall, probably leading to *septicaemia*? The cabin attendant didn't have a clue. You'd think that on a route like this one, the airline would insist on at least a smattering of tropical pathology, but my chit of a girl could hardly get the top off a wine bottle.

By this time I was feeling decidedly faint. Was it the onset of *viral encephalitis* with the consequent possibility of permanent *neurological sequelae*? Or was it simply the hallucinogenic side effects of my Larium tablets, caused by the marked resistance to chloroquine of the strain of *falciparum malaria* endemic in the Amazon Basin? It was difficult to tell.

Perhaps I should get some rest, try to reinforce my beleaguered immune system. I closed my eyes but quickly opened them again. Once the *onchocerciasis* took hold, the blindness would set in. I had better treasure my last moments of unimpaired vision.

In the end, I decided to fight back against the myriad infections I had contracted during the Raid Amazonie, using the powerful, broad spectrum antibiotic we know as *vodka*.

So far, it seems to have worked. But to be on the safe side, I plan to continue the treatment for the next twenty years.

In which I unveil the ultimate celebrity diet

WHEN I went to bed last night I found we'd run out of cocoa, so instead I ate 750 grams of Stilton and swilled it down with a bottle of Madeira.

Consequently, I was plagued by dreams with sinister and disturbing undertones. The transcript would have kept a university psychology department in business for years.

In one episode, I was so fat I got stuck in the flume at our local lido. The lifeguards poured gallons of sunflower oil down the tube in an attempt to free me.

It formed a blanket on the surface of the pool, completely suppressing the effect of the wave machine. Hundreds of children had to be rescued by the RSPCA and hosed down with anticoagulants.

This was followed by a dream in which I hacked a two-foot thick slab of blubber off the corpse of Moby Dick with a flensing spade and ate it between giant slices of fried bread.

Clearly, the subject of fat was engaging me on some deep, psychological level.

Some people lose weight so they can run faster. Others run in order to lose weight.

I belong to a third class — people who need to lose weight and should definitely run faster, yet do neither because they simply can't be arsed.

The other day, I came across an old photograph. It was taken at the 1984 Hampstead Heath Fun Run — probably the most inappropriately named event in the running calendar. I was so thin, I looked like a severed head on a pikestaff.

In those days, of course, I ran like a gazelle. I mean I finished every race on all fours.

The '84 Heath Run was no exception. The winners were all even thinner than I was. Many followed the Sheffield, or Stainless, Diet, which was fashionable among athletes of that era. It involved six meals a day — typically fish and chips, suet dumplings, pizza and boiled tripe, followed by sticky toffee pudding and deep-fried Mars bars. The idea was that you ignored the food, which helped to develop enormous mental strength, and ate only the cutlery.

Knives and forks contain infinitesimal amounts of fat but are rich in certain vital minerals. Like iron. And so while the adherents of the Stainless Diet were extremely slim — wiry, you might say — they were also immensely heavy. During the 1985 National Cross-country Championships, when 2.8 inches of rain were recorded in 45 minutes, three of them sank without trace in a particularly muddy stretch of the course.

The jogging boom of the 1980s was largely fuelled by the public's obsession with weight loss. This had unforeseen climatic consequences.

Between them, the participants in the third London Marathon lost almost three tons in weight. A huge cloud of lipids was borne northwards. As it rose, the fat condensed and was precipitated upon the eastern slopes of the Pennines. The moorland springs and streams were clogged with yellow fats.

The inundation coincided with the annual Bastard's Crag race in Wensleydale: hundreds of runners slipped on the glutinous deposits and slithered down the vertiginous hillsides (incidentally, the origin of the term, 'fell race').

As the running craze has proliferated, so the effects have become far more widespread. The term, 'Greenhouse Lards', has entered the vernacular. The presence of so much fat in the upper atmosphere has created a sort of inverted, global Bratt Pan. Our planet is literally being fried alive.

So if you're overweight and you're about to take up running, forget it. Switch on the telly, open a beer and tuck into another pork pie.

No need to feel guilty — you're saving the planet.

Never say diet.
How I failed to eat myself fit

MAN, THEY say, cannot live by bread alone. They're wrong. I know, because I've done it.

It worked just fine — except that three months in, they had to knock out the window frames and hoist me off my groaning bedstead with a crane.

There's nothing like simple carbohydrates for turning you into a grotesque parody of the human form, somewhere between a water bed and an elephant seal.

So when it became clear that I wasn't going to be able to wriggle out of Rory Coleman's awful Marathon Of Britain, I knew I'd have to downsize.

I gave up bread, beer and pasta. Instantly, my body went into shock.

The weight fell off me. For six weeks, I was the Incredible Shrinking Man. As the nutritionally-informed amongst you will have recognised, my regime was a sort of girl's blouse version of the Atkins Diet.

(I'm talking here about the real Atkins — not the diet pioneered by my college friend Dave Atkins who, at 21, was voted by the Junior Common Room 'Man Least Likely To Make 30'. Dave was the inventor of the legendary 'Amphetamine Sulphate & Cider Diet' which, in his case, was so effective that he eventually slipped into a crack between two paving slabs on Middlesbrough's Linthorpe Road and vanished into a parallel universe.)

The *real* Atkins Diet, of course, is merely the latest in a seemingly endless succession of nutritional fads, designed to exploit the unfeasible aspirations of the discontented and the gullible.

Old hands like myself will never forget the Macrobiotic diets of the Sixties, when the cardboard packaging of a Kelloggs' breakfast cereal provided more nutrition than the ingredients of your typical mess of brown rice, lysergic acid and boiled-to-buggery courgettes.

Or the Raw Pork Sushi Diet of Thatcher's heartless Eighties, which involved slicing rump steaks off live pigs and finger-feeding them to one's sexual partner from the bloodied pages of the *Daily Mail*.

Compared to these, the Blackford Girl's Blouse Diet is almost innocent. It works by depriving you of the opportunity to eat anything at all, ever. It's starvation by stealth.

After all, without fried bread or cornflakes or croissants, or brioches, or Danish pastries, what is breakfast?

Without beer, pasta or bread rolls, lunch is a ghostly, insubstantial affair. So you console yourself with wine which, on an empty stomach, quickly renders you insensible.

By the time you regain consciousness, you've missed dinner.

The effect on one's running is immediate and dramatic. It's like walking on the moon. You feel as if someone's lifted a hundredweight keg of lard from your back and grafted wings to your shoes. Your power to weight ratio has soared to that of the red ant. But beware — so has your calorific intake.

The organisers of the Jordan Desert Cup stipulate that you must take on 7,000 calories a day. This represents a stupendous amount of food. It exceeds the gross annual consumption of the entire population of Mali. To comply, you must lug around your body weight in filthy, freeze-dried risotto and energy bars of the size and consistency of breeze blocks. And still you lose weight over the course of the race.

With the Blackford, deprived of all the foods that make life even remotely bearable, you are in real danger of disappearing up your own fundament.

I arrived at the Nottingham finish of the Marathon Of Britain in shorts and a T-shirt that had seen me though six days and 175 miles. Having forgotten about the evening's Gala Dinner, I had to go straight into town to buy something to wear.

And the only thing I could find to fit me was a romper suit from Baby Gap.

It's gym life, but not as we know it

IT WAS my accountant's fault. 'You have far too much money,' he said. 'You need to get rid of it. For tax purposes.'

'How?' said I.

'Well, accountancy fees are tax-deductible. I'd be doing you a favour by doubling them.'

'Thanks,' I replied, warmly.

'But I'm afraid that's only the start. You need to embark upon some breathtakingly wasteful undertaking. Something to mop up all the spare cash that's currently slopping around in your accounts, driving the Revenue into a feeding frenzy.'

I frowned. 'Like what?'

'Well, how about privately financing a manned mission to the Sirius system?'

'I don't know the first thing about astrophysics,' I pointed out.

'Better still! There'll be lots of colossally expensive catastrophes to write off.'

'Can't I do something a little less… grandiose?'

My accountant was visibly disappointed. Then he brightened: 'You could always go for a course of reconstructive dental prosthetics, and join a gym.'

And that's exactly what I did. Looking back, now, from my packing case beside the Regent's Park Canal, I can't help thinking I might have over-cooked it a bit. Still, it certainly kept the tax man off my back, so I mustn't grumble.

First came the dental work.

When I was fifteen, I paid a visit to my dentist in Middlesbrough. This was remarkable in itself — back in 1965, dentistry hadn't really caught on in Teesside. It was regarded by the populace with the same scepticism as fortune telling and flying saucers.

As luck would have it, my appointment was on the day that my dentist had his nervous breakdown. I remember him charging manically about the surgery, covered in gore and uttering loud oaths. He tore four perfectly healthy molars from my gums, condemning me to a lifetime of discomfort and embarrassment.

So you can imagine that the prospect of possessing once again the proper complement of teeth was an alluring one. Like a lamb to the slaughter, I signed up for the orthodontic equivalent of the Sirius mission.

Only last month, my shiny new Hampstead dentist told me as I came round from the double bone graft, 'See you in February for the implants. Bring six thousand pounds.'

The grafts came from a bone bank in San Francisco (so I'm almost certainly HIV positive) and were granular. They're held in by little plates of Teflon, but they still hurt like buggery if I so much as get out of bed in a hurry.

Not that it's made much difference to my training, since the Alpine 78k has turned my hamstring into a sort of pain-sensitive stalactite.

In any case, I've joined The Gym. All chrome and mirrors and black leatherette, it's like something Damien Hirst might have dreamed after visiting a bondage club, then eating cheese too late at night.

There are no weights — just rows of diabolical machines, each wringing sweat and moans from its apoplectic victim.

As far as I can gather, the Code of Gym Etiquette forbids any verbal communication between males beyond grudging, testosteronal grunts.

Members of the opposite sex are to be completely ignored — even when they're contorting their lissom, lycra-clad torsos into impossibly provocative positions.

I find myself watching the others out of the corner of my eye, and wondering what they do during the rest of the day. My curiosity was rewarded when I bumped into a particularly finely-sculpted weightlifter outside the environment of the gym.

I'd often admired and (I admit it) envied him as, to an anthem of primaeval groans and grunts, he'd pushed twice his own considerable weight on the bench press.

Then, last week, I caught him writing me a parking ticket outside my local Waitrose.

I can't imagine why such a magnificent specimen of manhood should be reduced to such a humble occupation.

Perhaps he has the same accountant as me.

In which I dabble in a spot of anthroposophistonecromancy

FIRSTLY, THANK you, *thank* you. I have been deeply touched by the heart-felt support I've received from you, my Readers, over my continuing physical disintegration. I will treasure the letter forever. (Arthur: I wasn't going to accept the money, but then the bill came in for January's Deep Magnetic Regressive Hypnosis therapy so reluctantly I've been obliged to bank your cheque. Dr Yang: it should take four working days to clear.)

Meanwhile, I've resolved to suspend all treatment of an

orthopaedic character and to address my hip problem from the inside, so to speak.

As any half-competent pan-anthroposophistonecromancer will tell you (for £75 + VAT), diet is the key to healing.

It's little more than common sense: we are, as they say, what we eat. For instance: if, in the words of the Good Book, we were to live on bread alone, we would soon become soft, rectangular and white (or brown, depending on what type of bread we lived on alone). Our fellows would be inclined to butter us, and unless we slept in a sort of large equivalent of the bread bin, we would quickly go mouldy and attract the unwelcome attention of mice.

Since my last despatch, I have consulted a number of dieticians — some mainstream, others decidedly more esoteric.

A couple of initial observations: the price of Gazelle sperm doesn't justify its therapeutic properties; and when eaten in large quantities, runner beans are only efficacious in the sprint from the dining table to the lavatory.

A woman who lives on a barge with twenty-nine cats suggested what might be dubbed the Psychopatkins Diet. I was only permitted to eat raw pork — and this had to be carved from the living beast and consumed then and there, in the field.

Like many popular dietary regimes, this one proved impractical and terminated in a hair-raising car chase across the Home Counties. That is to say, I was in a car — the pigs were on quad bikes. As anyone who's seen the motion picture *Babe* (PG) will testify, the intelligence of the ordinary, domestic pig is vastly underestimated. Either my pursuers enjoyed an advanced knowledge of the road system, or else they'd somehow gained access to GPS technology.

Back in our village, I consulted the shaman who serves as GP, psychotherapist and marriage guidance counsellor, and also pumps out the septic tank. He has some unusual theories: one is that if you eat an athlete's running shoes, you become endowed with the owner's physical prowess.

I turned up an old pair of Seaton's that he'd accidentally left at our gaff after photographing me for the mag. It took six hours to force down the mud-spattered, sweat-soaked Montrails. I saved the laces 'till last, twisting them around my fork like spaghetti.

Next morning, in a state of high anticipation, I set off along my customary three-mile course. My hopes were soon dashed — I was so slow, I was overtaken by a traffic bollard.

Never one to give up, I shredded a pair of Mrs Blackford's wellingtons. The only way I could stomach them was to bake them in a sort of pastry parcel.

Next morning, I set out again along our lane. The boots worked significantly better than Seaton's trainers — but I was still nowhere near as quick as I'd been in my pre-injury days.

So in desperation, I've decided to self-prescribe. Forty years ago, my dad managed to arrest the rampant corrosion in the bodywork of our Ford Prefect. So I've just mixed my first cocktail of Wax Oil and red lead.

Bottoms up!

In which I limp through the outer suburbs of alternative medicine

I'M MAKING friends with my injury.

My Korean chiropractor insists that only when I learn to respect my chronic tendonitis will it respect me in return.

It all began, he tells me, when the dorsal metamorpholia of the pre-lumbar atrium were laterally destabilised by an acute trauma to the octavian marsupials of the left obstacle.

I'd suspected as much.

Running injuries, it seems, are governed by simple, logical rules. One of these states that the amount you spend on dodgy practitioners of Oriental complementary medicine varies in direct proportion to the incomprehensibility of their diagnoses.

My chiropractor examined me by standing me in front of a small candle and then observing it through my body. He was thus able to identify my problem by analysing the incandescent aura produced in my bone marrow by the candlelight.

This technique has taught me something rare and precious: that if someone tells you something, calmly and reasonably while keeping a perfectly straight face, and charges you more than £50 an hour for his advice, you will believe it — even if it's complete bollocks.

This conclusion is based upon meticulous research. I underwent six sessions with an acupuncturist from Macao. He scorched my thigh with a sort of cigar made from compressed pond weed. He jabbed a needle in my heel and made my chin wobble. He stuck such a forest of pins in my back that I would have passed muster in an am-dram production of *Hellraiser*.

Unusually for a Macaoan, he was passionately interested in Cajun accordion music of the early 1950s. While he punctured me, he would beat me about the ears with *The Best of Hank Merde et Les Elephants Foux*. This was more painful by far than the pins and by the end, I would gladly have swapped my course of torment for a nice, cosy cell in an Iraqi interrogation centre.

On the bright side, acupuncture definitely reconciled my Yin with my Yang and reorientated my meridian to a more favourable inclination *vis a vis* my planetary influences.

But my hamstring still hurt like buggery and I was unable to run three strides without collapsing like a drunken pantomime cow.

Meanwhile, I was getting as fat as Cracker.

I was intrigued by the notion of a combined reflexologist and cranial osteopath. How would she do my head and feet at the same time? Was she a giant, or a contortionist, or did she merely have praeternaturally long arms?

In fact, she turned out to be two women, not one. It was a bit like starring in a pornographic movie, except without the pornography — or the movie, come to that.

The reflexologist was trying to alter my frame of mind through my feet, while the osteopath attempted to fix my leg by rubbing my head.

The result was a head-on collision of soothing energies around my duodenum. For ten minutes it was profoundly unpleasant, and then I threw up.

I won't bore you with a complete account of my harrowing odyssey through the penumbra of alternative medicine. The low point, perhaps, was my ordeal at the hands of the White Witch of Wensleydale. For three days and nights I lay prostrate on a mattress of wholemeal bread while she dangled a quarter pound of mature cheese over the affected area and chanted excerpts from the Soil Association manifesto.

But a close contender was the Reptology session, which involved me squatting in a bog on heathland near Wolverhampton with a man in a frogskin hat. I emerged after almost six hours, chilled to the bone and thoroughly miserable. That I was able to mimic perfectly the call of the Midwife Toad (Lat: *bufo bufo*) was scant consolation. I had developed curious membranes between my toes and an unhealthy appetite for worms.

Back in London I slipped into a slough of despond. It was now six months since my hamstring had flared up and no cure seemed to be in sight.

Would there be no end to my suffering?

In which I try to stop looking at myself and BE myself instead

I'M INJURED. I never get injured, but here I am, injured. What's worse, I suspect that I got injured by congratulating myself on how I never get injured.

I'm plagued by this sort of thing. For instance, I used to lie awake at night, worrying in case I had hypochondria.

I get it when I'm meditating, too. I'm supposed to count out ten breaths while concentrating wholly on my breathing. If my mind strays to anything else — Ducati motorcycles, the size of mangoes, the Shania Twain video — then I have to go back and start again at one. What usually happens is, I get to nine and think to myself, 'Bloody brilliant! Nine!' And I have to go back to the beginning again.

It's as if I'm two people: me, and the Official Me Observer (OMO). The OMO likes me to live an exciting life because that's more interesting, I suppose, than watching me watching *EastEnders*.

So I often end up doing things I don't especially enjoy, simply because the OMO likes them. Running up Alps could be a case in point. I say 'could', because sometimes I'm not sure whether I'm genuinely enjoying something, or whether I'm simply pleased in a selfless sort of way because the OMO seems to be enjoying himself.

So being a double act can be a pain. Literally. When I'm running a marathon, for example, the OMO starts interfering at the first sign of discomfort. 'Oi!' he says. 'Have you seen yourself? You look knackered, mate. Bloody terrible! And you've still got seven-ninths of the race to run. I've just worked it out.'

The effect is immediate and disastrous. I started off imitating my favourite Ethiopian running heroes. Now, suddenly, I've switched to imitating Fats Domino.

Then, to relieve my pain and depression, my OMO pictures me at the finish line: there I am, breasting the tape just millimetres ahead of Ajdjiti M'bmti, reigning world champion, then collapsing into the enfolding bosom of Gwen Stefani.

Insane optimism is just as dangerous as leaden-footed self-flagellation.

I'm sure that really great runners don't have OMOs. They're just *them*. They're gathered, focused and single-minded. They don't have to share their energy and concentration with some disembodied, voyeuristic parasite.

And it isn't just runners. I bet it's the same with people who are tops at chess, bricklaying, double entry bookkeeping, you name it.

People who are *really* good are only interested in doing it — not in *witnessing* themselves doing it.

Whereas people who only do it for the benefit of the OMO are impostors. They can be quite convincingly good at whatever they do, but in the end, they're only doing a good *impression* of someone being good. Like Cliff Richard.

Do you know what I mean? Or am I completely mad? I don't think so. I think I might have stumbled on something fairly important here — the Secret Of Life.

The Secret Of Life is to *be at one with yourself*. Whatever you do, don't be at two with yourself. If you're harbouring an Official You Observer, kick him out.

You'll become a much better runner, I guarantee it. And a better double entry bookkeeper, too, should that be your burning ambition.

And you'll start to do the things you really want to do, instead of the things you want to want yourself to do.

So. My plan is to develop this, my new theory, in the self-help book to end them all. Entitled, *A Bi-psyche Made for Two,* it will explore the phenomenon of bifocal living and explain how, through a series of rigorous spiritual exercises, one can unify one's consciousness and achieve liberation from the vampirical OMO.

I will run workshops and travel the land with a roadshow, mesmerising audiences in concert halls and sports stadiums with my Secret Of Life.

Today England, tomorrow the USA. After a raft of appearances on TV chat shows, I'll top the bill at the Hollywood Bowl where, as luck would have it, I will have to share a dressing room with Shania Twain.

That ought to keep the OMO happy for a bit.

In which I am Thai'd in knots

'AH! MISS-AH Blackfor! Tha's perfec! Now put your light foo behine your head an' SLETCH! Thassit! SLETCH! Perfec!'

Amnuoy is a sunny, smiling sadist. Like many Thai people, there is something engagingly childlike about him. But even the sweetest children enjoy pulling the legs off flies.

I've always hated stretching. Warming up, it seems to me, is a waste of time. As far as I'm concerned, the first ten miles of the race is my warm-up.

Result: I am barely able to touch my knees, let alone my toes, and my field of vision is restricted to a 15 degree arc on either side of my nose.

Until I wrecked my suspension during last year's Swiss Alpine Sad Old Nutters' 78k Marathon, my only serious running injury had been incurred while stretching.

But now I was a prisoner in the five-star Chiva-Som open prison on the Gulf of Thailand, and my gaolers were determined that before I was released, I should be able to pick my toenails with my teeth.

I was subjected to an excruciating round of physiotherapy, massage, mobility sessions and Pilates classes, all designed to make me bend in places I hadn't bent since I was nine.

And this was my honeymoon, damn it.

Still, if you're going to be taken apart and reassembled without anaesthetic, it might as well be at Chiva-Som.

This exclusive health spa was based on an architect's proposal for an extension to Paradise. The plans were rejected by God as excessively luxurious, and lay discarded in the Archangel Gabriel's dustbin. Eventually, they fell into the hands of a Thai businessman who, not wishing to appear Spartan, added a few little refinements of his own. Then he bought up a stretch of sun-soaked, coral beach and turned the dream into reality.

After battling your way though Hua Hin, a dizzying explosion of humanity that assaults your senses with a barrage of noise and smells and primary colours, you pass through the gates of paradise into a willow pattern plate.

Mahogany lodges with steep, fish-scale roofs stand among koi ponds carpeted with sacred lotus. Sinuous paths wind through stands of bamboo and flaming bougainvillaea. Bright birds dart among the branches of camphor trees, as you sink thankfully into a featherbed of peace and quiet.

We found ourselves speaking in hushed tones, as if we were in Princess Diana's mausoleum. We were attended in our every need by flocks of tiny Thai girls, quick and pretty as hummingbirds.

Then we had our consultation with the spa's medical officer, I made the mistake of mentioning my chronic hamstring pull, and I was catapulted into an excruciating, week-long regime of pushing and pulling and bending and twisting.

The most cruel and unusual punishment of all was the Fitball class. This involved bending backwards over a huge, rubber ball like some early Christian martyr, until my vertebrae crackled in an excruciating concerto of agony.

My first Super Stretch class, a one-to-one encounter with Amnuoy, was conducted in the outdoor Tai Chi pavilion. But I screamed so loudly that subsequent sessions took place in a soundproof underground cell.

His laser-guided thumbs drove unrelentingly to the heart of muscles that had lain undisturbed for centuries. It seems that I've been cobbled together like a dodgy second-hand car from two entirely different people. My left-hand side is tolerably strong and supple, while my right-hand side dates back to the late Jurassic and has all the pliability of weathered limestone.

As Wantanee, my beautiful, almost microscopic physiotherapist, put it: 'You velly stlong man, Miss-ah Blackfo, but you stuck like statue!'

Tragic old fool prepared to take anything from statuesque Australian chiro

I SUSPECT that 99% of the population are injured. They're just not aware of it. In order to feel under the weather, you have to know what it's like to be *on top* of the weather. Moreover, one person's weather isn't necessarily the same as another's. Ask anyone in New Orleans.

This hip thing is ruining my life. It's driving me mad because for the last six months I haven't been able to run like I did for the last thirty years.

The people I work with probably have hip things, but because they wouldn't even dream of walking upstairs to the office when there's a perfectly good lift, they don't realise they're in excruciating agony and severely depressed through endorphin withdrawal and consequent loss of self-esteem.

First, I tried to fix myself. I reasoned that if I bought some new, extra-soggy shoes (a technical term) and ran off-road in thick mud, it would so reduce the impact on my joints that I'd be fine in a week.

It almost worked. I could manage an hour around the local fields before I began to list to starboard like a foundering trawler. But then my foot got stuck in a bog and I wrenched my knee so that it swelled up like a pumpkin.

By the time I sorted the knee out, the hip pain had begun to intrude into my non-running time. It would wake me in the night and my leg would suddenly go dead on me, halfway downstairs.

I hobbled the hundred yards to the gym every day, hammered myself to shreds on the stairs machine and developed — well, if not a six-pack, then a small keg — through my Pilates-style 'core stability' exercises. All of this helped, but only because I felt I was *doing something*.

When you're injured, it's the helplessness that really gets to you. If someone with enough letters after his name and sufficient personal charisma prescribed a course of French knitting, you'd hurl yourself into it with a pathetic degree of enthusiasm. Because at least you'd be *doing something*.

I went to a Harley Street chiropractor. She took an X-ray of my pelvis. It was wonky. She identified two seized joints in my lower back and set about 'adjusting' them. 'Adjusting' is one of those terms like 'precision bombing' that doesn't quite match the reality.

After a dozen sessions, the joints were noticeably more mobile. As were the other two dodgy ones she discovered halfway down my spine. I'm honestly glad about this. I'm sure, in the long term, it will benefit me in all sorts of ways. But as John Maynard Keynes once declared, 'In the long term, you're dead'. And unfortunately, it still hurts me to run.

She took another X-ray of my pelvis. (Good job I'm no longer bothered about breeding. Were I to sire another child, it would probably have six legs and weird, telekinetic powers.)

I am now one of the only patients in Harley Street's famously mercenary community to receive free treatment. I've become a medical challenge, a chiropractic *cause célèbre*. They *will* cure me, whatever it takes, whether I like it or not.

I only wish they would, and I still believe they might.

I'm worried, though, about the wear in my right hip that showed up on the last X-ray. My chiro says it doesn't look bad enough to explain my 'discomfort'. But she also says you can't always tell from an X-ray...

I'm beginning to wonder if my running days are done.

Meanwhile, looking on the bright side, I've heard some encouraging things about knitting in the style of the French.

2006. Sinking and resurfacing

PEOPLE KEEP wishing me a Happy New Year. I wish they wouldn't. There is no more dismal prospect than another 365 episodes of this global soap opera, clearly created by the writers of *EastEnders*.

I don't want a New Year. I can do without another graphic demonstration of man's inhumanity to man, man's inhumanity to Nature and Nature's inhumanity to man. 2005 was like a three-way tag match in which the weather took on two competing teams of morons. All against the cheery background of my declining mobility, thanks to my persistent hip injury.

What I want is a Used Year. 1971 was a good one for me — released album, voted *Man Least Likely To Make 30*, pulled supermodel, generally misbehaved on a cosmic scale. But I'd be more than happy to live someone else's Year instead.

For instance, Jimi Hendrix's 1967 would be amazing. As a matter of fact, I put in a bid for it on eBay but I was pipped at the post. They offered me 1969 instead. It was a lot cheaper, for some reason. And shorter.

For me, 2006 is likely to be not so much a happy New Year as a hippy one. Every conceivable kind of treatment has failed to alleviate my condition — including reiki, divination and a curious sort of voodoo from Java involving lugworms. So I'm gradually resigning myself to a hip replacement.

Fortunately, the price of the hardware has dropped dramatically since the discovery of 400 titanium ball-and-socket sets in Harold Shipman's attic (along with the plans for a crude but serviceable space shuttle).

Nowadays there's a wide variety of alternatives to your bog-standard replacement op. For instance, I've been offered the Birmingham Procedure — a less drastic solution than sawing off the top of your femur and shoving a big spike with a ball on it down the marrow.

Instead, they re-coat the surface of the bone with Teflon. I rejected it, reluctantly, on aesthetic grounds. I'm not even prepared to have the invisible bits of me associated with Noddy Holder. If they'd only called it the Seychelles Procedure, I might have felt differently.

Given that it's only my right hip that's affected, one surgeon has suggested that he simply swaps my legs over. In this way, the slightly worn ball part of one joint will fit into the near-perfect socket of the other, and vice versa.

I pointed out that I'd be left with my feet facing backwards. Running anywhere other than on the track would be extremely dangerous.

He beamed triumphantly. 'Ah! But we could re-orient your head through 180 degrees so that you'd be facing the same way as your feet! I pioneered the procedure myself. I call it the Slough Solution.'

Trawling the internet, I've unearthed an attractive low-cost option. The hip joint is designed to pop in and out so that a single leg can be shared by several individuals, on the same basis as a timeshare property. The system is ideal for relay runners. And providing they run around the track in the same direction, it doesn't even matter if they're of different heights.

The concept is marketed by Lego, the Danish toy company, under the name of Hippo.

So you can see there's quite a lot to consider when planning a major prosthetic adventure like this one. In the end, I shall probably settle for a sword stick and a wide-brimmed hat and cultivate an air of tragic dignity as I limp enigmatically down New Bond Street.

As I pass, people will whisper, 'Who's that dignified yet somehow tragic man with the limp?'

And some wag will reply, 'The limp what?'

In which I confidently predict that the new year will be even worse than the old one

THERE'S NOTHING quite so sad as last year's New Year's resolution. Nothing so eloquently sums up the Human Condition: namely, sunny, effervescent optimism perpetually condemned to dismal failure and disillusionment.

The resolution is a metaphor for life itself. Despite our most heroic endeavours, our finest intentions are ultimately doomed to wither and rot on the compost heap of eternity.

Sorry. I know this doesn't reflect the mood of cheerful anticipation that is conventional at the turning of the year, but I wanted to inject a sober note of realism.

For instance, you may think you're finally going to crack three hours in the 2007 London. But the truth is, you're not. And even if you did, so what? You're still going to die, and your medal will still end up in a Billericay boot sale in a job lot with a brass protractor and a rusty adjustable spanner. And of the three items, the medal will be the least useful.

Which is why, this year, I have decided to make only the most realistic of resolutions. Ones I have at least a faint chance of keeping.

Instead of resolving to train every day, I have pledged to set my alarm for 6am, to look out of the window at the horizontal sleet that lashes the Cambridgeshire tundra from October to May, then to turn over and sleep until 8am.

Rather than promising Seaton I will submit the copy for my column a week before his press day, I will scribble out my 600 words of frivolous gibberish in the snug of The Cat & Hacksaw after a skinful of Trappist duelling lager at 11pm on the night before my deadline.

Also, I have resolved not to enter the Trans 333. This is partly because of the general deterioration in world security. The race started out in Mauritania, which immediately became dangerously unstable. So they moved it to Niger. Ditto. So in 2007, they're planning to hold it in Regent's Park. To me, 90 laps of the boating lake just doesn't have the same cachet as the trackless wastes of the Sahara.

That being said, once the 333 boys move in, the open air theatre will probably fall to Taleban insurgents.

In any case, I'm not fit enough to run 333 centimetres, let alone kilometres. I weighed myself on the I-speak-your-weight machine on York station platform yesterday, and it actually whispered the result to spare my feelings.

This is because I had my hip resurfaced in the summer and then spent six weeks wallowing around the house like an elephant seal, trying to drain the EU wine lake.

When your metabolism has grown accustomed over thirty years to having its arse kicked daily around a five-mile agricultural assault course, and then you suddenly let it off the hook, it simply shuts up shop and eats pies.

Cross-trainers, boxing, spinning, free weights — they may reduce you to a dizzy, incoherent, sweat-soaked wreck. But they don't seem to make you any thinner. On the contrary, you put on great tumescent lumps of muscle which, unless you regularly get sand kicked in your face on the beach, are of no earthly use to anyone.

So now my hip is fine; but if it wasn't for the Evans Outsize maternity smock (the only garment I can get into) I'd look like a sumo wrestler on horse steroids.

And while I'd like to resolve to lose weight in 2007, such a resolution would contravene my new New Year's Resolution resolution, about only resolving to achieve the easily achievable.

So sumo it is. Sayonara.

Running is hard.
But not running is murder

HERE THEY come. The running wounded.

'Hello, John.'

'Morning, Jeffrey. Putting in the miles?'

'Getting back, you know. Slow process.'

'Injured?'

''Fraid so. The old trouble.'

'Not... ?'

'No, no. Achilles. Chronic. Muscle sheath shot. Permanently weakened. Went bang, just like that.'

'Nasty.'

'Yes. Of course, I over-compensated. Quads went into spasm, dragged the patella out of kilter, bloody agony, landed heavily, hairline fracture to the left foot, went sprawling, detached the right hamstring from the pelvic anchor point, bloke went up my back with his spikes. Physio said my spine looked like a camshaft.'

'Bad luck.'

'It's just life, isn't it? You can't grumble. How's the shin?'

'Not so bad since the bone graft. Trust me to find the only badger sett in Oxford Street. They heard the crack in Mothercare. And it was all because I got a blister from the new trainers. So I wore the old pair — the ones with the orthotic insoles for the tendonitis. 'Course, once the inflammation improved, the orthotics made me over-pronate and that aggravated the old business with the gluteus maximus by throwing the right hip out. So when I hit the badger hole I was wrong-footed and Bob's your proverbial.'

Now I'm a fairly unpleasant person at the best of times. But I turn into a real swine when I'm injured, so friends tell me. (Other people's friends. I don't have any.)

I get fat and ugly and aggressive. I snarl at runners in the street. If they're smaller than me, I may try to trip them up. They look so insufferably well-adjusted.

'When injured,' the books say, 'try swimming or cycling or a little easy stretching to keep your muscles in trim.'

Not me. If I can't run, it's Society's fault and someone's got to pay. I might go out and reverse my car down a pedestrian precinct at rush hour. Or set fire to a hospital.

There's no doubt that running makes humanity more tolerable. It files down the teeth, drains the aggression, defuses the impulse to creep up on one's fellow man and smack him about the head with a pipe wrench.

It's no coincidence that all the truly outstanding murders in history were perpetrated before the jogging boom. Take Christie, for instance. He was a handy 5,000-metre man before a groin injury brought about by over-training in hand-me-down carpet slippers.

And Heath, the infamous Acid Bath Murderer, won the National Cross-Country Championships so regularly, he was nicknamed 'Hampstead'. It was only a bad case of shin splints that got him dissolving women instead.

I'm off to see my physio now. I'm not injured — it's just that the off-road season has started and I can't afford proper shoes. So I'm having the spikes screwed directly into my feet.

Fit for purpose.
Confessions of a surrogate husky

IN THE beginning, running was my second-string activity. It was a means to an end — a way of staying fit enough to practise my chosen sport. Which was badger baiting.

I needed to be quicker on my feet than the local police, and the benefits of regular running soon became evident. I was soon fast enough to take up cockfighting as well.

Then, after a year of track work, and following the ban on hunting with dogs, I was able to hire myself out as a surrogate lurcher at hare coursing meets.

Following my example, Ethical Kev (the club vegan) volunteered to replace the hare. Unfortunately he was liberated by hunt saboteurs who bundled him away to an animal sanctuary in Orkney. Now he shares a walled enclosure with a three-legged pit pony and a blind pig.

Of course, it's all very well, running to get fit for another sport. But how do you get fit enough to run? You can so easily get sucked into an endless spiral of athletic pursuits.

In order to run, I joined a gym. To reduce the risk of a seizure on the cross-trainer, I bought a bicycle. I toned up for the bike with a daily round of golf — but only when I'd built up my stamina with a twice-weekly bout of table tennis.

That I was able to survive fifteen consecutive minutes of ping pong was purely down to my nightly shove halfpenny sessions down at the Frog In Formaldehyde.

By the time I got to bait a badger, I was spending twelve hours a day on sports. With no time left to earn a living, I was forced to sell the family home to pay off my shove halfpenny debts.

What's more, it became clear that I wasn't a natural golfer. My handicap stubbornly refused to shrink and in the end I sought the advice of the club professional. We played a round together, during which he studied my technique intently. Over a drink at the 19th, he advised me to saw six inches off my clubs.

'Do you really think that will help my game?' I asked him.

'No,' he replied, 'but you'll find it easier to get them into the dustbin.'

I was remarkably fit, for all that. It was the year I won 'the world's toughest foot race' — the legendary Marathon de Sade. I showed the flagellating monks a clean pair of heels and thanks to the weight training I was able to rip off the head cage before the rats did any real damage to my nose and ears.

Thankfully, my financial situation improved dramatically. The victories of the animal rights movement have worked to my advantage. Since my debut as a hare hound, I've stood in for several other breeds of working dog. Along with four huskies, I pulled a sledge-load of Norwegian explorers to the South Pole and only last week I fought an American Pit Bull in a disused quarry near Billericay.

So now I'm going to extend my repertoire to include other species. In fact, tomorrow I'm off to Andalucia to face El Cordobes, Spain's most celebrated matador.

Adios, amigos.

RUNNING IS NOT STANDING STILL

CERTAIN THINGS, you expect to change. I mean, you'd be unimpressed if your GP diagnosed an excess of the choleric humour and prescribed the application of leeches. [I'd be impressed if I got an appointment before next August – Ed.]

Indeed, it's hard to picture what the world must have been like before key innovations like electric starters and votes for women.

[I've never met a woman with an electric starter – Ed.]

[You haven't lived – AB]

But running? Running is such a basic human function – like breathing, or tax fraud. How could it possibly change?

New running rules 'will be law by 2009'

A leaked report reveals that the government's controversial overhaul of running will reach the statute book before the end of the decade.

One of its provisions will overturn running's most jealously-protected convention. In future, instead of first extending the right foot then superseding it with the left, runners will be required to commence with the left foot, then supersede it with the right.

A spokesman for the pressure group Right First, which opposes the change, commented: 'This is no way to run a country. In fact, it's no way to run, full stop.'

[Get on with it – Ed.]

[All right – AB]

The following section examines the changing face of our sport and wonders whether it has had cosmetic surgery, or if that was just a rumour put about by bitchy detractors.

Suffer, little children...

SEATON CALLED me this morning. 'Can you write me something about running for children?'

'Why ask me?' I replied. 'I've spent most of my adult life running away from them.'

'No, what I mean is, how do you get children to run?'

'Ah!' I said. 'Well, I could certainly write about that — but it'll make for an exceptionally short column. Because, in my experience, the best way to encourage kids to do something is to tell them not to.

'Alternatively, you could wear a severed pig's head and chase them around with a chainsaw. But the former is simpler and less likely to conclude in a gaol sentence. That's it. Job done. Ker-r-r-ching!'

He was clearly disappointed. So here, albeit grudgingly, are a few additional observations.

There are great arguments for starting young. Yehudi Menuhin performed the Brahms violin concerto at the Carnegie Hall when he was just four years old. Aged only nine, Fred Perry made it all the way to the semis at Wimbledon.

However, it doesn't always work that way. My mate Philip Baum displayed early signs of genius at both music and tennis. At the age of three, he was caught playing tennis in the street with his uncle Yehudi's Stradivarius violin. Now he's a clerk in an abattoir.

As for my own childhood, I quickly exhibited an unusual if not unique ability: I could run before I could walk.

The stress nearly killed my parents. I'd be lying in my cot, playing with my Tellytubbies mobile. Then they'd turn their backs for a second and I'd be gone. They'd find me lining up at the start of the South Downs 10, my gripe water bottle brimming with horse steroids dissolved in isotonic sports drink and an elite number pinned to my babygro.

Indeed, the notorious case of the four-year-old Indian marathon runner underlines the dangers of introducing youngsters to the sport too early. Children's joints are still only partially developed, and prolonged periods of repetitive loading, as in running, can produce permanent damage to these sensitive tissues.

On the other hand, kids' bones are remarkably flexible, which gives them a real advantage on the bends. So parents, use your common sense.

In the domestic context, a fit child can be an enormous boon to a household. 'Be a love, Ronan — just nip back and get my fags. They're on top of the jumbo pork pie beside the wine rack.' Or: 'See that gentleman over there, Lucretia? The one with the fat black wallet sticking out of his pocket? Wouldn't it be fun to run over and bring it back to Daddy?'

There was a time when a child's athletic prowess lent prestige to a family.

'How did Whitney get on at Sports Day?'

'Not too bad. She came third in the Three-Legged Javelin. How about Verona?'

'Same as usual. First in the Under-Elevens' Knife Fighting, the Underwater Wheelbarrow Race and the Iron Child triathlon. Oh, and her team won the One-A-Side Rugby. Bless her.'

Now, of course, any activity that is remotely competitive is considered politically incorrect. This, and the shameful sell-off of school playing fields, is strangling the grass roots of the nation's future sporting excellence.

At my daughter's school, they've got around this by integrating sport into the academic course work prescribed in the National Curriculum. For instance, when they did the Romans, her class built and raced their own chariots, and two of her friends were partially eaten by lions.

Just one of the many advantages of a private education, I suppose.

In which I give the London a long-overdue overhaul

I JUST watched the London Marathon on telly. Let's own up — it's hardly a spectator sport is it? For sheer, mind-numbing tedium, it's one rung below Crown Green Bowling and only just above Formula One.

By the way, have you ever wondered about Formula Two? It must be so cosmically dull, it has to take place secretly under cover of darkness, like badger baiting and sex.

As for the Marathon, the only interesting sections of the field are the first five runners and the last ten. There you will witness respectively the breathtaking, bestial brutality of high-level athletics, and the spectacular type of incontinence induced by a total lack of training and a diet of Pot Noodles.

They should equip the last 5,000 competitors with brooms or, better, those sticks with spikes on. If they insist on keeping the marshals hanging about till midnight, the least they can do is pick up the litter. That's a purely personal view, of course.

Talking of spectator sports, the spectators always seem to me far more interesting than the runners. They're even more pitiful than the vegetables who, like me, switch over from the Paint Drying Channel (number 136 on Freeview) to watch the race.

Imagine standing in the front row for three hours with your lumpy headscarf and no teeth, screaming, 'Gaworn! Get them knees up!' while you thrust pork pies and semolina pudding at dehydrated, near-delusional runners.

Then imagine being in the second row.

What makes them do that? What faint glimmer of counterfeit enjoyment can it possibly afford them?

All that being said, I did notice something very different this year. At first, I dismissed it as a hallucination. Then I looked again, more closely, and there was simply no getting away from it. There, flaunting herself to the world, was a runner dressed in shorts, trainers and — wait for it — *a running vest.*

I must tell you, friends, that I was shocked and appalled. Call me old-fashioned, but where was the rhinoceros head? Where were the stilettos and the tray of martinis? Why wasn't she running backwards in a clown outfit?

I suppose it was beyond the boundaries of her stunted imagination to don even the simplest suit of Thracian gladiator's armour? to knock up a rudimentary replica of Neil Armstrong's moon suit? Or even to crochet a bog standard Aztec chariot to drag behind her?

Standards have slipped since my day, I can tell you. Judging by the state of some of the competitors, you'd think this was a running race.

Frankly, turning up for the London in skimpy athletics kit is like attending a Royal garden party in a bikini.

In which I take a stroll along the catwalk. Or rather, catrun

IT IS with a sinking heart that I watch our once-noble sport descend into the candyfloss world of fashion.

When I took my first turn around London's South Circular Road, the total value of my kit did not exceed £2.50.

It consisted of Dunlop Green Flash plimsolls, paint-spattered tracksuit bottoms, an M&S vest and a bobble hat bearing the logo of a firm of electrical engineers in Macclesfield.

The shoes provided no cushioning at all but they did protect my feet from the broken hypodermics that served as route markers between Balham and Brixton.

While my skiing friends in the banking sector were crowning their Volvos with fibreglass coffins, my Ford Corsair was declared a technical write-off because the cost of mending the windscreen wipers exceeded its book value.

Running for me was a statement — two fingers up to the tennis players and the scuba divers and the golfers and the clay pigeoners. I wore the same shirt for weeks and the same shoes for years. I looked like a tramp and smelled like a goat in June.

The sports/casual movement was still just a gleam in Mr Nike's eye, so there were no fancy brands to aspire to. When your clothes became too filthy for gardening, you went running in them.

There were no women. Running was an excuse for morose,

disappointed men to slip the snare of domestic drudgery for an hour of monosyllabic grunting at their fellow misanthropes.

Gradually, the complexion of the sport has changed. In fact, it has undergone radical cosmetic surgery.

Twenty years ago, the accepted voice of running was *Athletics Weekly*, which more resembled a trainspotter's notebook than a magazine. For sheer glamour and aspiration, it fell somewhere between *Glass's Guide* and the tide tables.

Then along came *Runner's World* with its glorious technicolour photography. And while it wouldn't fit into the key pouch of your Ron Hill hurdling shorts, at least you didn't need a microscope to read it.

There were ads for shoes as technologically sophisticated as the Space Shuttle and slightly more expensive. Suddenly, you needed to be well-heeled to be… well-heeled.

The ads were sumptuous. To get juvenile delinquents in Middlesbrough to spend £100 on footwear made for £2 by juvenile delinquents in Jakarta, it had to look like a million dollars.

The global economics of the sports shoe began to resemble that of the cocaine trade, with a vast differential between the cost of production and the UK street value.

Then came polypropylene shirts and 1,000 Mile Socks and Gore-Tex jackets and heart rate monitors. The floodgates were open. Running has rapidly out-stripped golf and the gym as the healthy activity of choice among C-list celebrities. Anybody who's anybody does five miles a day (or *says* they do, dahling), it's so good for the sense of well-being, it's so like *totally* de-stressing…

Now it isn't just an economic model that running shares with Class A drugs — it's a clientele.

The gender balance has shifted. There are at least as many women running as blokes. Indeed, today, the delineation between sport and fashion is so blurred that Frank Warren is planning a lycraweight bout between Paula Radcliffe and Naomi Campbell.

Running's fashion revolution has extended even to the sleepy heartland of rural England. My own club has invested in a five-kilometre catwalk on Royston Heath and our chairman won't get out of bed on a Sunday morning for less than £10,000.

Where's it all going to end?

[Here — Ed.]

Out with the new, in with the old

IF YOU want a snapshot of what life will be like here tomorrow, look at America today.

This is as true, now, of running as it was of TV trials, designer drugs and the use of semi-automatic weapons by the under-nines.

The snapshot is a chilling one — perhaps most so when we look at the veteran sport.

The most serious disabled athletes have often chosen to have useless limbs amputated to enhance performance — after all, a non-functional leg is nothing but a weighty encumbrance.

But a grisly practice is now being adopted by increasing numbers of vets, who argue that the only bodily organs to be measurably and irreversibly *improved* by running are the heart, lungs and veins which together make up the circulatory system. (Brain power has never been associated with running ability — except in the negative sense that athletic achievement varies inversely to intelligence.)

And so these fanatical old athletes are having the greater part of their bodies removed, leaving only a huge pair of lungs, an enormous heart and a tangled mass of tiny, noodle-like capillaries.

The surgery, completely illegal in the United States, is carried out mostly in the old Soviet republics where the application of a sufficient number of dollars will procure virtually anything.

The result: the grotesque abomination which the American press has dubbed 'the Heart Cart' — a compact, four-wheeled buggy, driven entirely by the hydraulic power of the heart, sometimes to speeds in excess of fifty miles per hour.

Despite a horrified outcry from the public, the American athletics authorities have so far been unable to come up with a banning formula which wouldn't also disqualify cyclists who shave their leg hairs. And so the sight of these ghoulish little contraptions is becoming ever more common at race events around the nation.

It could never happen here, you say. No? Then let me remind you of last year's Frinton & District MegaVet Marathon, at which all the stewards were qualified geriatric psychiatrists, and private hip replacement clinics vied for business at the twenty-mile mark.

It was also the first event I can recall where the feeding stations offered free dental fixative.

At least the AAA has had the good sense to ban the use of Running Buggies. Inspired, perhaps, by elderly or obese golfers, some veteran runners claimed that the use of small, electrically-powered vehicles to transport them around the longer courses, was no more an infringement of the rules than travelling from green to green in a Golf Buggy.

It all ended in tragedy, of course, during the Saga Chelsea Hospital 10, when octogenarian road rage combined with myopic vision to produce a bloodbath of epic proportions.

Commentators say that the famous *Ben Hur* chariot race paled into insignificance as two hundred veterans, high on tonic wine and Night Nurse, careered round Hyde Park Corner, the clash of their sharpened Zimmer frames echoing harshly in the clear, October air.

In which I calculate the statistical likelihood of dying while running the marathon

IT ONLY takes one competitor to drop dead during a marathon and the nation resounds to the triumphal baying of the running sceptics.

'There! Proof that running's bad for you, and that eagerly pursuing obesity on a diet of lager, Capstan Full Strength and potato wedges in sour cream will ensure that you attain a ripe and robust old age!'

But just think about it: 30,000 people run the London. Assuming an average finishing time of four hours, the event takes up 2,000 person/days. So it's astonishing, statistically, that dozens of runners don't snuff it during the race. I'm surprised that there isn't a fleet of 'sweep hearses' coasting along at the rear to hoover up the cadavers.

Based on an analysis of the entrants' demographics, you'd expect the principal cause of death to be, not heart attack nor stroke, but plain old age.

These days, I feel old when I attend a business meeting, order a drink in a West End bar or watch *Top Of The Pops*. But not when I go running. Increasingly I'm surrounded by silver locks, skinny white legs and porcelain dentistry. And I'm not talking about shuffling geriatrics, late into their dotage. These characters are regularly knocking up times that put my 15-year-old PB to shame.

There was one bloke in my old London club, I remember, who took up jogging at 58 and a year later crossed the line in 2:50 — then collapsed with a cardiac arrest. A year later, he was back to pare two minutes off his time. At 70, he packed in running and taught himself to play the violin.

It was the fast movement of the Brahms concerto that finally did for him. (But did you hear anyone ranting on about the dangers inherent in German music of the Romantic era?)

Why is it that our sport so intensely irritates those who don't partake in it?

Simple. Jealousy. They suspect, secretly, that we runners have achieved immortality.

The marathon has only been a mass-participation event for twenty years. The full implications for runners' longevity are only now becoming apparent. But it's possible that an entire section of the population has earned everlasting life, unfading physical beauty, immunity to the ravages of disease and the degenerative encroachments of temporal decay.

Have we not run up Mount Olympus to join the gods? Are we not indestructible, invincible and unbearably lovely to gaze upon? No wonder the Lard Arses hate us.

Of course, we don't let on about the arthritic knees, the crushed discs, the bleeding nipples, the lost toenails, the compressed sciatic nerves, the ruptured Achilles tendons, the chronic hamstring strains and the varicose veins. Not to mention the stunted careers, wrecked marriages and neglected children.

But then, why let the truth spoil a good story?

Talking of children, mine have taken to asking me when I'm going to give it all up and behave like a regular, dignified old fart.

Never, I reply. But I suppose there must come a time when I'll decide to take up the balalaika or full-contact whist instead. It's just very hard to imagine. Will this be the last pair of shoes I cadge off Fishpool? Will I ever run across the Sahara again? Will I once more witness sunrise on the golden snows of Kancgenjunga?

The writer Jorge Luis Borges knew he wouldn't live forever when he realised that even if he started right away, he wouldn't be able to re-read all the books in his library before he fell off his perch.

Well, if you're over forty, just turn to the *Runner's World* Race Diary and you'll know what he means.

The last of the summer whiners

I ROSE early this morning, as I have done every Sunday for twenty years. The old hip was a bit stiff and a familiar twinge in the left calf reminded me that these days I ought to sit down before putting on my running shoes.

I sifted through a heap of faded T-shirts, finally settling for the 1984 South Downs 10. A moth had dined extensively on the course map, cutting Brighton off from Hove. Nevertheless, as I eased the fragile garment over my head, I could almost smell the wild flowers on the high chalk downs and hear the unceasing piccolo of larksong. Nothing takes you back like an old shirt.

There were no larks this morning. The day was veiled by a curtain of drizzle and even Oscar, the World's Fittest Dog, looked dubious as he sniffed at the open door. I noticed for the first time a peppering of grey about his muzzle.

As I limped down the hill, I was overtaken by a pack of athletic snails.

Nowadays it takes a good ten minutes before the sharp pain in my right knee subsides to a dull, manageable ache. In an attempt to work around this chronic injury I have devised a weird, contorted gait, like that of Quasimodo tip-toeing barefoot across a lawn of razor blades.

I shivered. An enormous percentage (I forget just how enormous) of the body's heat is lost through the head. And since my pate is now virtually threadbare, I really should invest in a woolly hat.

I glanced at my watch. If the boys were on schedule, they should pour out of Big Wood in around three minutes.

They were late, and when they did appear, they hardly poured. Three feeble old Harriers can't *pour*. Pouring was what we did in the Eighties, when thirty would show up for the Sunday Morning Run and there was a Fast Group and a Middle Group and a Slow Group, and the Slow Group was twice as fast as today's sorry bunch.

'Ah! Good morrow, Mister Blackford!' At least Norman managed a semblance of cheery bonhomie. Harry just grunted at the dog and Big Ron barely raised a grimace.

'You're slow today,' I replied, as I tagged on to their flank.

'It's me back,' muttered Big Ron. 'It hasn't been right since London.'

Good Lord, someone had actually run a race! Perhaps there was hope for us yet!

'You never told me you were doing the London, Ron. How did you get on?'

'Not this year,' he snapped. '1996.'

'1994, Ron,' corrected Harry. 'It was the year I did my Achilles.'

We wheezed and hobbled rheumatically along the little path by the river as we had done since before our children were born. The talk, once of weddings and christenings, was now of hospitals and funerals.

My mind drifted back twenty years to when dear old Welsh Rob would regale us with tales of his wild nights on the town with Psycho Terry. 'Trouble is, Terry can't take his drink. After thirteen pints, he just snaps.'

I caught sight of a small, wizened figure in the distance. 'Is that Brian?'

'What — Brian Baldry?'

'No, Brian what's-his-name. Hernia Brian.'

'Brian Bignull.'

'Hello, boys,' croaked Brian as he approached. 'Mind if I join you? I've just seen Malcolm Turby. Remember Malc? He's had to pack it in. Angina. He told me about Maurice.'

'What about him?' I asked, my heart already sinking.

'Gone! Just like that!' Hernia Brian snapped his fingers. 'Embolism, they said. Only fifty-eight.'

That did it. 'Oscar!' I called. 'Come on! We're going home.'

Harry smirked. 'Pace too hot for you, is it?'

'No, mate,' I replied. 'I've got a bloke coming over to install the stairlift. See you next Sunday!'

In which I embark upon a running tour de farce

QUICK UPDATE on economics and society and the role of the individual therein: nation in post-industrial decline, manufacturing base usurped by tiger nations, consequential growth of service sector.

That's what they tell us, and who am I to disagree? I'll tell you: I'm an averagely-intelligent citizen with a degree in economics. And I still don't get it. If we're just serving one another, where's the money going to come from? It'll just go round and round, getting gradually less as little bits of it get lost down the back of the sofa.

And this assumes that we can all come up with ways of serving. *Runner's World*, for example, provides a priceless service to you, its readers. But is it reciprocated? Ask not what your magazine can do for you, but what you can do for your magazine.

Anyway, some Italian running chancer has come up with a new service offering (or 'scam') that might give you lot the opportunity to 'put something back', as we smug, middle-class tossers say.

I've always maintained that running is merely tourism for the time-poor. And now this wily Continental has turned my theory into a business plan. For a mere £50, he will whisk you around Rome for an hour on a running tour of historic monuments.

It's a brilliant concept. You do your favourite pastime, then you get paid as if it's your job. Handsomely, too. Fifty quid an hour puts you right up there with Members of Parliament and benefit fraudsters.

Once I'm cured of the injury to which I have sworn never to refer again (but which has resulted from the degeneration of the cartilage buffer between the head of the right femur and the pelvic socket and which can be alleviated, though obviously not reversed, by regular physiotherapy from Alison in Hauxton near Cambridge) I plan to lead running tours of Machu Picchu on the same commercial basis.

However, until then, I'm experimenting with a few dry runs in Middlesbrough. I have recorded my commentary for training purposes, and I here present a transcript of a typical excursion:

Hi. I'm Andy, your guide for today. What's your name? How's that? Y-L-Z-C-G-N-C? Right, well, I'll call you Bob.

First, a bit of housekeeping. Sorry? *House... Keep... Ping.*

No, we're not going to iron clothes. It's a figure of speech. What? *Fig... Ger...* Look, forget it. I — run. You — follow. Savvy?

HELLO-O! Wait! Just slow down! Dear Christ! Try to stay within earshot, there's a good chap. Now, see that fine, imposing church over there? No, not that. That's the abattoir.

And see over... Bob! COME BACK!... That's the Arndale Centre. It's got a Matalan and a Costcutter and an Oxfam — the lot. What? Quite new, yes. 1976. Ish.

That? That's the river Tees. You get salmon in there nowadays. No, *salmon*. The fish. You're thinking of salmonella.

OI! YOU! STOP! This isn't a bloody race! Just wait there, please, while I have a little lie down. I mean, what's wrong with you? I was trying to point out the little grassy bit where the Cub hut was before Bagser McBride set fire to it, and you just charged off. Honestly, you've no idea what you're missing. I bet you don't even *have* Cubs in Slovakia...

Still, although it took a while to explain how the developers accidentally unearthed the mass cattle grave on the dockside and the smell forced the emergency evacuation of Teesside, it was worth it, just to see his little face light up.

All good practice for Machu Picchu.

In which I recall the birth of a noble and unique sporting institution

IF I had a pound for every time I've been asked the secret of a successful running club, I'd have three pounds.

The reputation of my own outfit has been eclipsed, unfairly, by the giants of the sport — the Haringeys, the Morpeths, etc.

This is partly a function of size, of course: Haringey currently has a membership of 1,230 compared to Numbskulls AC's three. Or four if you count Oscar the dog.

Consequently our trophy room is a little thin on Olympic medals. There's a chipped porcelain mug I won in the 1984 Hampstead Heath Race and a sort of laminated bone thing awarded to Oscar for finishing a dog-and-master event called the Canine 9k, in which the first vet to cross the line really was a vet.

Not a lot to show for thirty years of sweat, pain and humiliation.

Still a club doesn't live by gongs alone and all told, being a Numbskull has proved an immensely rich and rewarding experience.

This I attribute to the club's founding principle: that under no circumstances are members allowed to discuss running. Not training schedules, stress fractures nor groin strains. Not shoes, breathable polyester jackets, athletic support brassieres, 1000 Mile Socks, heart monitors nor isotonic energy drinks.

Also forbidden are tangential topics such as vitamin supplements, weight management, longevity, carbohydrate loading, Tartan track compound and the omnibus edition of *The Archers* (which inevitably clashes with the long Sunday run).

This leaves only a small number of approved topics. Historically, the most popular have been drinking, sex, *Little Britain* and drinking.

Founder Member Rob Wright sparked a controversy by introducing the subject of cycling. He'd once taken part in a road race, he said, during which he'd crashed through a fence and careered down a hill into someone's garden, finally bursting through a set of French windows and into their living room. Miraculously, he escaped injury. 'Funnily enough,' he told us, 'it turned out to be a friend of my mum.'

Then a bitter argument ensued among the membership (me and Roger) as to whether cycling constituted an acceptable topic of conversation. Roger said that as an athletic pursuit it was associated, if only obliquely, with running. My position was that since cycling didn't involve contact between the ground and the foot, it was profoundly differentiated from running and was consequently a permissible subject. Neither managed to persuade the other. Eventually, we got bored and the talk shifted back to drinking.

The Conversation Rule was formulated in response to my experience of joining a large London club. I'd turned up early for a weekend run, to introduce myself. I was comprehensively ignored.

Undaunted, I made straight for the front of the pack and insinuated myself between a couple of balding men in expensive designer kit. I bade them a cheery hullo, but they talked across me as if I didn't exist.

'How's your dorg?'

'Corinthia? She's absolutely fine. She's an old lady, of course, nowadays. She can just about manage five miles. And how's your dorg?'

'Barnaby's getting on a bit, too.'

'Aren't we all?'

'Not like Barnaby. He's 105 in dorg years. But he still manages a couple of miles around Sandy Heath of a Saturday.'

'Good show!'

Then there was silence, broken only by the wind whistling through forests of nasal hair.

'My dorg... ', I began. Their faces froze. 'My dorg's had his hind legs amputated. But he still enjoys a drag around the park.'

You'd have thought I'd advocated the compulsory debauching of nuns. I dropped back discreetly. This, I concluded, was probably not the club for me.

And the rest is history.

From string vest to sports bra. I meditate upon the rise of unisex running

RUNNING WAS invented by men for getting away from dinosaurs. It was a deadly serious business. Those who couldn't master this new skill, or spent their time moaning about their chronic hamstring niggles, were eaten. There was a satisfying, Darwinian inevitability about it.

Running remained an exclusively masculine affair for a million years. And then it suddenly occurred to some woman somewhere (probably California, home of all unnatural behaviour) that she could run, too.

There was no excuse. Not a velociraptor in sight.

Since then it's all gone horribly wrong. Men's role as steely-sinewed hunter-gatherers has been rendered increasingly risible. Compared to the lithe, fleet-footed nymphs who slip past us on gossamer wings at the 25-mile mark, leaving only an impression of elfin grace and a faint whiff of Issey Miyake, it is *men* who are the dinosaurs.

You lumber along, sweating and snorting in your string vest, your frayed athletic support chafing beneath your old Ron Hill hurdle shorts and your legs an intricate relief map of scar tissue and varicose veins.

You grit your teeth, silence your screaming tendons and press heroically on. And then you're swept into the ditch by an exotic hummingbird in tiny pink trainers, her svelte form caressed by a turquoise Lycra leotard that would pass muster in Stringfellows.

You mouth some half-hearted protest, but she doesn't hear you — she's listening to *Summer Of Love, Ayia Napa '06* on her iPod. Her immaculate hair sways in mesmerising counterpoint to her hips. Not a single drop of perspiration dares sully the radiance of her perfect skin.

Even were you so brutishly insensitive to her charms, so gruff and curmudgeonly as to demand why she'd cut you up and shoved you into a drainage culvert, she would likely turn with a smile more devastating than a rocket-propelled grenade and purr, 'Because I'm worth it.'

So where does that leave us blokes (aside from up to our necks in pondweed and old Stella cans)?

It seems to me that we have two options. We can either embrace (though not literally) the arrival of women at the start line and see it as part of Evolution. After all, when they turned up in the workplace, we gradually accepted innovations like functioning lavatories. And we don't really miss the pin-ups from *Peaches — For Lovers Of Huge Breasted Women* that once adorned every male's office wall. Do we?

Maybe you don't have to be a Neanderthal to enjoy running. Maybe the sport's transmutation into a linear version of Step Aerobics is merely part of a general process of civilisation.

Alternatively, we could dig in. We could resist the softening influence of the female and push ever outwards into a Gothic penumbra of the brutal, the punishing and the plain unhygienic.

We will race only in marshes. Or over the high passes of the Karakoram, barefoot, with only maggots for sustenance. To the bland, urban half-marathon, we will introduce an element of hand-to-hand fighting. The Cabbage Patch Garrotte and Machete 10 will become a regular feature in the running calendar of every male.

However, before we raise the stakes, we'd better be absolutely sure we'd win. I know women who are absolute naturals with a garrotte. They may look like butterflies in their pastel kit, but give them the slightest provocation and they'll kick-box your brains out.

Imagine being trounced in the Trans-Chechnya Razor Wire Challenge by some sylph-like domestic science teacher from Surbiton. It doesn't bear thinking about.

So pass the legwarmers, darling, I'm popping out for a jogette.

RUNNING AROUND THE WORLD

A RUNNING race can be many different things, depending how far up the field you start.

At the front end, it's somewhere between a ballet and a night at the dog track. Together, the first twenty athletes weigh less than John Prescott.

Pawing the ground and snorting, the pack impatiently awaits the start.

The air is sharp with Deep Heat and slick with Vaseline. Such is the tension that one twang of a taut hamstring is enough to trigger a false start.

At the rear end (sic) pantomime cows collide with chainsaw-juggling clowns and deep sea waiters. The gallows humour is raucous and intoxicating.

After six hours it will have subsided into the dumb misery of lactic cramps and the delirium of dehydration.

And this is only the Twickenham 10k — the outer limit of my own ambitions until 1994 when *Runner's World* secretly drew straws and told me I'd picked the short one.

From then on, whenever the organisers of some lunatic Ultra running escapade offered the magazine a free place, I would find myself volunteered for it.

I mustn't grumble. Yes I must. I've been to places no rational person would visit except at gunpoint.

The high point of one trip was seeing Papillon's signature in the cement floor of a punishment cell.

If he knew I'd gone there voluntarily, he'd have wet himself.

A bottle. Lips. Now.
In which I contemplate the heart of darkness

RIGHT, NOW I'm getting nervous. Tomorrow I leave for French Guiana and as usual I've left everything to the last minute. The list of kit seems to have stretched overnight.

It includes 250mg of ciprofloxacin hydrochloride, 10mg of Buscopan, 250mg of cephradine and two pieces of string.

Now the drugs aren't a problem — it's far too late to buy them now and I don't suppose I'll miss them until the first ghastly symptoms of Green Monkey Fever start to appear.

But the string is a real puzzle. I say 'string' but at a suggested gauge of 15mm, 'hawser' would be more accurate. You could moor an aircraft carrier with 15mm string. And there's no clue as to what it's for.

Perhaps it's for rigging up my hammock (kindly provided by the organisers). But equally it could be for strangling jaguars, abseiling down canyons or hoisting myself out of viper pits.

There's also a darkly enigmatic warning that aspirin is not available in Guiana because of Dengue. Who in buggery is Dengue? Some local warlord, I can only presume, with a penchant for misappropriating mild, over-the-counter palliatives.

My state of increasing anxiety has even permeated into my sleep, expressing itself in a series of strange and disturbing dreams. For instance, last week I dreamed that I'd written *Lord Of The Rings* — but when I woke up, I realised I'd only been Tolkien in my sleep.

Then last night, I dreamed I was lying on my back in a shabby hotel room, staring at a slow fan churning through a tepid soup of sweat and stale air.

The door burst open. It was Them, of course. One more mission, they told me. Just one. It seemed that our editor, Seaton, had gone up-river. He had failed to return and after some months, bizarre rumours began to percolate out from the interior: rumours of dark rites, of blood and sacrifice. Blackford, they said, you must run up-country into the very heart of darkness and persuade Seaton to give himself up.

For days I jogged along forest tracks with no sustenance except two pieces of string and a sackful of unpronounceable medicines. I was occasionally the target of poison dart attacks by fanatical followers of the execrable Dengue.

Eventually, I came across a clearing in the jungle — a place filled with a dreadful silence and marked out with human skulls. In fact, it bore an uncanny resemblance to the advertising department of *Runner's World*. In the middle of the clearing, on an ancient Aztec throne, sat Seaton.

Slowly he turned his enormous, shaven head towards me. The firelight danced on his oiled torso. My mouth was dry with fear and a terrible thirst. I fell to my knees and pointing to my mouth I croaked, 'A bottle! Lips! Now!'

We talked until dawn. He seemed genuinely pleased to see me. It seems he'd observed the big cats that are native to the Amazonian rainforest and, perceiving a commercial opportunity, had established Guiana's first jaguar dealership.

These restless nights have done nothing for my training. I keep telling myself that if I can run 100 miles across Jordan in 48 hours, then the same distance through a mere jungle and over six days should constitute an absolute stroll.

Still, I've made a serious effort over the past few days. For one thing, I've cancelled the cab that normally drives me the four hundred metres to the Effes Turkish restaurant for my lunchtime kebab and belly dancing demonstration.

In fact, my body is a temple. Unfortunately, I fear it may be the Temple of Doom.

Rats, bats and spiders.
One Amazon week

OVER THE years, I've recommended a handful of races that I've deemed suitable for the deranged.

The Raid Amazonie, however, is not recommended. It's compulsory.

When (not if) you finally complete this fantastic adventure in the virgin rainforest of the Amazon Basin, you will return filthy but purified, humbled and yet somehow exalted.

To a veteran of the Jordan Desert Cup — 100-odd miles in less than two days — the Raid had sounded like a doddle. The same distance, but spread over six days; your kit lugged from camp to camp by obliging Guianans in canoes; your food provided at the beginning and end of the day; the enveloping comfort of a hammock at night. But I hadn't taken into account the climate or the terrain. To give you some idea, the first 10k of Day Five took me over two hours.

Not that I was aware of that when we started out along the bank of the majestic Maroni River, the natural boundary between Surinam and French Guiana. Even at 8am, the heat was fierce and the humidity 95 per cent. The trail led us through rambling villages of huts, raised on stilts against the ravages of termites. Delegations of solemn, naked children watched us pass.

Who is 'us'? A handful of Guyanan nationals; some French expats (Guyana is still a colony of France); a seven-strong team in training for the forthcoming Raid Gauloises in Vietnam; a lone, plucky Portuguese woman called Celia; Scottish Jeremy; and myself.

On either side of the trail, there rose a solid wall of vegetation — palms and ferns and vivid, flowering shrubs. Then, abruptly, we veered off the track and through the wall.

The forest is a vast, natural cathedral. Shafts of dim green light penetrate the vaulted canopy a hundred feet above. Below, there rages a frantic, chaotic battle for survival. Each tree is a ladder to the light, entwined with creepers. And upon these arm-thick vines cling parasitic ferns, lichens and velvet carpets of moss. The air hums with the static of insects and resonates to the musical calls of invisible birds.

Jeremy peered up into the mysterious shadows of the canopy. 'You know those birds of paradise? They're supposed to be fantastically beautiful and everything, but I just think they look gay.'

'That's what 19 years in the TA has done to you,' I observed. 'Dulled your aesthetic sensitivity.'

Jeremy and I hadn't met before the race, but as the only two Britons in a sea of French and Guianans, we'd quickly formed a bond that strengthened, as bonds do under such extreme conditions, during our six days in the forest. And they were extreme.

At the end of Day Four, in the middle of a torrential downpour, we arrived by canoe at the village of Pin-Pin. The roof of the communal shelter leaked prodigiously, and so we poor old Brits were re-housed in a forlorn shanty on the edge of the clearing. We christened it Dengue Cottage, after the horrific haemorrhagic fever endemic to the region.

Alain Gestin, the race organiser, tried to make the best of things: 'One of you can sleep here, inside, and one outside on the veranda.' But his sales patter did not gain credibility from the bats fluttering about his head, nor from the corpses of the gigantic spiders that hung in ropes of web from the ridge beam.

We'd spent the day before the race in the town of St Laurent, the principal tourist attraction of which is the gaol that once contained Henri Charrière — better known as Papillon.

We visited his dank and tiny cell, and I can honestly say that it lay in the same real estate bracket as Dengue Cottage. (Though to be fair, Papillon was banged up for seven years — we just had to manage a single night.)

Jeremy sensibly elected to sleep outside. He inflated a number of balloons (I never did fathom why he'd brought balloons to the rainforest) in a futile bid to lend the shack an air of gaiety.

We spent the evening chatting to the locals around a spluttering oil lamp or bennie, in the local language of Tacki Tacki. At one point we answered a shout from the forest, and watched some men with torches and rifles trying to shoot a porcupine. It stared balefully down at us from its perch high in the mahogany, before eventually strolling nonchalantly away into the night.

We turned in at 10pm, only to be woken at 2am by a violent storm. Above the thunder of the rain on the thatch, I became aware of a furtive scuttling — the unmistakable sound of little rodent claws on rotten floorboards. Actually, not so little and not so furtive. Should I hoist myself upright in the hammock and switch on my head-lamp, I wondered. After some agonising, I decided that ignorance was bliss. It's a testament to the difficulty of the day's run that I was able to fall asleep, besieged as I was by rats, bats and plate-sized arachnids.

An hour later, at 3am, I was woken by an alarm call from an abnormally strident rooster. Had I not had four days of running in my legs, had I not been an aspirant Bodhisattva, and had it not been 3am, I would have strangled that bloody cock. Still, I felt its time would come.

Even the luxuries were extreme. Breakfast on the Raid is a fantastical thing, to be compared favourably with the miracle of the loaves and fishes. Only the French could engineer the arrival of fresh croissants and coffee at a location as remote as the frozen moons of Uranus. At one stopover, an abandoned military outpost deep in the forest, there appeared 40 chocolate eclairs.

It was all so very French. At the end of one day, after an arduous, hilly thrash along open tracks in the blistering sun, we pitched up at Camp Voltaire — a picturesque auberge with manicured lawns set in the loop of a cool, clear bathing stream.

The Camp sported a bar and a first-rate restaurant — decidedly surreal given its location, 40 miles from the nearest metalled road. It was the Gallic version of Hotel California.

That evening, we gorged ourselves on a magnificent duck terrine followed by a casserole. I asked Jean-Marc, runner and local GP, what was in the stew and received the halting reply, 'Not ze chicken, but ze fazeer of ze chicken!' I didn't understand until he fished out of the tureen the head of a cockerel, complete with coxcomb.

We slept soundly in our hammocks that night, in a large, open barn. I woke at dawn to the gibbering of baboons, punctuated disconcertingly by the joyful yells of a woman in the throes of coital ecstasy. I remember hoping sleepily that the sounds were not connected.

Later, Jackie — the proprietor of Camp Voltaire — stood before the huge and disarmingly frank mural of a Bacchanalian orgy that adorned the dining room. 'The British won't come here,' he grumbled. 'They think the place is alive with scorpions and poisonous snakes. They are mad. The forest is paradise.'

It was impossible to argue with him. You will encounter more discomfort running through a copse in Surrey than in the Amazon rainforest. There are no nettles, no brambles and precious few insects (although I was twice assaulted by *geppes* — vicious little wasps who adopt the view that attack is the best means of defence).

The one natural barrier that you won't encounter in Virginia Water is the *crique*. You'd think that the rainforest would be flat. But it isn't, it's heartbreakingly hilly. And at the foot of every hill is a *crique* — a sluggish, opaque stream — occasionally spanned by a narrow, mossy log, but mostly not.

My technique was to wade in until the mud reached my thighs and the water reached my chin. Then I'd swim. This was fine in the remotest reaches of the forest — but down by the Maroni, with its sprawling villages entirely innocent of modern sewage systems, the water took on a distinctly turgid quality. That I was probably wading through the ancient excreta of King Axapopacatel The Doubly Incontinent was scant consolation when the malodorous slime bubbled in my ears and nostrils.

The 'Long Day' followed our sojourn at Camp Voltaire. The day is long indeed. It's down as 45k, but all distances in the forest are immeasurable, and I'd put this one closer to 30 miles than a marathon.

I made the decision to walk the bulk of it. It was my first (and who knows, perhaps my last) encounter with a tropical rainforest. I knew I could either run it — eyes down, constantly monitoring the path for vines and roots — or adopt a brisk, striding walk and enjoy the luxury of looking up and around me, and of stopping to take photographs.

The forest presents a strange contradiction. It is a place of stately repose, of stasis, imbued with an almost architectural majesty. And yet it is at once poised in a state of hair-trigger readiness: there's a sense of breathless anticipation, as if the fragile calm were about to explode in a riot of primaeval violence. But at no time, even when alone, did it seem in the least threatening. On the contrary, I felt perfectly at home, somehow, as if I were quite where I ought to be.

Is it too fanciful to believe that, because our ancestors walked the woods, this unique landscape of shapes, smells and sounds is so deeply etched into our collective memory that it still seems hauntingly familiar today? After all, my Belgian Shepherd dog hasn't shepherded a Belgian sheep for ten generations at least, and yet he's wildly excited at the sight of anything cloven-hoofed and woolly.

It was with such philosophical conjecture that I idled away much of the final three days and the last moments before I slipped into an exhausted sleep at the end of the last day. A tide of celebratory rum cocktails gently engulfed me. The Milky Way seemed to dangle just inches from my face against a black, velvet sky. Nightjars cooed soothingly in the soaring canopy — while down below, in our shelter, an eight-inch venomous centipede climbed stealthily into Jeremy's rucksack.

But that's another story.

An epic tale of raw courage and resilience, set in the badlands of the American West.
Man vs Grass Seed

A WORD in your ear if you're visiting the USA: never accept advice from fat, back-slapping men in shopping malls.

Buying a pair of jeans shouldn't require a doctorate in the physical sciences. And yet I was persuaded by this… this garrulous, vastly-obese shit-fer-brains to sit for an hour in a bath of near-scalding water, wearing my new Levis.

Part Two of his advice involved me mincing and grimacing around our holiday location, a 'dude ranch', while the jeans dried on me. They were supposed to shrink until they hugged my contours perfectly. They never did — but they *did* dye my legs bright blue.

Being a Brit in a hot climate, the sun had burned my torso lobster pink on Day One. The longjohn of my diving suit had created a cummerbund of pristine white flesh around my middle. So that naked, I resembled a cylindrical version of the French flag.

Small wonder, then, that I spent as much time as possible alone, running in the high country around Walker's Basin.

The Rankin spread covers 30,000 acres near Bakersfield, California. The Basin is a modern Shenandoah — perfect little valley, oval and green, an oasis nestling among the scorched hills that enclose it on every side. A stream, clear and sweet, rises at the centre of the valley then tumbles musically away between the mountains down a precipitous creek.

I should've run along it. But being inextricably drawn to heights (though my legs turn to jelly when I stand on a chair) I struck out instead for the mountain tops. I followed a sort of trail up a ridge — it seemed to head in the direction of an old logging road near the summit.

Within half an hour, I was completely lost. The grass, scorched brown since the region's fourth rainless spring in as many years, came away in handfuls like hair from a mangy coyote. I slithered, cursing, down dusty slopes into the vicious thorn bushes that looked so cute and fluffy when I was reclining on the patio of the ranch with a cold beer in my hand.

As I was traversing one particularly filthy and treacherous incline, I was galvanised by a sudden crashing in the undergrowth. 'Be careful of them thar bears,' rancher Bill had grinned. 'Most of 'em are OK, but git yerself between a mother an' her cub, an' she'll rip yer guts out.'

It was a cow. Or more accurately, a steer. Rankin is a working cattle ranch. You can tell by the menu. Breakfast: beef sausages. Lunch: spaghetti bol, beef style. Dinner: paving slabs of succulent, barbecued beef or tortillas and shredded beef or chilli con beef or beef à l'orange.

Because you don't have to touch base with steers every day to milk them, and because the spread is the size of Greater Manchester, they don't meet a lot of humans. So they're as nervy as the pumas and the bobcats to whom this cowboy movie set is home, home on the range.

Another thing. The dead grass has a nasty little booby trap attached to every stalk — a seed with a barbed point, as sharp and hard as a tungsten steel needle. They bayonet your shoes, rip your socks to shreds and turn your shorts into mediaeval instruments of torture.

By the time I staggered across the creek into the ranch, I was bleeding, exhausted, severely dehydrated (the temperature was in the mid-nineties), and properly chastened.

It was all a far, far cry from the previous week's excursions along the shore path at Venice Beach, Los Angeles — more of a catwalk than a running track.

In which the Beach Boys meet Brokeback Mountain

'THIS IS WKLA comin' to you from the heart of beautiful downtown Santa Monica and it's another beautiful morning here by the ocean. Here's Steely Dan.' I turned up the radio and wound down the windows of the huge, grey 1965 Oldsmobile as it wallowed down Santa Monica Boulevard towards the ocean.

Strangely, I seemed to have become the star of a continuous Beach Boys video.

A light, warm breeze played in my hair as I pulled over and slipped on my running shoes. I set off along the asphalt track that winds for twenty miles along the beach. Even at 7am, the traffic was building up — mostly mountain bikers in radio hats and impossibly perfect girls on rollerblades.

I wish they all could be Californian, went the video soundtrack in my head. But actually, I didn't. California girls might be slim, athletic and that pleasing shade of golden brown, like lightly-buttered toast. But they were completely interchangeable.

As they sailed past the knots of wild, bearded derelicts who scattered the shore, it might have been a scene from an *avant garde* ballet in which Barbie searches for Ken, now a psychotic Vietnam war veteran in the final stages of alcoholic dissolution.

The elegant hotels of Santa Monica gave way to the bars and psychedelic facades of Venice Beach.

The henna tattoo merchants were setting out their stalls, the restaurateurs were brushing the night's accumulation of sand from the boardwalk. I would soon catch up with the runner in front of me — a tall, broad-shouldered type in shades and a red bandanna. If you're worried about your declining running performance, a trip to the States will do wonders for your ego. Nobody exceeds the national speed limit of the Ten Minute Mile, imposed during the fuel crisis of the 1970s.

Indeed, in New York's Central Park where the runners are exclusively short, spherical, middle-aged ladies, The Twelve Minute Mile Rule is generally observed.

Out West, of course, they're very laid back. In fact, there's fierce competition between Californians over how laid back they are. It requires great dedication and years of training to run that slowly.

I closed effortlessly on my quarry and pulled alongside him. 'Well, hi!' he greeted me. 'Where you headin'?' I hadn't a clue, I said. Could I just tag along with him?

His name was Alex. He turned out to be a tax lawyer and amateur ventriloquist who'd spent three years at RADA in London. He was originally from New York. His mother had taken up running — she was almost certainly short and spherical — and he'd kinda caught the bug.

Like everyone else in Los Angeles, he'd wanted to be an actor. But being a tax lawyer, he said, was the next best thing and actually very similar.

We jogged sedately along Venice Pier, past a tiny Chinese

woman with a twelve-foot fishing rod and past Ken, who was hanging out and drinking with a bunch of his psychotic veteran friends. They jeered at us good-naturedly as we ambled by, well within the speed limit.

It was now getting seriously warm. The sweat trickled into my eyes and I found myself envying Alex his shades and bandanna. Was I turning gay? Everybody else on the beach seemed to be. Except Ken, I supposed. And then again…

Venice is nicknamed Muscle Beach on account of the hordes of weightlifters who strut their stuff on the prom. In fact, there's a point halfway between Santa Monica and Venice where the Beach Boys video morphs into the Village People video. As we ran south, the biceps and tattoo counts rocketed.

Alex seemed more than ordinarily interested in a blond, six-foot gymnast with a Kiss Me T-shirt.

It was definitely time to turn back.

The wrath of God
(as meted out to your own Cape crusader)

WHEN GOD created Cape Wrath, he was having a particularly good day. 'I'll do a craggy, rolling sort of landscape', he decided, 'broken up by the odd, dramatic escarpment. Maybe a few boisterous gills, chattering down lush ravines of fern and foxglove.

'Then I'll bung in a stunning vista every mile or so — perhaps a tantalising glimpse of the sea between the ample breasts of two, purple-heathered fells, and for a centrepiece, an impossible stack of granite towering up out of the foaming brine. Just for good measure.'

When he'd finished, he looked down on the shiny new Cape and said, '*Damn*, I'm good!' But almost immediately, he began to worry. '*Too* good, perhaps. The minute those two layabouts get chucked out of Eden, they'll be up here, breeding like… like… ' (he hadn't created rabbits yet). 'It'll be wall-to-wall humans in no time. I'd better create something to discourage them.'

And thus it was that God invented The Midge. Just a couple, to begin with — but straightaway, they began to breed like... like...

Ever since, Cape Wrath and all of the loveliest parts of the Highlands and Islands have been preserved from human over-exploitation by God's tiniest and lowliest invention.

They were at their most vigilant on the day that the Island Race reached Durness — the little village that is the capital-in-exile of the Cape.

Some background necessary, here.

The Island Race has been a charity run of epic proportions — a 4,200-mile relay race around the coastline of Scotland, England and Wales.

Many hundreds of runners participated, many corporate sponsors donating many millions of pounds to excellent causes.

Seaton and I had travelled up to Sutherland to join one of the last stages — the race would end seven days later, where it began, at Gordonstoun, Prince Charles' old school.

As for the 'capital-in-exile', Cape Wrath was once inhabited by a modest population of crofters. It even had its own school.

Now, after the notorious Clearances and subsequent centuries of decline, it boasts just one permanent resident. A few weeks ago, John Ure moved into the old lighthouse-keeper's accommodation at the most north-westerly point in the British Isles — and the halfway point in the first ever Cape Wrath Ultra-Marathon.

John apart, there is no one in over 100 square miles of wilderness. The nearest village, a short ferry-ride from the peninsula, is Durness. And that's where the Island Race bandwagon, with its giant, Kwik-Fit juggernaut and its fleet of Ford support vehicles, pitched up for Day 97 of the event.

Let's cut to the chase: I came second. Second equal, that is, with Seaton. The security guards forced back the hysterical crowds as we raced, shoulder to shoulder, across the finish line and into the waiting arms of the Princess Royal. The helicopters bearing the world's press hovered above, making it all but impossible to hear Anne's congratulatory address.

As we took our places on the podium, the massed bands of the Scots Guards struck up *The Heroes Of Durness*, the anthem specially commissioned for the occasion from Sir Paul McCartney and J.K. Rowling.

Weighed down by gladioli, Caithness glass trophies and 24-carat medalry, we staggered back to the Roger Bannister Suite at the Durness Plaza for our complimentary sauna with the Ross and Cromarty Under-21's All-Girl Shiatsu Team.

That's bollocks, of course. But not *complete* bollocks. Steve Seaton and I really were Joint Second. Second out of eight. And while Princess Anne wasn't actually there to greet us in the car park of Durness Village Hall, we did receive a handsome scroll from Buckingham Palace, bearing her signature.

And although there may not be a Plaza in Durness, there is a Parkhill — the charming, homely establishment run by the extraordinary Dottie.

When we asked to settle up for our rooms and for the breakfast she had insisted on cooking for us at 6:30am on race day, Dottie was genuinely puzzled. 'Why would you want to *pay* to stay here?' she wanted to know. This was enough even to dumbfound Seaton, who accumulates eccentrics like Madonna attracts stalkers.

Should Durness ever declare itself an independent state (not as unlikely as it sounds), Dottie would be unanimously voted Queen.

The race organisers persuaded her to be the official starter. She held the starting pistol about six inches from her head, which invoked a flurry of panic among the officials. 'Not so close! Away! Away!' Following a host of complex and contradictory instructions, the pistol was eventually held very tentatively indeed at a full arm's length, as you or I might handle a plutonium fuel rod. Notwithstanding, she leapt a foot in the air when she squeezed the trigger.

But we were off, at any rate. It's two miles from the village to the little grey ferry that chugs across the sea loch to the cape. They took our times as we shuffled aboard. The water was preternaturally calm, unruffled even by the faintest breath of a breeze. This strange little interlude added to the special atmosphere of the run — dissolved the usual, neurotic apprehension that surrounds a race and invested the occasion with a dreamy, unhurried quality.

We would have lingered longer in the tiny, exquisite haven on the far shore, but the midges were having none of it. Clouds of them hung around our faces and drowned in the sweat on our arms and legs. Since they're unable to fly in anything more than a four-knot breeze, there must be precious few days on this gale-lashed promontory when they can actually get airborne. So today, they were making the most of it.

Of course, providing you ran faster than fifteen-minute miles, you created enough turbulence to keep them at bay. But as we penetrated further inland, the marshals were reduced to protecting their faces with nylon stockings, creating the surreal impression of an armed gang at large in a Victorian watercolour.

Although the hills grew sharper and longer as we neared the most north-westerly extremity of the cape, the miles passed quite pleasantly — largely because Seaton entertained me with an account of the EcoChallenge in Patagonia. Hearing about his ascent of an ice-face in a raging gale, his nocturnal ordeal in an impenetrable thicket of bamboo and his mild surprise at being caught on a high Andean ridge by the storm of the decade — it all combined to make our little ultra-marathon seem like a stroll in Hyde Park on a summer Sunday.

The miles flew by in this agreeable fashion until we reached John Ure's lighthouse. The light stands proudly and obstinately on a headland that manages to look exposed even in this, the most exposed terrain in the British Isles.

'If you sailed due north from here,' remarked the marshal reverentially, 'The first thing you'd hit would be the polar ice cap. Sail west and you'd hit Labrador.' I pondered these arresting facts as I scoffed a banana. It was a very big place indeed. The light had a far-away quality, like the look in the pale blue eyes of mountaineers.

We took a turn around the lighthouse, Seaton handed John Ure his scroll from Buck House and then we headed for home.

Out-and-back races get a poor press, generally, but I'm on the side of Flann O'Brien when he says that every road is really two roads. Even though we were treading the same tarmac, the landscape revealed a wholly new and different set of glories.

We were still in fair fettle when we reached the little harbour and could slump thankfully onto the ferry for a few minutes of good-natured banter with the leader in the ultra-marathon and a handful of relay runners.

It only remained to complete the two-mile home straight to Durness, which included a vicious little hill. We were preceded by the race organiser in his Galaxy who provided an impromptu commentary through his mobile Tannoy system, for the benefit of the local sheep and a handful of bemused children. We even put in a bit of a kick as we reached the village. If the sheep were impressed, they didn't betray it.

Hanging around the finish line, I felt so good it was uncanny. Perhaps I'd dropped dead on the way out and this was simply a mental aberration, the final paroxysms of my dying imagination.

But the feeling persisted (reinforced by the wine at the evening's ceilidh in the village hall). Seaton and I were even able to manage a brisk five-miler on the dunes at 6am next day, before setting off for Inverness and the flight home.

There's talk — wistful talk, so far — of making a regular event of the Cape Wrath Ultra. Possibly throwing in a beach run and a hill race, too, in the style of the Lanzarote Challenge.

If the dream ever becomes a reality, it should immediately become a compulsory event for every runner who is still able to feel awe, humility and gratitude in the presence of pristine natural beauty.

Perhaps they'll call it The Wrath Of God Marathon.

Devon and hell

DARTMOOR. 6:30am. Pitch black. We fumbled with our head torches in the carpark. The air was heavy with the autumnal fragrance of wet peat and purple heather. An invisible stream gurgled beneath a ghostly stone bridge. The shrouds of mist parted momentarily to reveal a few scattered stars. The billion-year-old light was enough to etch out the scarp of Dartmoor, grey-black against the deepest of blues.

Not for the first time since our 4:30 alarm call, I called into question the sanity of this expedition — to celebrate Sean Fishpool's 30th birthday by climbing around thirty granite outcrops, or tors, in one vainglorious circumnambulation of the Moor.

I'd explained the plan to the sceptical but resigned Mrs Blackford. 'It isn't going to be quick (*I won't be back until Sunday afternoon*). And it's going to very tough (*I don't suppose I'll be up to planting the tulip bulbs*).

'Seaton (*Steven, Editor, Runner's World*) is getting terrible gip from his knee after the mountain bike accident. And Ran (*Sir Ranulph Fiennes, hero*) has done his back again. And my Achilles is playing me up something rotten.'

'I can just picture it,' mused Mrs Blackford drily. 'Like an episode of *Last Of The Summer Wine*.'

The course encompassed the whole of Dartmoor in a wide, sweeping circle and was divided into seven 'legs', each led by a fresh, new member of the mountain rescue service. These were infuriatingly fit and enthusiastic young people — friends of the irritatingly youthful Fishpool, I supposed, as they bounded, gravity-defying, across the waterlogged tussock grass and the razor-wire heather while I stumbled and swore along in their wake.

Thankfully, they stopped at the summit of each tor for a photo call. Which gave me just enough time to catch up before they went bounding off like hyperactive gazelles across the next tract of filthy bogland towards an impossible horizon.

Seaton was supposed to be crippled. He confided to me, 'If I can't manage this, I can't in all conscience go out to New Zealand for the Completely Stupid Blindfold Ice Abseiling 500.' The CSBIA was just another in the series of suicidal ordeals that my editor undertakes each year, alongside the equally crazed Sir Ranulph.

It was humiliating that despite a tendon and cartilage injury which should have confined him to bed for a fortnight and kept him out of competition for three months, he left me for dead.

He dropped out at Tor 22, ashen-faced and cursing without prejudice the entire sentient universe.

Meanwhile, I sloshed and waddled my way across the waterlogged moorland like an amphibious Heathcliff. In the end, I gave up trying to keep up. I looked about me. The sun was fumbling its way through a veil of mist, sweeping the wilderness like a golden searchlight. A huge bird wheeled soundlessly overhead.

The guidebooks insist that the tors are natural, the products of countless millennia of wind and rain and frost. But it's easy to believe that they're made by men — Neolithic temples, perhaps, where virgins lost their hearts without the benefit of modern anaesthetics.

Then suddenly the mist parted to reveal a stone circle, still drenched (it seemed to me) in the sacrificial gore of maidens. I pressed my face against a rough-hewn, lichen-encrusted monolith in the hope of divining its arcane mysteries.

And I pondered the Eternal Question: what sort of silly bugger would freeze his nuts off killing girls up here in the arse end of nowhere, when he could do it far more comfortably down in Tavistock?

In which I hit the low point of my running career

'YOU'RE LUCKY!' called Malcolm, our Jewish neighbour. 'It's 82 degrees in Israel!'

'Thanks!' we returned smugly as our cab swept us away into horizontal rain, driven by a force eight gale.

'You're unlucky,' remarked Ari, our Israeli driver, as he swept us along the Tel Aviv–Jerusalem highway against the horizontal, gale-driven rain. 'We haven't had weather like this in twenty years.'

But I'm jumping the gun. The story of the Dead Sea Half-Marathon begins three million years ago, when the ground split and a big chunk of it dropped into the bowels of the Earth. The result was the Great Rift Valley which cleaved Africa and created Lake Victoria, the Gulf of Aqaba, the Sea of Galilee — and the Dead Sea, which promptly became the lowest spot on the planet.

Then, rather later (1982), the Dead Sea Half-Marathon was conceived as a memorial to local running Ron brothers, Giora and Tomer. One was killed by a sniper's bullet in Lebanon, the other in an accident in the local date plantation.

Every year, the race attracts a bigger, better field. This time there were around 250 runners. But this number included world-class athletes — a handful of sub-2:15 marathon men from Kenya and Morocco and Russia, and Helena Barocsi of Hungary, first lady home with 1:16. It was especially tough this year, thanks to the wind. In fact, by the six-mile mark, I'd renamed it 'The Half-Dead Sea Marathon'.

The 'sea' was salty from the start, but it has become saltier by the millennium. Today, it is 28% mineral in composition. In the intense heat of summer, when the temperature often soars to 45 degrees, the water evaporates at the waterline and the salt encapsulates stones and jetsam in a blinding, crystalline lichen.

Higher on the shore, the beach appears to consist of round stones. But prod them and they collapse: they're just bubbles of mud, encased in brittle shells of salt.

Hot sulphur springs bubble up, staining the foreshore with delicate pinks and yellows.

Other significant events of the past three million years:

1) Lot's wife turns into pillar of salt.

2) King Herod the Great builds palace on top of a mountain at Masada. It is occupied by Jewish Zealots at the time of the Great Revolt. Then the Romans build a siege ramp as big as the mountain. The Zealots draw straws and ten of them kill the rest — then one of the ten kills the other nine, then he kills himself.

3) Sodom is founded, is fun, is knocked down.

4) The Sea rises and covers the scrubby tamarisk trees that grow on its shore. Then, six hundred years later, the Sea retreats and the trees re-emerge, embalmed in salt.

5) King David stops at pretty little oasis on the shore called En Gedi. So does Solomon, who stays long enough to write some songs.

Today, En Gedi is a kibbutz perched on a spur of land between the brutal slabs of the Judean desert and the weird, petrified beaches of the Dead Sea. The name means 'the Place of the Goats'.

It was founded in the 1950s on the western shore and was served only by a rough dirt track until after the Six Day War, when the road was built.

Before anything would grow, every ounce of soil had to be washed to rid it of salt. Now it is a tropical garden of breathtaking beauty, visited by dragonflies and bright, darting birds — an outdoor hothouse, more lush and more urgently fragrant even than the crystal palaces of Kew Gardens.

The house lights go down and the theatre is filled with an unearthly music. But the curtains remain closed. Then a girl in a leotard skips and pirouettes out of the wings and flits a feather duster over the front row of the audience, as though they were ornaments.

I jogged at dusk along luscious avenues of palm and banana, past gigantic cacti, massive trunks from the islands of the South Seas with rattlesnake seed pods and branches dangling dreadlock air roots; royal bougainvillea, adventurous vines and bright creepers, almost animal orchids and death-pale lilies — and, like a chaste thought too late, a sweet Edwardian rose from an English garden.

And then, abruptly, the dream ends in a concrete wall and an electric fence. Beyond, an old tank moulders on a mound of rubble, its gun pointing blindly into the precipitous valley behind the kibbutz.

There can be no better metaphor for mankind's flimsy hold over Nature than En Gedi. Its lush acres are a testament to the determination and creativity of its people. But if they were all to quit and go back to Jerusalem and Kiev and New York, it would wither and die in days under the terrible hammer of the heat and the salt, and the desert would simply absorb it once again into its merciless bosom.

The girl leaps effortlessly onto the stage: the curtains part to reveal six, abstract sculptures in vibrant red, pink and orange. She runs her duster over their sinuous curves, until they begin to sway like sea anemones in the current of the music.

The evening before the race, the wind soughed uneasily in the trees above our chalet. The mountains of Jordan, only a few kilometres away across the water, dissolved in a strange yellow mist. Dust devils whirled ghostlike along the chemical shore.

'The pessimists say the weather will be bad,' said Ari, 'But in fifteen years, I tell them, we have never had bad weather for the Race.'

That night the soughing became a miserable moaning and then a full-blown howling. Tables and chairs bowled about the kibbutz, the torn limbs of trees crashed to the ground, a tumult of brown water thundered in the wadi below, fingers of rain forced their way beneath our door. Sleep was impossible.

Next morning, the wind had abated a little — but only a little. I overslept, missed breakfast and had to hitch the four kilometres to the start.

The race is an out-and-back from En Gedi Spa along the coast road towards Masada. I should say *races*, because there's a 10k, too, and a handful of kids' events.

The outward leg was hard, hard, hard — uphill and straight into the teeth of the gale. A bunch of six elite runners separated off more or less immediately, leaving the rest of us battling on against the elements.

I quickly found my pace, which was of the type favoured by arthritic tortoises. Nevertheless, I took some pride in the fact that I managed to stay ahead of a contingent of Viennese vets — until I realised that they were merely sheltering from the storm behind my monolithic bulk. Come the halfway mark, when wind and hills turned in our favour, they sailed past and left me for dead. You see, they were bastards.

The dancing statues grow hands as they gyrate upon their plinths. Like butterflies emerging from their pupae, the girls wriggle off the clinging tubes of Lycra that bind them to the ground. These are living statues of skin and muscle, a surreal mix of sensuality and comedy, expressed with strange grace.

Why is it that no matter how many races you run, you always forget how horridly, interminably foul they are until the starter's gun sends you waddling off on the next one? My running life has been a repetitive nightmare, punctuated by periods of pathetic self-delusion.

I managed the last two miles only by holding in my mind's eye the complimentary dip in the hot springs at En Gedi Spa. I finished half an hour behind the Kenyan victor, Bernard Boiyo (1:07) and dragged myself to the steaming pool of yellowish water with its endearing stench of rotten eggs. I lowered myself thankfully into the water, then scrambled hysterically for the side, screaming in nerve-searing agony.

I had forgotten to apply Vaseline to my inner thighs before the race, and now they were raw. The effect of the hot, saline water upon my sores defies description. It was like having your nerves individually teased out with white hot pliers.

And so begins the En Gedi Half-Marathon Gala Evening, an hour of magical and breathtaking dance. Out Of The Blue is only a local amateur troupe; but such wit and precision, such sheer, blinding creativity, is rare enough on the professional stage. That's Israel at its best — fresh, wonderful and surprising.

We were to fly home next day. We watched a slide show on

the flora, fauna and archeology of the Dead Sea. 'The trouble is,' explained the speaker, 'the Jordanians over on the other side of the Sea put fresh camel shit on their land. That's why we have so many flies at En Gedi.'

My heart sank at this — just as it did last year in Jordan, when our taxi driver told us that Jewish tourists always stole the pillows from the hotels. Attitudes like these are endemic to the region. Nor are they the preserve of fundamentalist bigots — you're as likely to find them in otherwise kindly, intelligent, educated individuals of both races.

A prejudice must be deeply ingrained indeed if you can, in all seriousness, blame the flies on the Arabs.

But you should run the Half next year. The Dead Sea is an incredible place, like nowhere else on the planet. And at 400 metres below sea level, it will mark an all-time low in your running career.

Greenland.
Run by heroes, named by an estate agent

THE ROAD east from Kangerlussuaq is easily the longest in Greenland. It winds up through a dry, glacial valley for twenty miles before it hits the ice cap. And then for another 130 astonishing, frozen kilometres, it penetrates one of the most forbidding and desolate wildernesses on Earth.

At the far end, they say, is a secret VW testing station. But it could just as easily lead to Superman's Ice Fortress.

The road is unlikely to wear out through over-use. A handful of hunters haul the carcasses of reindeer and musk oxen along it in a race to reach the abattoir. (If it takes longer than six hours, the meat freezes solid and must be dumped.)

It's trodden by the odd geologist — the road is lined by some of the oldest rocks on the planet.

But on a certain Sunday in September, the route reels under a veritable explosion of traffic.

The second Polar Circle Marathon attracted 65 runners. Most were Danes although there were a heartening number of local Inuit and one madwoman flew in from Sydney for the weekend.

We all descended upon Kangerlussuaq because it boasts the only runway in Greenland long enough to accommodate a 757.

Kangerlussuaq has recently been awarded city status, although the name is bigger than the place. It looks exactly like what it is — an abandoned air base. Until 1992, it was home to around 1,400 US servicemen. Those with poor disciplinary records, you have to conclude, or else just plain bad luck.

We were billeted at the Old Camp. We slept in little rooms in a hut. I was considerably longer than my bed. I must say, I did wonder as I fidgeted through the endless Arctic night why Greenlanders build accommodation that would induce claustrophobia in a Borrower, given that the island is two thousand miles long and supports a population of just 60,000.

In the centre of the camp stands a gigantic tepee, the venue for our pre-race barbecue. Despite near-zero temperatures, an army of cooks sweated over griddles piled high with steaks of reindeer and musk ox. I can report that both are quite edible, though apt to get stuck between your teeth.

The Greenland Vegetarian Society must have a hard time of it. When I asked what variety the jam was at breakfast this morning, Jan replied, 'Reindeer'.

The government in Copenhagen is pushing Danes to eat at least five portions of fruit or vegetable every day. They're running the same campaign in Greenland, which is barmy. Anything that isn't red meat has to be flown in, so that in Kangerlussuaq an apple is worth its weight in cocaine.

In fact, there's a surprisingly low incidence of heart disease in Greenland, probably because the natives chew seal fat and eat their livers raw — a diet from which a heart attack would provide a welcome release.

The day before the race, a couple of old, yellow school buses rattled and groaned up the valley for the mandatory course

Inspection. The organisers insisted that we knew what we were in for.

Twenty-five miles in, the road changed abruptly from dirt track to bobsleigh run.

I tiptoed gingerly onto the ice (which at this point was three kilometres thick) with a bunch of shivering, disconsolate runners. I fell over instantly. This was ludicrous. It was like… like walking on ice. And tomorrow we would be expected to run on it.

Kangerlussuaq is at the head of a fjord. But when the water stops, the valley doesn't. There's at least another thirty miles of dry river bed to the east, scoured out during the last Ice Age and as arid and pointless as a desert wadi.

To complete the illusion, sand drifts over the road and whirls in furious little eddies across the plain. If it weren't for the bitter cold, we could have been in the Sahara.

When I left London, it was hot. It was very hard to imagine 10 degrees below zero — that's without the wind chill. So I arrived in Greenland hopelessly ill-equipped for the climate. I bought some gloves and a fleece and a hat inscribed with the euphemistic motto, *Greenland: The coolest place on earth.* In November, the temperature in Kangerlussuaq can drop to minus 60. Think of it this way: if you threw a cup of boiling water in the air, it would freeze before it hit the ground.

The sun doesn't venture above the horizon for three months (if I were a sun, neither would I) so the Greenlanders exist in a state of perpetual twilight. On the plane back to Copenhagen I sat next to a Danish psychiatric nurse who'd been seconded to a hospital in Nuuk, the capital. 'When they commit suicide in Greenland,' he said with a degree, I thought, of reluctant admiration, 'they do it with a great deal of determination. No cry for help. Just a rifle bullet through the brain. I mean, they're *serious.*'

By the time we assembled at the Start on race day, I was almost looking around for a rifle. I got off the coach and within seconds, despite two polypropylene shirts, Gore-Tex top, pants, Lycra shorts, tracksuit bottoms, woolly hat and gloves, I was shivering uncontrollably.

The starter's gun (a rifle, interestingly) meant that at least we could get moving, even if it was up a 20% incline into the teeth of a vicious wind.

Within half a mile, I was reduced to walking. Encouragingly, I was still overtaking those who for reasons of mental illness had elected to jog.

Within half an hour, we'd reached the bobsleigh run. To my infinite relief, the ice was now covered by three inches of snow. It was eminently run-able.

Then you round a bend in the canyon and the three-billion-year-old rocks and the bonsai birches end abruptly at the foot of a thirty-metre ice wall.

This is the polar ice cap. One millimetre you're in Greenland — the next, you're in the Arctic.

It's faintly ridiculous. Something from a schoolboy's diagram of the planet. Like finding that the Equator really *is* a thick black line, drawn around the globe by a clumsy draughtsman.

The face of the ice is disappointingly mucky. The demonic winds that lash the landscape whip up the dust from the moraine and blast it into the ice cliffs. However, behind the grubby face of the glacier are gaping chasms of a radiant, depthless turquoise.

This alliance of ice and light is heartless, impossibly lovely, dangerously seductive. It's the very antithesis of life and yet you stand rooted, hypnotised by its promise of scintillating oblivion.

And the strange beauty of this awful place hits you with all the force of a religious conversion. Or a truck. And you raise your face to the bitter, alien sky and cry, 'What the fuck am I doing here?'

In which a bad idea is made to seem like divine revelation by the intervention of industrial grade lager

IT'S NO good. I can't put it off any longer. Everest casts a long shadow at the best of times, but even in May's unseasonable heatwave, a distinctly Himalayan chill reminds me that a monstrous challenge is only a few months away.

I have a theory about pubs. While they are widely accepted to be the fount of every social evil from cirrhosis to wife battering, they are also the incubators in which are hatched mankind's noblest and most extraordinary achievements.

For instance, it is a little-known fact that Sir Alexander Fleming discovered penicillin after a couple of snakebites at The Two Geezers in Beak Street. He turned to his mate and said, 'Y'know, Dave, I've half a mind to leave a bit of wet bread on me bench tonight!'

'Go on!' replied Dave. 'You don't care, do you? You're a regular hellraiser you are, Sand!'

To arrest the sad demise of the on-trade, the breweries should exploit the wonderful sense of optimism that is generated by an open fire, a friendly crowd and ten pints of premium lager. As a campaign line, I modestly suggest:

Anything's possible in the pub.

The Himalayan 100 Mile Stage Race is another case in point. Less than a year had passed since I brought my feet home in a body bag from the Sahara to give them a decent burial on Hampstead Heath.

I vowed that in future, if it was longer than the omnibus edition of *Brookside*, I wouldn't run it.

But a man's capacity to moan about his discomfort is matched only by his ability to forget how discomfortable he really was.

October found me at my customary place at the bar of The Cat & Hacksaw, listening to the same old training lies from the same sad crew with whom I'd limped across the wilderness.

'Yeah, I'm only knocking off around fifty miles a week nowadays. Maintenance mileage, y'know. Sometimes manage the odd track session, just to keep that edge.'

'Me, I like to put in a few hills. Nothin' like hills to keep up yer basic fitness level. Oh, yeah, cheers mate — I'll have another pint of Guinness.'

'My rule is, I only run with a rucksack with a twenty-pound

brass pig in it. Even on the track. It takes a while to come through, but after about six months you really begin to feel the benefit.'

In reality, of course, none of us had run anything more than a dizzy, flatulent five-miler the morning after the week before.

I don't know who it was who first brought up the Himalayan thing, but I have a horrible suspicion it may have been me.

At any rate, I remember mentioning that the previous year, Seaton, my editor, had run just one stage of it before succumbing to pneumonia.

A strange light had glowed in Eadie's eyes: 'Ah! Sounds like our kind of thing!' (Eadie, you may recall, had been doing rather well in the Marathon des Sables until he'd lurched off in the direction of fundamentalist Algeria and had been snatched by helicopter from the jaws of death).

By the time we'd teetered from the snug into the street, we'd sworn solemnly to enter the race. As always in these cases, the full enormity of what we'd done didn't strike home until the following morning — as, with a shaking hand and a mounting sense of impending doom, I set about tailoring a training schedule that would culminate in my scaling the roof of the world:

SUN: Gentle 4 mile run/walk on flat.
MON: Talk loudly at work about Himalayas in hope women will overhear and question me further.
TUE: Go to gym. Attempt 5 sit-ups.
WED: Send off for Black's mountaineering equipment catalogue.
THUR: Make big colour-coded training wallchart.
FRI: Talk loudly about Himalayas in pub after work in hope women will overhear and question me further. Especially Samira from Accounts.
SAT: Buy magic markers/coloured sticky paper for wall chart.
SUN: Gentle 5 mile run/walk on flat.
MON: Use office computer to design brilliant little icons for wall chart.
TUE: Read Black's catalogue. Put big ticks next to particularly rugged bits of kit.

WED: Go to library. Borrow copy of *A Short Walk In The Hindu Kush*.
THUR: Go to gym. Try for 10 sit-ups. Hurt neck.
FRI: Drop out of egg and spoon race at daughter's nursery school.
SAT: Burn wall chart.

I know it may not seem much to the casual observer, but one cannot overestimate the psychological importance of *making a start*.

In which I find that under the wrong circumstances, Hampstead Hill is harder to run up than the Himalayas

THERE ARE now just 64 days before I board my flight to India — a flight that, for the most part, will be conducted at a lower altitude than the start of the race I've got to run when I get there.

During the past week, thanks to overwork, indolence and my accidental discovery of the tequila slammer, I've only managed one run. In a freak storm, I ran along the River Dollis — a quaintly-named open sewer that overflowed and flooded the adjacent path with the unspeakable detritus of our non-biodegradable civilisation.

So today, I was determined to put in some decent training. I set the radio alarm for 6:30am. When I awoke, it was if I'd been dozing inside the treble bin of Metallica's PA system as the gig started. My pre-race nerves were already so frayed that my arm shot out like a piston to cancel the alarm — and knocked my glass of water onto the radio.

A jagged blue bolt shot from the stricken device, straight up my arm. A giant hand grabbed me from the bed and hurled me into the air. I landed, limp as a golliwog, in a pile of dog poop.

I came round under the soulful gaze of the culprit. For one disoriented moment, I thought I was drowning in the River Dollis. Then I put Number Two and Number Two together.

I snatched up the nearest offensive weapon and made to beat the canine about the head with it. In a feint that would have impressed Errol Flynn, he ducked, snatched my shoe between his slavering jaws and ran downstairs with it.

I snapped. 'You bastard!' I screamed. 'Who feeds you? Who takes you running? You fat, incontinent ingrate! I'll sell you to the Koreans!'

This woke the baby.

By the time I'd pacified her, made her toast and sat with her through two episodes of *Teletubbies*, I was late for work. Perhaps I could kill two birds with one stone, and run to the office?

On with the rucksack, up through the woods, doing well, making good time — until I hit the Hampstead Pavement Artists' Competition.

One day in the year, impelled by the knowledge that if Damien Hirst made it, anyone can, hundreds of rat-haired, layabout ne'er-do-wells with pierced eyebrows and forged housing benefit cards crawl up to the Village with their bags of chalk and their cans of fighting lager, to daub the thoroughfare with formularized depictions of threatened species and the Mona Lisa.

I just happened to pick that day.

I tried running in the road and, to a cheer from the ragged creative elements, narrowly escaped being reduced by a McDonalds truck to the same consistency as its cargo.

I jogged home and took a cab to work.

Still, there was always lunchtime. I'm only five minutes from the park — so at noon, I changed into my kit. And then, just as the alarm sounded for the fire drill I'd forgotten about completely, I realised I'd also forgotten my shorts.

Five minutes later and I'm in the street in my boxers, trying to pull my T-shirt down over my privates, only making it rise like a dawn mist over my backside. The scenario dimly recalled an insecurity dream from my adolescence.

The fire was real — caused by a short in the alarm circuit. I scuttled across the road to my gym. The running machine, thank God, was free. I whacked it up to 20kph, and burned off my frustration and embarrassment in a flat-out sprint.

Then the fire over the road blew the power supply for the whole of the West End, the running machine stopped dead, I didn't, and I crashed through the wall into the Ladies' Changing Room.

I was pursued for ten miles through Central London by security staff and hirsute female weightlifters.

It was the best training I'd had in weeks.

In which I develop a curious list to starboard

'SIT DOWN, Mister Blackford,' intoned the doctor. 'What seems to be the problem?'

'I have a hip injury,' I replied.

'Ah!' he said significantly. He leaned back on his chair and frowned at the ceiling. 'Then you certainly *do* have a problem. And contrary to what you might imagine, it is a problem that afflicts the spirit, not the body.'

'I'm sorry?'

'It is symptomatic of a spiritual sickness, a moral malaise if you like, that has reached epidemic proportions in our sick and twisted society.'

'But I don't... '

He rocked forwards suddenly on his chair and fixed me with a fierce glare. 'I've been a doctor for twenty years, Mister Blackford, and believe me, there is no such thing as a "hip" injury. Nor is there anything "sexy" about heroin. These are simply the posturings of a morbid, decadent, self-obsessed generation and I, for one, will have no truck with them!'

'No, no!' I protested, 'I mean I've injured my hip! Accidentally! By running! I haven't made it up or anything! It's perfectly real and I want you to cure it for me!'

He stared at me for a long moment. Then he stood up abruptly. 'Right. Well, we'd better take a look at you then. Hop up on the couch.'

I really had injured my hip, of course, and in the most absurd way. The nagging pain had spread and increased in intensity over the course of two or three weeks, until I abandoned any hope of 'running though it' and descended into black and ugly depression.

Some of the most horrible crimes in history were committed by injured runners. The psychopathic tyrant Vlad the Impaler, for instance, was a harmless clerk at an insurance company until he pulled his Achilles in a cross-country. Henceforth, he found he could best express his frustration and disappointment by driving stakes through the breasts of innocents.

But I digress. I was on the phone to Seaton, my editor, moaning about my predicament, when I noticed that the conversation was punctuated by little hissing sounds. They seemed to coincide with my shifting from foot to foot (a nervous habit I developed during the long years in Rampton).

An inspection of my right running shoe revealed a small puncture in the air chamber. I once drove my dad's Jaguar for fifty miles with a flat tyre. The effect on his wheel, brake discs, track rods, axle, suspension and, as it turns out, chassis, was similar to the effect on my hip of running for a fortnight with a flat shoe.

Worse, just like dad's Jaguar, I wasn't insured.

In which I buddy up with an abominable training partner

ALL IN all, if pressed, I wouldn't recommend running with an invisible Yeti. Yetis are uncomfortably large, ill-tempered and indescribably smelly.

My particular Yeti, Lobsang, arrived in London last week to begin training for the Yetminster 5. It's his personal protest against my running the Himalayan 100 Mile Stage Race in November. He says however grumpy and malodorous he might be, it's nothing compared to the karmic dislocation caused by two hundred Westerners charging around the Eternal Snows like hyperactive puppies.

He's invisible because Yetis usually are. Indeed, a Yeti is visible to humans only during the morning after its birthday. And since a Yeti birthday ceremony requires the Yeti to drink one horn of fermented yak milk for every year of its age, and since the lifespan of the Yeti can exceed three centuries, Yeti sightings are exceedingly rare.

The reaction of my fellow runners to Lobsang's arrival has been consistent and predictable. I've run on the Heath with Roger for fifteen years. I've nursed him through two failed marriages, a disastrous affair with a Danish dental hygienist, a bankruptcy and a strained Achilles.

We go back, Roger and I. Our friendship was forged in the white heat of agony. Together we have endured raging thirst, exhaustion and hypothermia in the Hampstead area.

And yet, when I introduced him to the invisible Yeti, he fixed me with a rheumy eye and suggested, 'Bog off, you stupid bastard'. As he trotted away on his ruined legs, a hopeless tangle of varicose veins and ruptured sinews, he flung back a final, encouraging word: 'You stink, you do.'

'What a tosser,' Lobsang remarked. 'Don't worry, he's coming back as a nematode.'

'What's a nematode?' I asked.

'It's a kind of little worm thing that lives up pigs' bottoms.'

'How do you know?'

'I did an Open University course in zoology.'

'No, I mean, how do you know Rog will come back as one?'

'Trust me,' he smiled slyly. 'I'm a Buddhist.'

The Yeti business apart, my training has been going quite well. You may recall that my hip injury was caused by a puncture in the rear air chamber of my right shoe. At the sports clinic, I was advised to throw away the shoes immediately and buy a new pair. (By the way, I can really recommend the doctor at the clinic. His name was Mr Nike. He had a charming manner and drove a Bentley.)

My shoes were only six months old, so rather than throw them out, I simply punctured the left one as well. For a week, I had *two* hip injuries. Then they cleared up, which only goes to show. (However, now I have no feeling in my right hand and I've developed an audible defect of the foot called Squeaky Heel. The only other recorded incidences of this rare illness are among Canadian lumberjacks who steered giant fir trunks through the rapids of the St Lawrence River.)

Nevertheless, I've started a programme of races to prepare me for the Himalayas. The first was a 19-miler in Devon. It was organised by a psychopath and involved drinking many pints of *Some o' That*, a local blend of treacle and Semtex.

My next is a gruelling event, dreamed up Numbskulls AC to rival the notorious *Tough Guy* race. The *Big Mincing Nancy* is run in high heels over five laps of a tidy garden in Penge (but only if the weather's nice). There's a pillow fight at the half-mile mark and a dandelion-and-burdock drinking contest at the finish.

Meanwhile, my evenings are spent immersed in books about the Himalayan region. My favourite so far is by an escaped German prisoner of war, Max von Vonn, who hid from the British for nine years in the tiny, closed kingdom of M'ngnx. There he was initiated into the secrets of the Fidgeting Monks of Qng. He learned to tie his shoe laces with his ears and to fly short distances without mechanical aids. He taught himself the language of the plant world and struck up a physical relationship with a larch. (Their friendship was soured many years later when upon their return to Heidelberg, the young tree refused to sign an oath of allegiance to the State. Eventually, von Vonn tired of his arboreal lover and had her turned into an occasional table. However, she enjoyed her revenge in 1962 when one of the table legs gave way, tipping a cup of boiling Bovril over the now ancient von Vonn's genitalia.)

The region abounds with such tales, and I can hardly wait to experience these wonderful places for myself. However, I am under no illusion about the severity of the task I face. For instance, much of the run takes place in what is technically outer space: at such altitudes, the entire Albert Hall could be contained in a small jar. And so much of my training involves holding my breath.

Quite handy, I have to say, when you're running with a Yeti.

The Himalaya 100 Mile.
I leave my toenails on the Roof of the World

IF YOU'VE ever had to write a CV, you'll know that life isn't a smooth curve on a graph. A gradual, ordered personal development is what we invent when we try to persuade the world that we know who we are and what we're doing.

In reality, of course, that's bollocks.

You can spend twenty years cocooned in a state of comfortable inertia, then go off to the Himalayas for some madcap, five-day experiment in vainglorious stupidity, and come back utterly and irreversibly different.

You mix with people you'd never even get to meet under normal circumstances, you go through hell with them, you realise that like most people, they're the finest, noblest people in the world, and it reminds you how small you are.

But then you've just run a hundred miles up and down impossible gradients at brain-withering altitudes, so you realise that you're also a demi-god.

These two realisations are hard to reconcile. I wouldn't recommend introducing yourself at dinner parties as 'small demi-god'. Nor entering it under 'Profession' in your passport.

Nevertheless, epic runs *do* alter you forever. And the Himalaya 100 Mile Stage Race is no exception.

One day, I was dragging myself up a six-thousand-foot hill with heavy legs and a heavier heart, agonised by the doubts and fears that assail everyone at the beginning of a big endurance run. Just six days later, purified, proud, transformed and completely shagged out, I was experiencing what it must be like for extra-terrestrials, visiting the planet for the first time.

The bus rattled and battled its way along the pitted, molten road to Bagdora, a twenty-mile ribbon development that unreeled like celluloid. Just watching this real=time anarchist manifesto made your eyes ache with sensory overload.

Stacks of hemp teetered on rickshaws; pale, angular cows sauntered mournfully in the path of gaudy Tata trucks, half transport, half temples, from the Hindu Design Centre, Blackpool.

Every foot of frontage supported an enterprise in miniature. Here they patched the holes in alloy pans while next door they cut and pasted passable tread onto twenty-year-old tyres.

This was raw, desperate existence-ekeing at the hopeless end of the global food chain.

With a scream of gears, we edged across a tenuous-looking Bailey bridge. Below, between the meanders of a sulky little stream that would in April explode in a torrent of Himalayan meltwater, gangs of women and children toiled, sieving, grading and shovelling stones.

Eadie nudges me. 'Look at that. Bloody wonderful.' I drag my eyes away from the lowest of the low, performing this biblically menial task, to see a woman, richly endowed with the sensuous elegance that is the spring of Indian femininity, reclining in an ancient rickshaw. She smiles enigmatically as she fondles a little goat upon her lap.

'Bloody marvellous,' Eadie breathes as he toys impotently with his camera. 'Never capture it on film, of course.'

To me, in that seething place, in that weird, smokey, yellow light, she seemed like an Indian *Madonna Of The Rocks*. But then I'd just run a hundred miles at a mean altitude of 12,000 feet with a bunch of ultra nutters, so what did I know?

Still, Eadie was right about the elusive nature of the place. There was no way you could capture the tattered veils of diesel smoke, the mingled reek of cesspool, boiling tar and tired old dust, the cacophony of motor horns and rusty engines, the scream of tortured springs, the declamations of thin brown dogs and strutting cocks and the incessant, futile bawling of the populace.

After the six-day silence of the Himalayas, it simply failed to compute.

The Himalayan 100 Mile is not a race against runners, but against the illness and injury that are inevitable when the human system is made to perform shattering tasks, day after day, at unaccustomed altitudes.

That first evening, for instance, left us 6,000 feet higher than the morning. But then we'd also descended 2,000 feet during the 24-mile course, which we had to regain, so our total ascent was 8,000 feet. And this over a ragged track of stones that demanded continuous concentration to avoid torn ligaments or worse.

The higher you went, the steeper and stonier the path, the colder and thinner the air.

The giant bamboo of the rainforest gave away to moss-draped pines and finally to heathers and bright alpine flowers. Cloud shrouded Sandakpu, our destination, a huddle of rude huts in a saddle of the hills.

I made it only because it would have been unthinkable not to.

Dinner appeared at 3pm — quite how was a mystery, since the outpost enjoys neither electric power nor running water. By 5 o'clock the sun was gone, the temperature was dropping through the floor and we were all in bed.

In spite of an Arctic-rated sleeping bag, a quilt and a blanket, underwear, a sweater and a *Runner's World* bobble hat, I was freezing.

I blame the bobble hat.

That night, the wind howled and moaned around our cabin — and yet the air outside was perfectly still. Something to do with the altitude, I expect.

Dawn found us huddling together on a rocky knoll like Druids at the Solstice, watching the first rays of the sun strike the snowy summit of Kanchenjunga. Every col and crevasse was etched to divine exactness by the amazing clarity of the light. What little breath was available to us was well and truly taken away.

Meanwhile, away to the east, an innocent quill of cloud clung to the peak of Everest. One of our support party, a Gurkha mountain guide, squinted critically at the highest point on the planet. 'Storm,' he said eventually. 'Anyone up there now in serious shit.'

Running at altitude is a frustrating business. Running downhill feels like running on the flat. Running on the flat feels like running uphill. And running uphill is just plain horrible. The paths snake upwards forever, 1:4 straights punctuated by 1:3 hairpin bends. The best I could manage was a sort of 'scout's pace' of twenty paces jog, twenty paces walk, which at least reduced the searing muscle pain to finite limits.

Even the downs were awful. Especially the final stage of the (alleged) marathon on Day 3. We tipped over the edge of a barren, twenty-mile ridge and plummeted into the emerald maw of a great ravine. Misty miles below, a thread of silver glittered. Our path (a dry stream bed) tumbled towards this distant goal with a rough exuberance that on several occasions nearly killed me.

I skipped and skidded down the dusty channels, my toes and heels vertically aligned like a ballet dancer's. I knew straight away that the price of this barely-controlled descent would be paid in toenails.

Bryan, the landscape gardener from Somerset, was better on the down. I'd coaxed him up some of the more vicious hills when his CD-sized blisters had filled with blood and burst. Now he helped me to override the excruciating pain in my toes as I kicked and cursed my way down the mountain.

Down and down we dropped, through fire-scarred forests, mossy glens and parched heathland, then through the uppermost outposts of humanity — tiny farmsteads, monasteries with prayer flags flying, schools of corrugated iron.

By now I was so tired, I could no longer control my feet. Navigating this demented helter-skelter required total concentration, but now I stubbed my toes with every step, or else my feet would slide down my shoe and crush my nails against the toe-caps.

Eventually we reached the 'final' checkpoint — only to find that there were still nine kilometres left to run. Worse, our route took us across the river (the silver thread was now a sizeable river) then up a further fifteen hundred spirit-breaking feet to the finish at Rimbik.

A glorious, life-restoring beer in the sun, then I dragged myself to the Sherpa Tensing Guest House and ordered a bucket of hot water for my self-administered shower.

They led me to my accommodation — a cramped wooden structure, glued to the edge of a terrifying precipice. I was expected to sleep on a single, wooden pallet with some other competitor.

I garnered up the last fragments of my energy and tried to convert it into assertiveness: 'No. I do not wish to share a bed with another man.'

In an uncharacteristic display of impatience, our minder snapped, 'This isn't a five-star hotel, you know!'

In an uncharacteristic display of murderous violence, I nearly punched his stupid lights out. Instead, I apologised: 'I hadn't realised this is only a four-star hotel, where one would naturally expect to spend the night with some hairy-arsed bloke you only met last Thursday. Now, find me a bed of my own, mate, or I'll… ' Then my momentum ran out — until, in a moment of inspiration, I blurted, '… or I'll tell Mister Pandey!'

It worked like magic.

The name of Pandey struck terror, or at least the most pointed sort of respect, into the hearts of everyone who worked for him. For he is the reason why the race exists. It is he who has carved this amazing event out of some of the most difficult and inhospitable topography in the world — he who, for one week of the year, succeeds in impressing a rigid schedule upon a culture which barely acknowledges the existence of time — he who provides food and water of unfailing purity in the country that invented gastroenteritis.

Mr Pandey's unflagging energy and enthusiasm swept us all along and made even the toughest moments of the run seem less like an ordeal than a fabulous adventure. By the end of the race, he had won the admiration and affection of every one of us.

In fact, during that amazing week, admiration was one commodity that was not in short supply.

Noel Hanna, a dog handler with the RUC, had only ever run one race in his life — a half marathon, back in 1992. And yet he won this one. He covered the 100 miles in around fifteen hours — a feat which simply defies comprehension.

He was raising money for a charity founded to research into the causes and treatment of brain tumours — a subject far too close to his heart, since his wife has suffered for six years from such a tumour. And yet the wild exuberance he shared with his fellow Ulsterman, Craig Johnston, inspired the entire party. Even the Americans went home with Belfast accents and a repertoire of extremely dodgy jokes.

By the time of the race, Noel and Craig had already raised £15,000.

As the days went by, story after story unfurled: so many of my comrades' lives were touched by tragedy, and now they were fighting back for all they were worth for the sake of sick loved ones, lost children, dying friends.

There was a lot of plain, ordinary courage around, too: Eric lost the sole of his foot, turning awkwardly in a mad downhill dash on marathon day. But he made another one from Second Skin and bits of string and mud and stuff, and ran the 13-mile stage next day. Beat me, too.

Barry the fireman damaged his ankle so badly that you could have mistaken it for a giant aubergine (if it hadn't been attached to the end of his leg, that is). He hobbled on for another three days, finishing the race and notching up a very creditable time.

Then Lisa developed pneumonia and the altitude made Bryan as sick as a pig. But they all battled on, uncomplaining to the end. To me, their amazing determination was more impressive than a score of dawns on Kanchenjunga.

When we finally dispersed after twelve days (or an entire lifetime, depending which way you looked at it) it seemed almost inconceivable that we shouldn't be together again next morning, and the next, and forever, at some bleak start line on the roof of the world.

And I was left again with that strange loneliness you feel in the absence of people you hardly knew, yet with whom you shared a huge and life-altering experience.

Flat and dead in the middle of the road. Just another morning run, really

YOU CAN tell a lot about a country by the quality of its roadkill.

In Britain, for instance, it consists mostly of pheasants — slow, dim birds, imported from China because English aristocrats were too slow and dim to shoot anything of local origin.

I've run in countries where there isn't any roadkill: either because intensive farming techniques have long since eradicated even the faintest folk memory of wildlife, or else because any creature unlucky enough to be run over would be sizzling on a griddle while still in mid-death rattle.

Barbados, on the other hand, has just the sort of exotic roadkill you'd expect from a tropical island paradise.

On my first morning run, it was the only thing that kept me going. The combination of jet lag and 98% humidity reduced my pace to a sweat-sodden slouch.

The road wound up from the coast through canyons hewn from ancient corals and draped with curtains of vines.

Ten minutes on this modest little hill and I was gasping. My legs were cast from something stolen from a church roof and my lungs felt like the inflamed scrotums of small rodents.

Then I saw the crushed carcass of the giant millipede. Six inches long, its yellow blood played a pleasing counterpoint to the lustrous black and red stripes of its fragmented carapace.

With renewed vigour, I averted my eyes from the grinding incline ahead and concentrated on the road immediately before my feet.

I was soon rewarded. Fifty yards up the road was the toad. The size of a silicone breast implant and bright green, the reptile offered no obvious sign of traumatic injury.

Perhaps, assailed by the baking sun and the remorseless gradient of Mile-And-A-Quarter Hill, he had simply lost the will to live. I could identify with that.

Now I was staggering past files of ladies in immaculate hats and suits. Each proffered a cheery, 'Good mornin'!' It was Sunday, I realised — they were on their way to the Seventh Day Adventist chapel in Speightstown. Most Barbadians go to church — even the teenagers, says my Barbadian friend, Patrick. 'It's why there are nine murders a year in Barbados and six hundred in Jamaica.' He added, 'If I won a ticket to Kingston, I'd trade it for a beer. They're crazy over there.'

The hill degenerated into a meandering series of Surrey-esque undulations. High stands of sugar cane rustled ominously on either side. The sun, still only a couple of hours old, was squeezed through the lens of the morning's tropical deluge and beat me about the head and body like a soggy, boiling towel.

Just thirty minutes into the run, I was starting to hallucinate. A huge cat lolloped across the road, barely ten yards ahead of me. Even in my dazed state, the creature's long, whip-like tail struck me as unusual, even for a Siamese.

A minute later, the 'cat' assailed me with a welter of abusive chatter from a rotting tree stump, egged on by its wife and two, whip-tailed infant horrors. I chattered back at the family of green monkeys. The 23rd Psalm had no effect whatsoever, but the weather report for UK offshore coastal stations shut them up good.

Two days later, I visited the Barbados Wild Life Reserve — a bewitching oasis of ancient, mahogany forest commanding fantastic views of the island's Caribbean and Atlantic coasts.

The green monkeys gather there, daily, at 3pm to gorge on mounds of fruit. It's a protection racket — they desist from ravaging the plantations of local farmers and the government pays them off with free bananas.

It was now 8am and the temperature was in the mid-eighties. In two weeks, I would be embarking on a 105-mile non-stop run across the Jordan desert with a full pack and a 62-hour deadline. And here was I, close to collapse after just forty-five minutes of gentle ascent in the world's most rapturously inviting climate.

It didn't bode well.

How a simple linguistic misunderstanding can ruin your entire life

I REMEMBER discussing Life with a University friend, back when there was time to think about anything more cerebral than the expiry date of the house insurance and the health of one's prostate.

'Everything we do', he'd declaimed through a cloud of cannabis smoke, 'is subject to the Rat Shit Effect.'

I'd been impressed. In those days, I had joyfully embraced cynicism as synonymous with realism.

My favourite book was Jean-Paul Sartre's *Nausea*. Three months previously, it had been *Edward The Red Engine*. In the ways of the world, I was on an almost vertical learning curve.

So the notion that all human endeavour could and should be equated with rodent excrement struck an immediate resonance with me.

I adopted this new philosophy with a manic ferocity that manifested itself, paradoxically, in a kind of mumbling, round-shouldered despair. I hated The Smiths for their naive optimism and their irrepressible *joie de vivre*.

It was twenty years later when I accidentally encountered my old college pal. I was a mortuary assistant and he was paying his last respects to his grandmother, a celebrated juggler who is credited with the invention of pole dancing.

He hadn't changed much, except that his face was etched with laugh lines, like a relief map of the cheerier bits of Afghanistan.

That evening we reminisced about the old times over a

drink — he sipped a glass of champagne, I necked a bottle of gin. When I reminded him of his 'Rat Shit' analogy, he seemed genuinely shocked. 'No, no! I said *Ratchet* Effect! R-A-T-C-H-E-T. As in screwdrivers.'

I realised I had wasted half my life.

Anyway, I expect you're wondering what this has got to do with running. So am I…

No, hang on — it's this: that once you begin to run for any other reason than to lose a little weight or to 'de-stress' or to put one over on your rapidly deteriorating contemporaries, you are subject to an inexorable Ratchet Effect.

You start off with a five-miler and you stagger across the finish line in your Green Flash tennis shoes, ashen-faced and coughing blood. Within a year, you're togged up in polyprop and Lycra, nipples taped and crotch an inch deep in Vaseline, high-fiving with ten-year-old delinquents in the London Marathon.

A few weeks later and you're watching coverage of the Marathon des Sables with a speculative eye. Twelve months on, you're out there with your power bars and venom pump, kicking and cursing your way across the most beautiful and forbidding landscape under the sun.

And then you're stuffed. Like an addict, you can't stop. But unlike the addict, you can't book yourself into The Priory for an 'Ultra-Marathon Detox'. The only way is down (or in my case, up) — from the desert stage race to the Alpine 78k to the Himalayan 100m to the Guianan rainforest 105.

Now comes the big jump — from stage race to non-stop, and the Jordan Desert Cup.

In a non-stop race, you can stop. You've got to, in fact, unless you're a demi-god and you're in with a decent chance of winning.

What doesn't stop is the clock. So if you sleep, you lose time. Perhaps so much time that you fail to hit a checkpoint and they disqualify you.

I have six months to train. Believe me, I'll need every minute.

In which I totter through the landscape that inspired Bram Stoker's *Dracula*. And *Heartbeat*

WHY I should have imagined that a fourteen mile run along the Cleveland Way in August might be good training for the 105 mile Jordan Desert Cup, remains a mystery.

Perhaps I reasoned, not unreasonably, that August = Summer = Heat and that the combination of sweltering temperatures and rolling hills might in some way mimic the experience of shuffling across Wadi Rum with a sack of anvils on my back.

As usual, I had deluded myself. For one thing, I'd failed to take into account the commencement of the new Ice Age. Only days before, a tornado had cruised majestically up the Humber, and Hull was buried under hailstones the size and weight of hedgehogs.

With Oscar The World's Fittest Dog at my side, I climbed out of the sleepy fishing village of Staithes and hit the coastal path to Runswick Bay. The moment my torso rose above the protecting parapet of the cliff, I was chilled to the marrow by a fierce nor'easterly. This in spite of the big, happy sun that was rolling around above in a blameless blue sky. It was like being stabbed in the back by a smiling man.

The Cleveland Way is 'undulating'. In the recent Euphemism Olympics, 'undulating' took Silver — outclassed only by 'discomfort' (as in when the doctor says, 'you may experience a little discomfort when I do this').

The path hurls itself gleefully at vertical climbs, then thunders directly down dead drops. There are no 'gently winding sections' or 'gradual ascents by means of easily-negotiable hairpin bends'.

This is Yorkshire. The course was clearly designed by Geoff Boycott after a bad day.

I knew within two minutes of setting out that it was going to be awful. My lungs were full of pond weed and my legs weren't properly attached to my pelvis. As the quaint cottages of Staithes fell away behind me, even calling the dog left me breathless.

The coastline between Saltburn and Whitby was once the arena for an extraordinary burst of economic activity. Almost equalling the

Klondike Gold Rush for naked greed, the shale cliffs were literally torn down in the quest for alum — an all-purpose Philosopher's Stone, used in the 18th century for absolutely everything.

The alum secret was stolen from the Chinese by Italian merchant adventurers — then from the Italians by Yorkshiremen. Why was it so important? A hundred years on, nobody can rightly recall. However, great mounds of shale were ignited and burned for years on end to crack out the alum.

The alien landscape thus created, albeit mellowed a little by time, looks weirdly prehistoric. No wonder Bram Stoker had Count Dracula flit over Kettleness Point in the guise of a bat.

But today, as I heaved and wheezed myself over The Undulations, I was oblivious to all except the burning need to stop.

As I gasped out of Runswick Bay, along a path I used to skip up as a kid, I let Oscar off the lead. He grinned at me as if to say *You must be bloody mad!* and launched himself back down the hill. He'd clocked a half-eaten sausage outside a tent on the beach, and the image had etched itself indelibly upon his simple, canine cortex.

Although I was gasping from exhaustion, I had no alternative but to surrender the four hundred feet I'd already climbed and stagger back down to the beach. Where the dog, licking his lips, greeted me like a long-lost twin.

For the next five miles, the stiles had no dog gates and I had to hoik the smug Belgian sod from field to field.

Eventually we reached Sandsend, where I gratefully embraced the prospect of a flat, two-mile jog along hard-packed sand to Whitby.

But the sand wasn't hard-packed and it soon dawned on me what Jordan would really be like. Within minutes, we were reduced to Scout's Pace.

By the time we reached the Station car park and the blessed ministrations of our loved ones, we were nearly dead. Oscar drank three pints of water.

'This desert thing,' ventured Mrs Blackford diplomatically. 'Is it something you *really* feel you *have* to do?'

A Surrey state of affairs

IF 'THE World's Toughest Foot Race' were merely a race to develop the world's toughest foot, I'd be laughing. I'd do a couple of weeks' firewalking in Haiti, soak the old plates of meat in permanganate and bingo, I'd be quaffing my Special Brew from the Jordan Desert Cup by Christmas.

However, there's rather more to the event than the description suggests. Most alarming of its many alarming features is that it's non-stop. So within a few hours, the runners will be strung out sparsely across the desert — and instead of simply following the bunch in front, I shall be forced to navigate for myself.

This would be fine if I weren't directionally dyslexic. I couldn't land a kite on Africa. If I'd been Captain Cook, I'd have tried to colonise the Isle of Sheppey. And don't wave your maps at me — you might as well show me hieroglyphs from the Rosetta Stone.

Profoundly insecure in this knowledge, I decided to practise with a modest orienteering event. Twelve miles through the tame, gently undulating heathlands of Surrey, I decided, might just awaken the migrating bird in me — fan into life the primitive homing instincts that must surely smoulder among our folk memories.

I directed a confident, cheery wave to the loved ones as we trotted away from the prosperous little commuter town into the leafy lanes and neatly manicured paddocks of the Green Belt. The sun smiled down. Martins darted under eaves of immaculate thatch. Dragonflies sported over serene streams, caressed by the fronds of stately willows.

This was going to be a doddle.

Eight hours later, I was crashing, wide-eyed and breathless, through a thicket of malevolent brambles. My arms and legs were ripped by thorns, spotted with the burning Braille of nettles.

The sun, apparently, had smiled on Surrey enough for one day. There was a damp chill in the air and a malicious breeze was rattling the dry sticks of the coppice.

Something stirred, off to the left in a dense stand of birch.

'Hello?' I called, 'is that Checkpoint Three?' It wasn't. It was a muntjac — a dwarf deer imported recklessly from exotic parts and now bent on devouring the rare plants and treelets that your decent, British deer wouldn't stoop to.

Exhausted, I slumped against a tree and rummaged in my rucksack for the map. I stared at it with my most rugged and eagle-eyed outdoor look.

It smirked back at me and stuck its tongue out. I turned it upside down — or was it downside up?

I refuse to be intimidated by a pattern of wiggly, coloured lines. So I smoothed the map over a log and with my index finger traced random routes across it. I thought it might make more sense if I frowned and bit my lower lip, the way the Professionals do.

Eventually, I picked it up and tore it into approximately three hundred pieces. These I stuffed down a rat hole.

Now in my view, *The Blair Witch Project* doesn't have a great deal to tell us. But it's right about one thing: when you're lost in a wood, it's not a good idea to throw away the map.

It was dark, now, and I was very, very edgy. Don't believe the conservationists when they tell you all the interesting animals are extinct. The woods are crawling with stuff. Stuff that bites you, stuff that stings you, and stuff that just crashes around and scares the shit out of you.

(It's a fact that many thousands of wild animals have escaped from the private zoos of Surrey's obscenely rich. My friend John Mundy once nearly ran over a wallaby on his bicycle.)

And here's another thing: given that you can't organise a test match or even a bloody barbecue without it getting rained off, how come, when you're really up against it, you can't find a single cubic centimetre of water to drink?

By the time morning began to filter through the birch trees and the wolves retreated to their secret, Surrey lairs, I was almost dead from thirst.

Still, as I reasoned later to my distraught wife, there are no woods in the Jordan desert.

She seemed strangely unreassured.

I thought Petra was the dog from *Blue Peter* until I ran The Jordan Desert Cup

SLOWLY AND painfully, bent against the freezing wind, two small, grey figures wound down off the mountain towards the lights of a village.

Above them, the fantastic canopy of the stars was dissolving in a gunmetal dawn. The three hours after moonset had been especially trying: the way was steep, often precipitous, and littered with stones. The feeble, orange beams of their headlights were hopelessly inadequate and the exhausted runners stumbled and cursed their way down the track, jarring their blistered toes and turning their ankles.

The concentration required to avoid serious injury had killed all conversation but now the second runner made a determined effort to catch his companion. As he drew level, he gasped, 'I'm shot! My feet are killing me and I'm frozen to the bone. We've got to stop and get some hot food down us.'

The other nodded. 'I have to get out of this fucking wind. There must be somewhere to shelter in the village.'

The call of the muezzin drifted eerily over the blue-grey gulf that still separated the runners from the lights...

I dropped back again and fixed my gaze on the village: it seemed to drift in the half-light like an elusive, ghostly galleon. But after an age, we tottered from the path into a scrubby little olive grove, coaxed rucksacks from battered shoulders and lowered ourselves painfully to the ground. For a while, we didn't speak — just drank in the sacrament of silence and stillness, the simple bliss of not running.

I looked at David. Dishevelled and unshaven, covered with the patina of a hundred miles' desert sand and road dust, he made a sorry, sorry sight. 'Has it really come to this?' I wanted to know. 'We're just a couple of down-and-outs. Tramps. We're... the underclass.'

David pushed his camera at me. 'Here. Do us a favour. I want to record what is undoubtedly the lowest point of my fucking life.'

In one respect, he was right: that poor gruel of rice pudding and sultanas, reconstituted over the sooty flame of a miniature stove, did mark the nadir of our Jordan Desert Cup. We'd been running or walking for the worst part of a hundred miles through baking desert heat and the fierce, freezing winds of the high mountain passes. We had slept little, eaten less. We'd burned, blistered and shivered our way across some of the most hostile landscapes in the world and now we wanted nothing so much as to stop, to lie down, to go home.

But the restorative powers of rice pudding must rank among life's great mysteries. As warmth and energy seeped into our ragged sinews and the promise of a golden dawn suffused the eastern sky, we were visited by a new optimism. Only ten miles to go, after all — a mere stroll for superheroes of our calibre. After binding another slab of Second Skin to my bleeding feet, I rose and experimented gingerly with the walking thing. It hurt — feet, knees, thighs, hips and back, mostly — but at least it still worked.

A few minutes later, the Underclass was on the move again.

The Jordan Desert Cup is organised by Atlantide Organisation International — those wonderful folks who brought you the Marathon des Sables. In fact, it claims to have superseded the MDS as 'the world's toughest foot race', for although it's shorter it's a non-stop event. You set out from Wadi Rum and you finish at Petra — within 62 hours, or you're disqualified.

As for 'the world's toughest', that's a claim veterans of the Death Valley Race would dispute, I'm sure. But it's certainly hard work. For one thing it isn't, as AOI claims, 105 miles long. On this all the contestants were agreed. The legendary marathoneer Rory Coleman had run the test race in '99 and he'd warned us with his customary cheeriness at the Start that we were in for at least 120 miles. 'They must have measured it from a spy satellite.'

'By the way,' he added, 'you'll be needing your space blankets. It's going to be minus fifteen in the hills. And the first seventy miles is through soft sand. You'll be lucky if you run more than 300 yards of it.'

Oh, joy. This only served to deepen the sense of pre-race gloom that had set in upon meeting the Brit contingent at Heathrow. They looked young, bright-eyed, clean-cut and, above all, supremely fit. In stark contrast, I was old, slightly hung over, inadequately equipped and conspicuously under-trained.

I couldn't bear to listen to their accounts of eighty-mile training jogs and back-to-back sub-three marathons. Quietly, I took myself off to the Business Class lounge and mixed myself a serious Bloody Mary. 'This is it,' I reflected. 'You've really done it now. For twenty years, you've scraped by on the bare minimum. But this is Armageddon, matey. Escape now, before it's too late!'

My mood didn't improve as, some eight hours later, I was shoved out of a jeep into a makeshift campsite in the sand. I found a skimpy strip of unoccupied carpet in a communal bivouac and tried to sleep. The air vibrated to the snores of twenty congested Spaniards. I was lonely, cramped and gripped by a dark foreboding.

If I could have pressed a button and been transported instantly to my comfortable bed in Hampstead with its beautiful built-in wife, I would have pressed it then, without a second's hesitation.

At 5:15am, the Spaniards stopped snoring and started jabbering. Why do the Latins always sound as if they're arguing over the ground rules of a duel to the death?

Blearily, I dragged myself from the tent and then stopped short. We were camped on a plain of sand, enclosed by sheer walls of golden sandstone that glowed in the morning sun as if lit from within. This was Wadi Rum — a place of such stark, alien majesty that all my misgivings momentarily evaporated. The defile opened out to the south to reveal a limitless desert, punctuated by more of these astonishing monoliths, like stone battleships on a shimmering sea of sand. 'That's where we're going,' said a voice at my shoulder. 'Due south.' It was Liam, an ex-Marine from Somerset.

'Speak for yourself,' I wanted to reply, 'I'm going north and I'm not stopping till I reach the snug of The Cat & Hacksaw, Great Titchfield Street, London West One.'

The feeling of doomed isolation returned. Looking round, it was as if all the other participants had been best friends since infant school. There was a sickening air of happy anticipation abroad.

Liam, it turned out over the next few days, was good at north and south and all that technical stuff. (This was just as well, because I have a blank spot about compasses. Despite twenty years of diving and ten of trail running, I still need a refresher course in basic navigation before every event.)

Later, as we queued for our emergency parachute flares, he revealed more of his practical side. 'We had these in the Gulf. Standard issue. We used to rip out the parachutes and fire them at people.'

In fact, there was a lot of queueing that day. Each runner's pack had to be opened in front of the race officials, compulsory items of equipment displayed, emergency reserves sealed, calories counted. One Jordanian was in a right old state because he was 500 calories short of his minimum. A helpful Italian offered him a chunk of sausage. Unhappily, it turned out to be pork, and the Jordanian's wails of anguish were audible throughout the camp.

That afternoon, Liam appeared in my tent with a pot of impact adhesive and two buffs — tubes of elasticated material that fit around the neck and cover the mouth and nose in the event of sandstorms. Under his instruction, I glued the buffs around the sides of my shoes, where they formed highly-effective sand-proof gaiters.

Thanks to this brilliant piece of inventiveness (originally conceived by Coleman, I think) we were spared seventy miles of shoe-emptying and the worst sort of blisters.

Later, Liam and I became quite good friends. I'm sure he thought I was a softy London wuss — there were the occasional muttered remarks about handbags and whingeing — but we were stuck in the same boat and were able to contribute equally to the stream of banter that sustained our spirits across the weary miles. Nevertheless, he had a rare talent for conversation-stopping remarks. I asked him if he'd rejoin the Marines if he had the chance.

'Like a shot,' he replied.

'Why?'

'Because nothing — *nothing* — beats the sheer exhilaration of firing live rounds at people.'

The second night was tough. We'd breathed a sigh of relief when the fine sand finally gave way to a firm path. But after a catnap and a dehydrated Chicken Korma at Checkpoint 10, we were faced with a three-thousand-foot climb into the mountains on rocky, rutted trails.

Coleman and Liam had struck out an hour earlier and as David and I left the camp behind in the encroaching dusk, the air turned suddenly chilly.

The hills were a maze of footpaths and rough roads, and we relied heavily upon the occasional chemical lightstick to guide us. So imagine how we felt when we approached a dozen drunken Jordanians, cavorting in what looked like Superman's crystal lodge, but which actually consisted of thirty or forty stolen route markers. 'Hey! Come! Come!' they shouted, beckoning wildly and staggering about in the eerie green light like pissed wizards at a disco.

We declined politely on the pretext of a pressing engagement.

As we climbed ever higher the breeze became stiffer. Two hours later and it was a no-nonsense, full-on gale, unceasing and bitingly cold. Checkpoint 11 was like a wind tunnel, but we managed to snatch an hour's doze before the cold woke us and prodded us onwards. For half the night we fantasised about Checkpoint 12 — an oasis of warmth and comfort, we promised ourselves, snuggling in the lea of the mountains.

In fact, CP 12 had blown away. A few, sorry individuals huddled miserably behind a rock. We knew that if we joined them, we'd never get up. So grimly, wordlessly, we pushed on.

I found myself looking back with real nostalgia on the last desert stage when the temperature had hovered in the thirties. What I wouldn't have given, right now, for a touch of heatstroke.

Then the moon dipped below the hills and the night began in earnest...

The Jordan Desert Cup ends, with a well-developed sense of its own importance, at Petra — one of the wonders of the ancient world.

4,000 years old, it is an entire city of caves and temples carved from the red sandstone of a deep canyon. One of the most dramatic facades was commandeered by Spielberg as Indiana Jones' *Temple of Doom*.

The route drops into the valley from the wall of the mountains. As David and I scuttered down a slope of loose scree, I reflected how lucky we were to be negotiating it in daylight. Others were not so fortunate, as a host of cuts and bruises, even a broken arm, would later testify.

The place is too downright, bloody extraordinary to run through without proper acknowledgement. We tarried, gawked, chatted to tourists, took snaps. Then David glanced at his watch: we had just ten minutes if were to finish in 48 hours-and-some-thing, instead of 49. And so our last kilometre was consumed in a frantic and undignified dash through the serpentine canyons of Petra, barging past tour parties, panting and wheezing like a couple of broken-winded old pack horses.

We made it with seconds to spare.

I'd like to describe the feeling of sheer relief that overwhelmed us as we collapsed onto picnic chairs in the sunshine with a litre of cold water, no pack to carry and nowhere to run. But I can't.

The English language simply isn't up to the task.

In which I'm tempted to take a chainsaw to the International Family Friendship Breakfast Jog

I GREW up on Teesside, where the landscape consisted largely of slag tips — bleak, bare hills of cinders, the by-product of iron smelting. Teesside did not enjoy a vigorous tourist trade.

On the other hand, I've just been to Lanzarote where the landscape consists entirely of slag tips — bleak, bare hills of cinders, thrown up 200 years ago in a volcanic catastrophe. And the whole of Northern Europe is queueing up to visit.

The difference is the sun, which spends 364 days in the Canary Islands, and the rest of the year on Teesside.

On the east coast of Lanzarote bloats Puerto del Carmen — a five-mile wilderness where grotesque, pink parodies of the human form in lard and polyester heave their swollen cadavers from *Burger King* to *Dunkin' Donuts.*

On no account go within a stone's throw of Puerto del Carmen — except to throw stones.

However, on the windward side of the island, where the unbridled power of the Atlantic explodes against towering, misty cliffs and tangles of jagged magma, the lard gives way to svelte, bronzed bodies, the shell suits to Gore-Tex and Lycra.

Here, perched upon a fragile archipelago, is Club la Santa — winter quarters to Danish triathlon stars, German swimming relay teams, heavyweight boxers, Norwegian pursuit cyclists and Linford Christie.

Architecturally, the club falls somewhere between the Odeon, Ongar, and a badger sett. Like every building on Lanzarote, it's green and white. The rooms are basic but comfortable, the food adequate, the hot water plentiful — and the sports facilities unrivalled anywhere within a four-hour radius of Gatwick.

What's more, the outdoor Olympic pool is heated. Lanes, no kids. The track is tartan, the punchbag still carries the impression of Bruno's right, the sheltered lagoon cajoles you into booking windsurfing lessons with frightening Germans.

Then there's the five-a-side soccer pitch, the first-class gym, the day-long stretch and aerobics classes and the volleyball and tennis courts.

If they don't yet do Formula One Bull-Baiting, it's only a matter of time.

What better venue for the Lanzarote Challenge, timed to hit a narrow window of opportunity at the end of the summer, just before the energetic bit of Europe vanishes beneath the ice cap and every half-decent athlete from Trondheim to Munich descends upon the island?

The race series was conceived ten years ago by Vince Regan (an Irish ex-marathon star) as he watched the Tour de France on TV.

The event was to consist of four races, short, hard and different. The idea was to test a runner's versatility, rather than flat-out speed or endurance.

The concept remains unchanged. The 10k is still a bloody nightmare, as I'm sure it always was — three laps around the lagoon on a course which allows you to see every runner before and behind you, all of the time. I'm not saying it's psychologically gruelling, but Amnesty has filed a formal complaint.

The only downhill stretch puts the wind behind you, so you boil and gasp and beg for a breath of air. Then you turn the corner over the bridge and the 'breath' is a force five gale, turning your vest into a billowing mainsail as you wind up the interminable hill to the start (again).

Worse, you're far from fresh, even at the start. The moment you arrive at the club, they seduce you into a series of 'non-competitive fun runs'. If it's not the 'Wake-Up 4k', then it's the 'International Family Friendship Breakfast Jog'.

Then there's the stretching sessions. As you turn up at the track, you're recruited by some bronzed example of athletic Danish gorgeousness into making an aerobic prat of yourself by pulling the muscles the funruns have missed.

I've never been a great one for learning by experience, but I've always tried to bear in mind that in twenty years of running, my only serious injuries were incurred while stretching.

The second race is the Ridge Run. This starts on tarmac then splits off up a dusty track around the rim of an extinct volcano. (At least it's extinct. Just five miles away, the most famous restaurant on the island will grill you a steak over a hole in the ground.)

Once again, you must come to terms with the awful realism afforded by a panoramic view of the course. You know it hurts like buggery, you know you're not Kenyan, but do you *have* to endure such a stark, uninterrupted view of the leaders, climbing the ridge two shin-shattering miles ahead of you?

Perhaps this is the ultimate challenge — total transparency. You can't pretend you're doing better than you are, because you can see precisely where you lie in the field. You can't fantasise about being nearly home when you're not, because the green and white towers of Club la Santa are depressingly visible from every point on the course.

Still, when you burst, gasping, across the finish line in the stadium, it's only a hundred yards to your room and a life-restoring bath. Then a further fifty to a beer at the Sports Bar in the Square. Then a final, heroic six feet to the restaurant where you'll eat anything they tell you to while Vince presents the prizes to superheroes who were already showered and dried while you were still spitting blood, three miles out in the lava fields.

That night, I contracted tuberculosis, our three-year-old daughter ran the kind of temperature you could grill meat over, and the Club's resident instructors, the Green Team, decided to stage a Drunken Bellowing Contest outside our door at 2am.

Sante.

I would happily disembowel all the competitors and spectators at the UK's best-loved running event

EXHAUSTED BY my millionth London Marathon, I collapse into bed. After what seems like seconds, I wake with a start as my radio brays, 'It's 5:30 and today is Marathon Day!'

Cursing, I drag my aching limbs out of bed and just like every other morning, pin my number on my vest and smear vaseline between my toes...

Trapped in a vortex in the fabric of time, I have spent all eternity running the London.

At first, I loved the special atmosphere of the event (generated by 30,000 runners telling each other how special the atmosphere is).

I loved the warm sense of solidarity which attends all such expressions of mass stupidity.

I loved the fleeting nanosecond of enjoyment on Westminster Bridge between the agony of running and the crushing anticlimax of stopping.

But after my five-hundredth race, these small pleasures were etched away by the acid of repetition.

What remains? The sense of doom as I wake, as if I'm about to sit an economics exam I haven't revised for.

The aches and pains and the plain, physical weakness that so cruelly mocks the weeks of training.

The breakfast I take like medicine, which sits stubbornly in a ball at the foot of my oesophagus.

The sullen driver from the second cab company (the first didn't show up, so I'm late and shaking with panic and impotent rage).

Bowel worry.

The concourse at Charing Cross, heaving with happy gangs of comrades, all infinitely fitter and better prepared than I am.

The inane chatter of the Hinderwell Joggers: 'When d'you think you'll hit the wall?'

'I'm not going to hit the wall. I'm saving all me energy for runnin'.'

174

As I hang on the strap in the cattle truck, the sharp stink of liniment like fear in the air, I realise how much I hate people.

Oh, individually they're all right. But herd them together into a group, or worse, a crowd, or worse still, a crowd with a common interest, and I must fight the urge to address them with a scythe.

The impulsion comes most strongly upon me when a short, barrel-chested, bow-legged pillock with an iron-grey number one haircut and a Wirral Strollers vest shouts 'OGGEE! OGGEE! OGGEE!' And a hundred identical little pillocks return, 'OI! OI! OI!'

Now language, after all, is the crowning accomplishment of *Homo Sapiens*. It gives us sway over the beasts of the field. Not only does it allow us to express complex constructs of logic, to describe and define the world outside us and the abstract concepts that shape our inner lives, it has recently been suggested that language actually precedes thought — that it is the *sine qua non* of humankind's unique self-consciousness.

And all this ricket-ravaged little retard can manage is OGGEE! OGGEE! OGGEE!

Pass the scythe.

I don't know what drives people to line up to watch a marathon. I suspect it's the same ghoulish fascination that once attracted them to public hangings.

Once, the Isle of Dogs was an empty desert. For seven blessed years, it was free of snot-encrusted urchins exhorting you to 'get them knees up' and toothless hags thrusting food at you. (On various occasions, malodorous East End crones have offered me jellied eels, steak and kidney pudding and chocolate fudge cake with custard).

And I assume it's beer that deludes fat men with grey beards and Union Jack bowler hats into thinking that by playing *When The Saints Come Marching In* on battered trombones, they will propel me to the pinnacle of athletic achievement.

For their legendary Cockney hospitality and good humour, I would happily murder them all.

Meanwhile, the cab hasn't shown up and I'm beginning to worry about the bowels.

I'd better get on.

In which I run the modest Kingston 16 and learn that short races are just as awful as long ones

LIFE, I have concluded, is more like a fartlek session than a marathon.

It jogs along for years at a decent, steady rate — and then it passes the second lamp post after the church and *vroom*! Its head goes down, its stride lengthens and suddenly it's thundering along at five-minute-mile pace.

The scenery fairly flies by: *Oh, look, the kids have grown up. Wasn't that my career back there?*

There's no predicting exactly when Life's going to take off, but when it does, it's both exhilarating and alarming.

It happened to me last week. On Sunday night, I was gloomily contemplating another Monday morning. It was as if my first two periods were going to be double maths with Mrs Fellowes followed by a French vocabulary test, then Logger Goodwill was going to beat me up behind the cadet hut.

Ridiculous, I mused — that was all thirty-five years ago. Mrs Fellowes is probably dozing her days away in a twilight home somewhere, while Logger serves five consecutive life sentences for genocide.

Meanwhile, I'm the Creative Director of a West End advertising agency, with an infinitely-elastic credit card and an air-conditioned motor car.

Still, this didn't stop me resigning at 9am next day.

Why, you ask. I can't really say. Suffice it to say that I was sick of school, so I bunked off. It was the sort of madcap decision I might have made on a Friday afternoon with a skinful of good, Spanish fighting wine. But this was Monday morning, I'd run five miles on the Heath and I was as sober as a fish.

In the time-honoured tradition of my industry, I was out within the hour.

So I'm writing to you as a free man. I gaze out between sentences and next door's flowering cherries to where the silver meadows of Hampstead Heath beckon seductively. I mention casually to Oscar, my delinquent Belgian Shepherd dog, the possibility of a run and he stares at me disbelievingly: *Are you completely mad? This is the afternoon. You don't go running in the afternoon. In fact, you shouldn't be here at all. You're an optical illusion. Bugger off.*

He's probably right. With the Marathon ten days away, I'm fighting off a cold. For a while, I was winning. I woke in the night and felt as if I was trying to swallow sawdust cake with bayonet tacks. So I gargled with salt and TCP — a recipe developed by A&E charge nurses to induce vomiting in overdose cases — and it seemed to do the trick.

Then I ran the Kingston 16 and knackered myself so comprehensively that the cold has come swaggering back in through open gates.

The race was a Learning Experience. The first thing I learned was, don't add the price of a first class stamp to the entry fee just because you can't be arsed to stick one on your SAE. If you do, the organisers will simply bank your cheque and send off your number without a stamp. It will then turn up two days after the race, plastered with official threats and insults.

I also learned that two-lap races are more than twice as hard as one-lap races. (Actually, this is something I've always known, but always forget.) In a one-lap race, you can always fool yourself that the finish is closer than it really is. But after the halfway mark on a two-lap course, the horrible truth is always there, staring you in the face, sneering at your feeble attempts at positivity so that even your best running buddy is dragged down into the pit of your despair.

Oh, Christ!

What's up?

That cat!

What about it?

I saw that cat last time round. There's miles to go after that cat.

There can't be.

There is. I'm telling you. I was feeling great when I saw that cat first time around. And I was only feeling great for the very first bit. The cat must be really near the start.

How do you know it's the same cat?

Don't be stupid! Because it was near the wheelbarrow.

Oh, God — it wasn't, was it? I remember the wheelbarrow. The wheelbarrow was only about ten minutes in.

Are you sure?

I'm sodding positive. Just shut up and run.

Bloody, sodding cat...

Anyway, I can no longer resist the Call of the Heath, so I'm off to put in my final long one before the Marathon.

Last month, I was sober. This month, I'm sober and unemployed.

Next month, no doubt, I'll be sober, unemployed and disappointed.

In which my genetic incapacity for team spirit is emphatically confirmed

I TOOK up running because I hated team sports. Still do. They demand a degree of respect and responsibility for your fellow man who, in my experience, is a moron.

Team Man is an oaf with a head conjoined directly to his body without the intervention of a neck, who only joined a team in order to legitimise his need to beat the living shit out of men whose only fault is to wear a different colour shirt.

I used to play hockey. I was the fastest man on the field because I was possessed of an urgent desire to be as far away from the ball as possible. Hockey is a game so dangerous as to teeter on the brink of the suicidal. The ball is dense and heavy, and is propelled at the kind of velocity that occurs only when initial might is amplified exponentially by the leverage of a long, flexible club.

But more compelling still was my dread of letting down my teammates.

That's why I like solo running: if you screw up, you have nobody to blame but yourself. Take the case of poor old Basher Burbage who took a five-hundred-yard detour during the Bogota Anti-Personnel 100. We were lucky to cut him from the wire before the vultures made it unnecessary. But at least he had the (brief) consolation of knowing it was his own fault.

Not so in a relay race, where your teammates depend upon you in the most burdensome way.

Before last wekend's *Long Short* (Pinner to Royston) event, I'd only competed in two relays.

The first was in Reading. I was cajoled by a 'friend' into entering a bunch of useless amateurs in a race against the national teams of several East African countries.

I got lost during my leg, strayed into a field and was chased by a bull. I say bull — DNA tests revealed it to be a lesbian cow. But believe me, you wouldn't have wanted to stick around to argue the case.

My second relay was the Numbskulls 50, where the runners were picked at random from a hat. Our first leg runner turned out to be just that: he had one leg.

Anyway, for reasons too complicated and stupid to explain, I agreed to run in the *Long Short* (Pinner to Royston) event. I airily agreed to do the 12.8-mile stage. But I felt far from airy when, twenty miles down the A1(M), a passenger in my neighbour's car, I realised I hadn't packed my running shoes.

Jayne turned the car around and headed home. 'Don't worry,' she said sweetly. 'One day, you'll chuckle about this over a glass of wine.'

Bile, more like.

Picked up the shoes, had half an hour to drive the thirty miles to the swap-over point in St Albans, chose the motorcycle, touched 150mph on the motorway, got lost, couldn't call race organiser because mobile in Jayne's car, finally reached start, late, with all four indicators mysteriously flashing, ran like demented hare, returned to bike, battery flat, had to jog home.

Some sound advice: never mistake a hilly road marathon for a supermarket trolley dash

SEVEN LAPS round Tesco sounded like my ideal event. Supermarket Dash meets indoor track race with the added bonus of Clubcard points at the final checkout. So I accepted the invitation with alacrity.

Three months later, my features locked in a wild, demented stare as I dragged myself up the fourteenth 1:5 hill, I had cause to regret my habit of speed-scanning my email at midnight without spectacles.

For Tresco, situated 28 miles off Land's End, was the venue for the Isles of Scilly Marathon — an event so surreal that Salvador Dali himself wouldn't have looked out of place on the start line.

For one thing, I little imagined when I descended blearily from the sleeper train at Penzance that, within a matter of hours, I would be engaged in a public fencing match against a beautiful Olympic gold medallist.

But first, Tresco. Imagine if you will a tropical island torn from its moorings in the Grenadines by some natural cataclysm and borne across the Atlantic on the Gulf Stream, finally coming to rest beside the Cornish riviera.

Next, imagine this island annexed by the director of *The Prisoner*. Cars, crime, litter and The Poor are quietly spirited away. There prevails the eerie equilibrium of a painted smile.

If one feels the slightest stirring of unease, it is quickly dispelled by the glory of the surroundings.

Water of an unfeasible turquoise gently caresses blinding white beaches. Palm trees sway languorously amidst mats of amaryllis lilies and white and purple agapanthus, huge-bloomed natives of South Africa.

Cacti the size of caravans thrive amidst Chilean flowering succulents, Australasian tree ferns and blazing banks of bougainvillaea from the Mediterranean.

While beside the shell-strewn shores, tens of thousands of

purple-pinnacled echia reach for a sky that is only one degree less dazzling than the ocean.

Tresco's legendary gardens were founded in the 19th century and lovingly husbanded by generations of Dorrien-Smiths, the present owners of the island.

They were decimated in January 1987 (the gardens, not the Dorrien-Smiths) by the first snow to settle on the island in living memory. But thanks to a worldwide horticultural grand tour by Tresco's Head Gardener and his team, their splendour has been entirely restored. Visitors flock from five continents to admire this miraculous natural anomaly, a mere twenty-minute chopper hop from the British mainland.

When they arrive, they're piled along with their luggage onto a trailer towed by a farm tractor — one of the handful of petrol-powered vehicles permitted on the island. Most of them are deposited (the visitors, not the vehicles) outside the Island Hotel — an establishment occupying the kind of position God would choose for his holiday home in Heaven.

It is sheltered from the worst excesses of the weather by wildly romantic outcrops of the type described by Wordsworth. A path winds from the conservatory onto a manicured croquet lawn and thence to an immaculate beach.

It is the hotel's head chef who is to blame for the Isles of Scilly Marathon. Peter Hingston's small daughter Jade suffers from Cystic Fibrosis and he'd always intended to raise money to fight the disease by running the London.

However, since the race falls in one of his busiest seasons he decided last year that the mountain must come to Mohammed. If he were going to run a marathon, it would have to be on Tresco.

To enter the race, you must pledge to raise money for the Cystic Fibrosis Trust. In this respect, as far as I know, it's the only event of its kind. The 2000 event raised enough to keep Steve Smith, a top research scientist with the Heart & Lung Foundation, in business for an entire year. And this year he returned to the island to run the race for himself.

It is this kind of intimate involvement and personal dedication that makes the race so special.

Example: Bob Brown had just returned from running 3,000 miles across Australia in 65 days. (No, *you* work it out.) But he turned up on Tresco and donated his shoes to the CFT auction. Then he went and won the bloody race.

Now you may not think that a piddling little rock off Penzance would hold much terror for a veteran of the endless, scorching Outback. But the race is tougher than you'd think. There are three hills on Tresco — two short, sharp, vicious little buggers, and one long, enervating slog. But since the course is over seven and a half laps of the island, you end up climbing... no, *you* work it out.

Among the other guests at the Island Hotel was the British Olympic Women's Modern Pentathlon team. Given the dreamlike quality of the weekend, I wouldn't have been surprised to bump into Dr Jonathan Miller, too, along with Jacques Chirac, the Black Dyke Mills Band and Sooty.

We'd hardly had time to explore our split-level room with its panoramic view of the shore and a bed that would qualify on acreage alone as a Scilly Isle in its own right, when we were summoned to the croquet lawn to watch a display of fencing by two of the pentathletes.

Dr Stephanie Cook and Kate Allenby, gold and bronze medallists respectively, explained the rules to a small group of bemused spectators. Most of the terms are in French, but as far as I could make out, you just wiggle your wrist limply for a bit, as if flicking the cockroaches off a trifle, then charge screaming at your opponent, slashing and hacking and stabbing like a homicidal maniac.

So I challenged Stephanie to a duel. They wired me up to the electronic hit sensor, shoved an épée in my hand and off we went. I lasted about thirty seconds. As I lunged and swiped wildly at the air some considerable distance from her torso, she slipped easily through my guard. Had it not been for the little button on the end of her sword, she would have reduced me to

Gruyère. My humiliation cost me a pound in the Cystic Fibrosis box.

Not to be outdone, Mrs Blackford took up the fight, donning a ridiculous fibreglass bustier and acquitting herself far more respectably than I.

Finally, the wonderful Kate Allenby knelt to spar with our six-year-old daughter, who has since developed an unshakeable ambition to become an Olympic pentathlete.

'I can swim, I can run, I can ride a horse and now I can fence. When can you buy me a gun, daddy?'

Kate and Steph hurled themselves into the spirit of the marathon, manning the marshalling points and even running a couple of laps themselves.

Their presence was a welcome distraction in a race which was as challenging psychologically as it was physically. On a point-to-point course you can kid yourself you're nearer the finish than you really are. In this event, the brutal truth stares you in the face throughout. You tick off the laps like the years of a life sentence.

In a field of eighty, there's no safety in numbers, nowhere to hide. You're on your own. You fix your gaze on the runner in front, panicking when the gap grows, rallying when it shrinks.

Without the customary human traffic jam of the London, I went off too fast. Fortunately for me, so did everybody else. By the halfway mark, I was feeling better and beginning to pick off the odd straggler. I worked slowly through the field, and eventually staggered up the final hill and across the line in fifteenth place.

The finish was ten yards from our room and the hot, deep bath in which I promptly fell asleep.

The thin cloud that had kept us cool throughout the race rolled back, now, and the sun shone down on the island's little community centre and the medal ceremony. Rosie Inge, one of the big spirits behind this extraordinary event, managed a few kind and appropriate words about every single runner while the pentathletes dished out the gongs.

There can be no other marathon in the world quite like

Tresco. This year, it was held on the same day as the London — and while four hundred times as many runners set out from Blackheath as from the Abbey Gardens, they'd have been hard pushed to enjoy their day as much as we did.

In which I realise that there's no Spain without pain

I HAVEN'T run a road marathon since that grisly business in the Isles of Scilly — seven laps of an island, three hills per lap, and the same hooting gauntlet of spectators you had to face the next time around, and the next, *ad nauseam*.

Nevertheless, Seaton has cajoled me into running Madrid.

His technique is always the same — we go to that nice, airy little Italian place, roughly equidistant from our respective offices; the ravaged old waiter asks with his ironic, toothless smirk whether I want to eat 'Sophia's bosom' (Pollo Sophia Loren, chicken breast cooked in cream with mushrooms). I reply in the affirmative.

He doesn't even bother to ask about the Pinot Grigio, after a bottle or so of which Seaton suggests with that deceptive casualness he reserves for such occasions that I sign up for something enormously stupid.

This time he used a new technique: 'How about Mongolia in July?' I hum and I ha — this is a big, tough race in what is, after Teesside, the planet's last great wilderness.

Eventually, as the Pinot finally storms the last trenches of common sense, I agree. And then he slipped in the Madrid thing which, compared to running a hundred miles across a desert in the merciless heat of a Central Asian summer, sounded like a gentle stroll along the prom at Eastbourne with a girl on your arm.

It's the same trick they pull at electrical superstores when they get you to buy the TV, then slam you with the three years' extended warranty.

Anyway, I haven't trained on a road for months. I don't possess any shoes that aren't soled like a JCB.

It's not that I'm addicted to mud — it simply isn't safe to run on the roads around Royston.

The average age of a driver in these parts is fifteen. Once he's forced you off the road, arms flailing, into a ditch, he'll career into a lay-by in the TWOC (*Taken Without Owner's Consent*) with his seven mates and set fire to it with an incendiary device combining a quart of Red Bull with a good-vintage sniffing solvent.

At the other end of the scale are the farmers, weaving their way home from market day in their 1964 short wheelbase Land Rovers after nine hours of badger baiting and strong drink in the copse behind The Two-Headed Goat.

So I now have six weeks to transform my legs from the flaccid, lard-filled prophylactics they are today into sturdy towers of steel-riven muscle, resilient enough to withstand twenty-six miles of tarmac.

The worst of it is, I can't even toughen up my quads in the gym. Interesting commercial conditions have compelled me to forgo my sessions with Gary, my sadistic personal trainer. The result on my overall physique has been swift and dramatic — like a cartoon of Popeye swallowing spinach, run in reverse.

And even if I were to achieve anything like the degree of fitness necessary to run a fast road race, what possible pleasure will I derive from it?

This isn't the Costa del Sol, remember, where the spectators are the very same, warm-hearted Cockney criminals who once cheered you around the Isle of Dogs.

Seriously, I can live without ten-deep crowds of well-meaning Spaniards thrusting *patatas bravas* in my face as I hobble by.

And I've heard a rumour that anyone with a finishing time of over five hours will be herded into an arena before a jeering mob of sherry-soaked louts and goaded by men with capes and pointy sticks.

The whole affair is too ghastly to contemplate. Oh, in the name of my poor, dung-encrusted Montrails, what have I done?

In which I experience the excitement of the Pamplona Bull Run. Except with no bulls and not in Pamplona

FRANKLY, I won't get out of bed nowadays for anything less than a long-haul all-expenses-paid trip to somewhere you can only reach by quadruped. A place where the parakeets outnumber the paramedics, and there are more infectious diseases than honest politicians.

I ran the Madrid Marathon because when Seaton suggested it, I was three-fifths drunk and I could have sworn he'd said 'Madras'.

By the time I'd realised my error, he'd booked my flight and my lightless cupboard in the Hotel Splendificanza del Las Vegas.

Still, I reasoned next morning, what's a mere 26 miles to a veteran of the Baffin Island Bastards Invitational and the Gaza Strip 200k?

How wrong can you be?

As I teetered, delirious, down the final cobbled straight to the finish, I honestly thought I was having an aneurysm. My temples were pounding, my legs had decided to sever relations with my torso and I moved like a marionette operated by someone with Parkinson's.

I was so desperately dehydrated, I felt, looked and smelled like a sun-dried otter.

But I'm racing ahead, here — in strict antithesis to my performance in the race.

The Madrid calls itself a 'Maraton Popular'. I take this to mean that the organisers have no ambitions to attract international, elite athletes, nor to break any records. A sensible strategy, given that it takes place just one week after the London and the hilly, bendy course is unlikely to produce world-beating performances.

It was pretty popular, all the same. I was one of 12,000 runners — mostly male, mostly Spanish, this demographic alleviated only by a modest French contingent.

The Hotel Splendificanza was situated just five hundred

metres from the start — which was decidedly popular with your correspondent, who was able to rise at eight, down a civilised breakfast then amble along to join the action just fifteen minutes before the gun at 9:30.

I was struck by the lack of razzamatazz (a Spanish word meaning 'bullshit'). Given the unashamedly expressive personality of your Mediterranean type, I'd expected more of a carnival atmosphere.

Last time I was in Spain it was to shoot a commercial. I'd briefly left our location at 2am for a breath of fresh air, to be confronted by a thousand silent, torch-bearing ghosts in white robes and what appeared to be Ku Klux Klan headgear.

A woman in a blood-red dress wailed a weird, Moorish dirge from a balcony and a huge tableau, depicting the spearing of Christ by a mounted centurion and apparently levitated solely by the willpower of the ecstatic onlookers, was swaying ominously down the high street.

So can I be forgiven for expecting a little more street theatre than was afforded by the Maraton? There wasn't so much as a pantomime bull in sight — and this from a nation that ritually slaughters whole herds of the real thing every year, in their infatuation with dramatic spectacle.

That being said, there were parachutists. On the one hand, they didn't carry coloured flares — on the other, they landed bang on the start line, then actually ran the race. That's pretty cool, by anyone's standards.

But there were no steel bands playing *Hot, Hot, Hot*, no brass ensembles playing *Midnight In Moscow,* no amateur DJs playing the bloody theme from *Chariots of* bloody *Fire*. Nor were there armies of toothless East End hags pushing plates of jellied eels at you. To this extent, it was a huge improvement on the London.

I'd like to add that every spectator you passed didn't yell, 'Good job!' or 'Way to go!' But they *did* yell what sounded like '*Animaux!*' I know little Spanish, but according to my schoolboy French, they were calling us animals. This did little for my sense of self-esteem — but in retrospect, I think it was only the local equivalent of 'Get them knees up!' Or indeed, 'Way to go!'

The best thing about the Madrid Marathon is that you get to see most of Madrid. Run London and you miss out on Crystal Palace and Hampstead and Chiswick and Clapham and Kew. But the Madrid course is a convoluted, serpentine tour of the city that gives you a pretty good snapshot of the place and its inhabitants.

The people are friendly and urbane, as befits modern citizens of the Eurozone. But the buildings express a darker, altogether madder side, suggestive of a dream life mired in frustrated megalomania and lost empires. General Franco meets the Inquisition.

You sit and sip your San Mig in a seductively shady plaza. You just happen to glance up and you realise that the architecture is bearing down on you, grinding along on its monumental foundations with murderous intent: monolithic piles that might have been commissioned for Moscow by an 18th-century Stalin.

Another minute and you'd have been mashed between the molars of two malign apartment blocks.

There's a disconnect between the place and the populus, as if the present inhabitants had accidentally wandered into a city built by a different race then exterminated by an alien deathray.

On the Saturday, Race's Eve, I ventured into the vast cathedral that struts presumptuously beside the rococo royal palace. It was probably built in the 1920s — a last, agonised homage to the supremacy of the Roman church. It had all the scale of a great mediaeval monument, but without the obsessive decoration and the sheer, lunatic extravagance that can elevate Catholic kitsch to something almost magnificent. It might as well have been built of breeze blocks.

Its solitary concession to visual impact was a huge, painted montage involving a nun — the only reason I didn't mistake it for a Bollywood film poster.

And yet, you see, you can't buy a dish in any restaurant in

town, however humble and unprepossessing, without wishing you could take it home and marry it.

Now why is that?

By the time I tottered through the Palace Square next day, I was in no fit condition to ponder anything so cerebral. On the rim of a great plain, a range of barren mountains shimmered in the sweltering heat of this May morning. The water stops seemed almost pointless: the more I drank, the more thirsty I felt.

I'd glanced at the 'ups and downs' chart in the race programme. It claimed unequivocally that the second half of the route was downhill, and consequently that the Finish was several hundred metres lower than the Start. In fact, the Start and Finish were within spitting distance of each other, on a level stretch of road outside the Prado museum. And the last five kilometres were relentlessly uphill. They felt vertical.

I collapsed over the line in a pitiful 3:47.

Still, I reflected as I sat under the cold shower in my room, at least the city was great and I was taking home the best goody bag of my entire career. It contained more running kit than Ron Hill's attic, including a showerproof jacket and a pair of sports shades.

It was just a shame about the race. I suppose every silver lining has to have a cloud.

In which I discover Malta — home of the fabled Knights Of St John. And, one can only assume, Maltesers

UNTIL I was dispatched to cover the 6th Malta Marathon Challenge, I'd only seen the island by the alien glare of sodium lights as I was whisked at midnight from the airport to the Gozo ferry terminal.

My companion at the time (a dour Yorkshire fell runner) had stared balefully out upon the rushing tableau of limestone ruins and parched grass: 'It'll be nice when it's finished,' he'd remarked.

Yet for the past 5,000 years, there just hasn't been *time* to finish Malta. The place has been ravaged every ten minutes by tumultuous mobs of, respectively, Sicilian Neanderthals, Roman legions, Greeks, the Tarxian Cemetery People (honestly), Carthaginians, Saracens, Normans and various Napoleons. In fact, I doubt if the Maltese have ever had time to properly digest their dinners, let alone lay down a nice patio.

In 1566, the Knights of St John resisted a siege by the swarthy infidel hordes of the Ottoman — but only by the skin of their teeth. (Nowadays, the Order's most militant wing is the St John's Ambulance Brigade.)

Until then, the Knights had hung out in Mdina. And Mdina is where the first leg of the Malta Marathon Challenge started and finished.

The Malta Marathon Challenge is indisputably held in Malta. It is certainly challenging. But it isn't a marathon. It's the marathon distance, run over three days and comprising a 10k race (approx), a three mile (ish) hilly sprint, and a longish run of whatever's left over from your 26 miles and 385 yards.

Mdina rejoices in an almost unpronounceable name — unlike most Maltese place names, which are completely unpronounceable. Witness: Xewkija, Xlendi, Xrobb il-Ghagin, Ta'Xbiex and Ghaxaq.

The language was cunningly devised by the Maltese International Scrabble Team. Then someone told them proper nouns didn't count.

The town, though, is fantastic. It's a walled city, with streets as narrow as bowling lanes, blank-faced, introverted convents and a lovely cathedral church in St Paul's Square — which the stuffy old guidebook damns thus: 'Its pleasing Renaissance harmony is disturbed by only one intrusion of Victorian Gothic'.

There has been a church on the site of St Paul's since the 4th century. And there has been a circular 10k race at Mdina since 1990.

I was sent to cover the event but, inevitably, I ended up running it. The smell of liniment, the joyous flapping of little pennants, the pompous strutting of marshals — it was all too much for an old war-horse like me, and I heaved my bloated, white cadaver around a course that was either 'violently undulating' or 'gently vertical', depending upon which school of race invitation writing you subscribe to.

I tried to introduce myself to the organiser, but he was on his mobile: 'What? You mean they're deliberately moving the route markers? The little bastards! I'll be there!' And he dived into his car and tore off through the ancient citadel in a cloud of scorched rubber.

Call me an old hippy liberal if you like but in my opinion the moving of race markers should be punished by public castration. Of course, it isn't such a serious offence in Malta — you can't run more than ten miles in any direction without falling into the sea — but when the Humorous Wing of the Saharan Bedouin tried it last year during the Marathon des Sables, we had to call out the helicopters.

The view from Mdina is like a frame from *Ben Hur*. The land falls steeply away on every side, bathed in a misty, golden, biblical light.

It was pleasantly warm, although the Maltese shivered beneath layers of thermal mountaineering gear. If you can't cook a pizza on the bonnet of your 1973 Austin Allegro, you qualify for severe weather payments. In high summer, the daytime temperature hovers around gas mark eight.

This was November. Shorts and T-shirts for the Brits, Italians and Dutch who made up the bulk of the 200 or so entries. I scanned the competition with a practised eye. Mostly around the forty mark, decent club runners, lots of ladies, a larger-than-usual contingent of craggy old vets (that is to say, even craggier and older than me).

Norman was in his late sixties, retired, craggy to an alarming degree. His face looked like an aerial photo of the Sierra Nevada, the arid brown relieved only by a pair of eyes like glacial tarns. He introduced me to his companion, who was female, thirty, lissom and not in the least bit craggy. 'Personally,' he muttered at the start line, 'I hate running. It's just that me and Moira are married. But not to one another. The only way I can ever get to see her is by entering bloody races.'

Another old campaigner was John. At home, he runs with the Hash. Last year, he organised a Halloween event in which all the runners dressed as ghosts and witches and hobgoblins. 'We shut down Barnet for two hours,' he smiled darkly. 'The town centre looked like the set of *Night Of The Living Dead*. Marvellous.'

The route dropped smartly out of Mdina onto a rural plain where the air was slow and thick. Within minutes I was regretting the gung-ho, can-do mood that had led me to join in. Then we were climbing steeply towards the soaring cliffs at Dingli — fresh, sea air and screaming muscles.

We passed a signpost indicating in various directions Mgarr, Zebbug and, surreally, Clapham Junction. The Junction is named after the deep, parallel ruts that score the rock in the area. The origin of these is mysterious: Professor Themosticles Zammit believes 'they were cut on purpose by Temple People for use by wheeled carts transporting rubble for the construction of terraced fields.' And who are you to disagree?

I'd spotted the winner at the hotel, within minutes of arriving in Malta. An Italian called Walter Durbano. He was a dead ringer for the little whippet-like Russian bloke who always wins the MDS. You know the type — seven stone nothing, physique of a National Hunt jockey and three thousand pounds' worth of running kit with special, camera-seeking logos.

Sure enough, he streaked across the finish line while I was still throwing up over Dingli Cliffs. He went on to win the entire event, just pipping Wales's Dale Rixon at the post. (Unsurprisingly, since Dale had run a marathon in 2:13 a mere six days before).

Jacqui White won the ladies' race. English, brilliant, lives in Turin, one of running's late starters. She accidentally entered a triathlon a couple of years ago and has just qualified for the Hawaiian Iron Man. Malta was just a little training run.

That evening, we strolled among the quietly rotting hulks on Manoel Island. Malta is like the limestone it stands on: layer upon layer, laid down by history. Push your hand into the ground, part the blossoms of the bougainvillaea, look behind the ruined wall — the past is everywhere, broken, rusted, decaying, rising from its grave, insinuating itself through shattered spars and fractured stones into the flimsy fabric of the present.

In the quietest corner of the abandoned fortress or the crumbling plague hospital, you can sense the bloody resonances of carnage and atrocity, cross and crescent, cannon smoke and wild heroism, villainy and victory.

Saint Paul was shipwrecked in Malta on his way to Rome, and stayed long enough to enthral its populace forever.

In the Second World War, the same weight in high explosives that fell upon Coventry during that city's entire, terrible ordeal, rained down upon Malta — every eighteen hours for three months.

The final, sixteen-mile leg of the Challenge took us along the coast road. The ocean gleamed on our left; golden limestone bluffs rose away to the right. We tracked around the hotels and restaurants of St Julian's Bay, through the abandoned barracks of the Cambridge Battery, along the tourist promenades of Sliema, until we climbed finally to the foot of Valletta's inscrutable fortifications.

Past the auberges of the Knights of St John, past incongruous jumbles of churches and gun emplacements, past statues of saints and generals chipped by musket balls and shrapnel, past the fantastic, baroque cathedral of the Order and finally, after our own, desperate battle against gravity, to the great central square with its triumphal gateway.

For the contestants in a race which was always just one step away from a dream, a finish fit for heroes.

Man versus Hearse? How very appropriate

I STRONGLY recommend Man v Horse. You'll enjoy every moment — the long sweeps along remote forestry tracks between stands of dark and silent pine; the soaring leaps across sucking bogs;

the exhilarating scrambles down steep, broken ground into the enfolding arms of valleys, impossibly green after the stony austerity of the moor.

This is assuming you're a horse, of course. Humans should avoid it like a plague of Dale Wintons.

However, as a born-again-and-again Buddhist, I know that pain is merely a passing illusion, and that my athletic ability is constrained only by my habitual expectations of myself. So last Saturday, I ran the race.

On Monday I had to get a stairlift installed. In 22-miles gruelling miles of potholes, vertical descents and bottomless marshes, the only muscles I didn't pull were the ones I pushed.

Man v Horse is run annually in Powys, Mid Wales. It starts in the rain at Llanwrtyd Wells and finishes a mile away in the rain at Victoria Wells after a bracing wade through a thigh-high torrent.

This washes just enough mud off the runners to render them identifiable to the coroner.

A little history: the race came about as the result of a bet between an 18th-century Welshman called Guto Nyth-Bran and a piebald cob called Drummer. Both had consumed large amounts of the fiery, local coal spirit known as Llwdyffch when an argument arose over which was faster over open country — man or horse.

The argument was overheard by Gordon Green, 18th-century landlord of the Neuadd Arms, who organised the first race in 1979.

Horses, having twice as many legs as people, invariably win — despite compulsory vet inspections. This is just as well for William Hill, the sponsors, because they're offering £20,000 to any runner who beats the horses to the finish line.

Last weekend's race (the twentieth) was undersubscribed, with only 250 solo runners. But each peat bog would accommodate at least four grown men, standing on each other's heads. And the raging meltwater cataracts could happily sweep away a score of runners at a time, thus opening up the trail for yet more enthusiastic, gullible chumps.

The horses had more sense. Only seven were sufficiently misinformed or stupid to show up, and one of those had the good sense to pack it in halfway round.

As tradition demanded, the official starter was Monster Raving Loony Party icon, Screaming Lord Sutch. His impromptu rock 'n' roll medley at the post-race party turned out to be his last public performance: he was found dead at his London home a couple of days later. Lord Sutch was a national treasure, and Man v Horse (not to mention the next election) will be a duller event without him.

I'm sure he would have approved of the Numbskulls, Britain's most exclusive running club. Back in 1984, two thirds of the membership entered Man v Horse — i.e. myself and Rob Wright.

Rob went off fast, slicing through the field like a Stanley knife through a Millwall supporter. At Mile 20, he was swaying dangerously from side to side of the track. Summoning my last erg of energy, I trotted past him, waving gaily, only reverting to my leaden-footed slouch once I was safely round the next bend.

It was half an hour before he staggered over the line, ashen-faced and wall-eyed. 'Get us a pint in!' he croaked.

I bought the beer, watched it go flat and finally drank it before going in search of Rob. I found him stark naked in the freezing chicken coop behind the Neuadd Arms that passes for a shower. He seemed quite unconcerned as he introduced me to the stark naked female mountain biker with whom he was engaged in conversation. 'Andy, meet Rita!'

Yet be warned: the ordeal of Man v Horse is seldom alleviated by such entertaining diversions. It's a tough run and if you're seriously thinking of following in the footsteps of a bodhisattva like myself, you should start training early.

Start with something more modest — say, Man v Guinea Pig — then work your way up through the animal kingdom.

Good luck. Or *ddiddorol o drefytedaeth gwrthdaro,* as we say in Wales.

In which I discover that our memory of physical discomfort only lasts for eleven months

I'VE RUN Man v Horse now, on and off, for sixteen years and I've come to the conclusion that it's the most ill-named event in the running calendar.

For a start, you don't run against a horse — not in any real sense. All right, so you might catch an occasional glimpse of an hysterical pony, galloping on the spot in the main square of Llanwrtyd Wells, as you hang around at the Start.

Then an hour or so later, high on some barren, mist-sodden moor, you might be lucky enough to hear a cry of 'Horse!' before you're bowled off the track into a ditch. And if you're still conscious, you might see a great, snorting sweat-flecked beast go thundering by — or even the horse she's riding.

But that's about it.

The race should really be called Man v Mud. Or Man v Common Sense.

This occurred to me as I loitered outside the Neuadd Arms before this year's race, in the interminable, penetrating rain that passes for weather in Wales. I felt lifeless and heavy, as if the water had soaked into my bones.

Somebody muttered, 'It wasn't like this when Lord Sutch was around.' But it was. It was always like this, and always will be — wet, cold and profoundly uninviting.

Still, there was definitely something missing: this was the first year that the race's legendary First Marshall, Screaming Lord Sutch, would not be surveying the field from the starter's podium. How an ageing rock 'n' roller from Harrow ever got mixed up with a mountain marathon in Powys, it's hard to imagine. But his untimely death last year has left an unmendable hole in the fabric of an event that is almost as eccentric as he was.

My friend Fordham ambled over to me. He looked cold and glum. 'I don't feel at all good,' he declared. 'I'm in half a mind not to run.'

Fordham always does this immediately before a race.

Sometimes, if he can't persuade me that he's coming down with viral pneumonia or anthrax, he'll deliberately engineer an accident to sprain his ankle or tear a hamstring. Then he'll spend two hundred pounds on ultrasound and prosthetic supports and hobble around the course in a perfectly respectable time. It's just his way.

'I haven't felt good for about twenty years,' I tell him. 'But I'm not going to let it stop me having a thoroughly miserable time for the next four hours.'

'Shhh!' hissed an unfeasibly short but smartly turned-out runner. 'I'm trying to listen to the briefing!'

He was clearly a first-timer. The pre-race briefing was conducted as tradition dictates by Gordon, landlord of the Neuadd Arms, and as always it was entirely incomprehensible. 'And the runners... er... run along *here*.' He waved vaguely at a grey blur — a bad photocopy of a small-scale map, characterised mainly by thick bunches of contour lines. 'And you've got to be very, um, careful... *here*... no, *here*, I mean, sorry...' And so on. Frankly, it could have been a map of Madagascar for all we knew or cared.

We started at 11am — and a braver little knot of bandy-legged idiots you'd be hard pushed to find north of the Brecon Beacons.

The rain was thin, cold and utterly relentless. Up on the first hill, it merged with the mist and became an all-saturating wetness. It smelled of damp sheep and soggy peat and dripping bracken. It turned the rough track into a treacherous quagmire in which a hapless runner might be swallowed whole and digested. I ran 22 miles with my toes curled, just to keep my shoes on.

Worst were the forestry trails, for they had already been mashed to buggery by the giant tyres of logging vehicles. It took me twenty minutes to traverse one particular hillside where a generation of firs had recently been ripped out of the ground. The landscape resembled the Somme in 1915 as I slithered about in a soup of mud, bark chippings and razor-sharp flints.

What are usually dry stream beds had become raging torrents

during three weeks of incessant rain. On two occasions, I had to wait for another runner to come along so that we could link arms and cross in tandem.

One especially interesting aspect of Man v Horse is that although it's a circular course and ends up where it begins, you go up far more hills than you come down. I know this defies every natural law, and I can offer no rational explanation. Perhaps natural laws don't apply in Wales. Which would explain the weather. And the language.

To make things worse, the few downhill bits are even more horrible than the up. The mud is refined to a light, glassy paste that reduces friction to a negative value. It's like skating down a glacier of KY Jelly on graphite skis.

I was glad I'd worn my trusty Nike off-roaders, but I really needed crampons.

During the latter part of the race I overtook increasing numbers of walking wounded. You could tell they'd come a cropper because they were covered in a ghastly slime of blood and earth. I stopped for one poor old soul who was staggering ashen-faced down a particularly daunting KY bobsleigh run. 'Are you all right, mate?' I enquired.

He looked at me, but his eyes were focused on some far-distant galaxy. 'Nottingham Forest,' he replied mildly.

Here's another thing about Man v Horse that sets it apart from the norm: the average age of the runners who overtake you increases steadily throughout the race. This is an event for grizzly old mountain men. During the latter stages, one's view is restricted to throbbing maps of varicose veins like aerial photos of the Amazon — calves that might have been sawn from Victorian dressers — mail order shorts from the Sir Stanley Matthews Centenary Collection.

The T-shirts, too, reflect the special character of the participants. None of your *'I'm Running For Rupert'* or *'Support Yo! The Hampstead Mid-Life Crisis Drop-In Centre'*. Most of these old boys run in string vests, where even the holes have holes. Occasionally, you can just make out the legend, scrawled in biro across the back of a National Service issue sports shirt: *'Grimsdyke Grinders. Take No Prisoners.'*

The last mile was distinctly Welsh — that is, at least two miles long. We slithered down a hill, waded through a century's accumulation of cow shit to sway dangerously along the hard shoulder of a major road, struggled up a slurry-filled gully to the top of a moderately-serious hill, then slithered down said hill, mostly on arse, negotiated a white water cataract and finally hauled up a nasty little incline to the finish.

I looked around me. The sense of universal relief was palpable. We'd been up to our necks in Nature in the Raw. We'd cursed and kicked our way though some of the most beautiful countryside in the realm. We were filthy, knackered, cold, hungry and magically fulfilled.

As I set out to jog the mile back to Llanwrtyd Wells (a feature of the race that almost certainly contravenes the UN Declaration of Human Rights as 'cruel and unusual punishment') I reflected with great satisfaction that Man v Horse was indeed the finest event of the year.

If you're a man, you simply have to do it.

If you're a horse, even better — the race is sponsored by William Hill and next year they'll be betting £22,000 that you'll win.

Think about it. That's an awful lot of oats.

Rory's revenge. Wily old poacher turns gamekeeper

6pm. THE sun, relenting after its scorching assault upon the day, cast a benevolent glow upon the golden stone of a handsome Cotswold church — and in its peaceful graveyard, a nervous little group of ultra runners.

Rory Coleman, characteristically, was neither peaceful nor nervous.

'First of all, welcome to the first ever Marathon of Britain! For twelve months, this has been my dream — and now I want it to be *your* dream!'

He spread his arms in a wonderfully inclusive gesture, which embraced not only the thirty-six bemused guinea pigs who had signed up for this extraordinary ordeal, but the whole of Worcestershire — starting with the gently rolling lawns of Coombe Park.

This venerable estate, centred about an uncompromisingly geometrical 18th-century house, is most renowned for its artfully-landscaped grounds — the first in the portfolio of Capability Brown.

There were the Brits, a handful of Germans (a *handful* being the collective noun for any number of Germans greater than two) and Cyril.

'And let's also welcome Cyril, who's from Ireland!'

There was a pregnant silence — then, in an especially aggressive brogue: 'Have you got a *problem* with that?'

Cyril was to be my tent-mate, apparently.

I was already slightly frayed. I'd turned up at Evesham railway station, expecting a shuttle to spirit me in the style due to a senior media celebrity to the MOB encampment.

Two hours of merciless sun in the station car park elapsed before I was forced to seek urinary relief at the Railway Hotel. Which was deserted. I sidled to the gents where, bizarrely, a loudspeaker was relaying a recording of Bernard Manning.

Rory was right about the dream thing. The inaugural MOB was about to become the most surreal event of my running career.

As we waited for dinner — the first of many miracles, up-conjured twice daily from thin air by the mobile caterers — we circled warily around the neighbours whose personal idiosyncrasies, bodily odours and mood-swings we would have to endure for the next six days.

Thankfully, one of these turned out to be Luke Cunliffe, with whom I had charged around Dartmoor two years earlier to celebrate Shaun Fishpool's thirtieth.

Unaccountably, he was fat. I say unaccountably because he's a personal trainer. And only a few months earlier, he'd been the only Brit to complete the dreadful Trans 333, just before turning in a sterling performance in the Grand Union Canal 145-mile race — the one where they castrate you with a rusty hacksaw if you sit down for more than five minutes.

He moaned a lot about being overweight. He needn't have worried. Six days later, despite the caterers' best endeavours, he was thin. We all were.

Cyril was thin already. He resembled a spectral projection of Richard Harris after an eternity spent in Limbo, deprived of all sustenance.

But he was amiable enough for a spectre and displayed an early enthusiasm for tidiness which the rest of Tent 4 quietly conspired to encourage.

The rest were mostly Malcolm and Del, proprietors of Tortoise & Hare, the legendary Surrey running store. They looked horribly like Proper Runners.

Malcolm had dark, burning eyes of the sort that stare wildly ahead as they streak across the finish line twenty minutes before the next bloke.

Del radiated the icy calm of the hard-bitten ultra runner — the professional who has seen things that would make your orthotics shrivel in your Montrails, but who elects to keep his own counsel.

They reminded me of bounty hunters in a Western B movie.

God knows what they thought of Luke and me. Well, me, then. They already knew Cunliffe — together they formed the Flame Health Team, handsomely equipped with gleaming new kit and branded shirts, courtesy of an imaginative and far-seeing sponsor.

While I, the ageing privateer, was clad in exactly the same kit I wore in the 1962 Middlesbrough Boys' High School Cross-country. When I came second from last.

That evening I laughed intemperately, consumed by a kind of gallows humour that had its roots in my inability to provide a satisfactory answer to the question: What in fuck's name am I doing here?

We went through a rather perfunctory kit inspection: needless to say, I'd left everything to the minute just after the last one, then raced around town in a frenzy, loading up with kilos of unnecessary stuff — cast iron fire dogs, mahogany table lamps and an impressive Druid headdress cast in phosphor bronze and emblazoned with a hundred leaden figurines representing the elfin spirits of the forest.

In the excitement, I had quite forgotten my whistle.

Fortunately, this oversight was rectified by the redoubtable Stephen Partridge — a key figure in the MOB's translation from ill-conceived fantasy to ghastly reality.

Only Partridge would carry a spare whistle.

Next morning, we were woken at 6am by a pitifully poor impression of a cockcrow. Rory mustered us for a final briefing. It was already hotter than the Sahara was when I ran the Marathon des Sables (the model for the MOB).

He surveyed us slowly, nodding and grinning evilly. He took us through the day's section of the road book. He illuminated some of the more arcane convolutions of the course. 'This race is 98% off-road. I've run every inch of it. It took me twelve months. It's a bastard, frankly.' He displayed all the self-satisfied sadism of the poacher turned gamekeeper.

'Lastly, a warning. It's about the stiles. Many of them are rickety. Some are slippery with moss. Be extremely careful on the stiles.

'Now — the bus is waiting to take you to the start. Good luck, everyone, and God bless.'

We turned to go, but Partridge intervened dramatically. 'Wait, everyone! Before you go, there's one thing you should know. It's about the stiles. Many of them are rickety. Some are slippery with moss. Be extremely careful on the stiles.'

Rory stared at him blankly. 'Thank you, Stephen. Now, before we leave — any questions?'

Mimi of the Tuff Muthers team piped up, 'Yes. We thought your wake-up call was pathetic. Next time, please can we have a real cock?'

The bus took us to the charming town of Malvern, a celebration of 18th-century prosperity. Winding streets, clinging to the side of that astonishing geological aberration, the Malvern Range.

A few elegantly-chosen words from our glamorous starter, Floella Benjamin (surrealism was already taking hold, notice) and we were off.

The race literature makes no bones about it: *Competitors must have considerable orienteering skills to complete this event successfully.*

Three minutes in and we were all completely lost. 'Chickens' and 'headless' were the terms that sprang most readily to mind as we careered for ten precious minutes around the roads and tracks that were supposed to lead us to the ridge of the Malverns.

I suppose propelling us up a 1:4 incline bearing 10-kilo rucksacks at the height of a heatwave was Rory's idea of a joke. And we responded, I think, with admirable good humour. So far there were no blisters, stress fractures nor obvious cases of heatstroke. And the view from the top was simply stunning. Across the Vale of Evesham shimmered the misty ridges of the Cotswolds. Little did we know it then — the course was a well-kept secret — but we could just have made out the destination of the third day's run.

Back down the Malverns and 17 miles ex-Floella, we broke the tape by the elegant private church at Coombe Park. Luke Cunliffe and I had notched up a creditable joint sixth place. I was privately amazed. Mr Banks, my high school gym teacher, would have eaten his mortar board.

My success was largely down to Cunliffe's excellent map-reading. He ran with his head buried in the road book.

AB: Look! Muntjac! Dwarf deer originally introduced by private collectors for their private zoos, but now breeding successfully in the English countryside!

LC: Hard left, then right in 150 meters.

AB: Ah! Now this is a really ancient track! Hooper's Law enables one to date a hedgerow by counting the established species therein, then attributing one hundred years for each species.

LC: Across the field, then a 30-degree turn east-nor'east, passing the sewage works on the right.

Cunliffe ran from Malvern to Nottingham through some of the most beautiful countryside in all of fair England and I swear he saw about six feet of it. He endured this without complaint and it's the primary reason why we did so well. In rueful retrospect he called it 'the plight of the navigator'.

I'd have loved to have helped, of course, but the road book was designed by The Borrowers and was indecipherable to anyone with eyes more than 40 years old.

I've made the point to Rory who has promised to produce a 'talking book' version next year for the infirm.

That evening, I extended the hand of friendship to the Bounty Hunters — tentatively, as you do to men with guns.

I asked Malcolm how he'd come to own his own running shop. To cut a very long story short, he'd tried to get a proper job. During the psychometric test the HR director had asked him what frightened him, and he'd replied, 'Giants'.

Tortoise & Hare is founded on unusual principles. It's miles from anywhere, it doesn't open until noon, but it doesn't close until eight. Its customers have names like 'Spikey Al', and are expected to spend several hours there. They are received with more or less enthusiasm depending on how many doughnuts they bring.

Next day, England lay in a state of shock under a sun like a sledgehammer. Malcolm succumbed to a virus and Del dropped out in a heroic gesture of solidarity and drove him home.

Not a breath of breeze stirred the wilting junipers as we trudged and jogged along the scarp of the Cotswolds. On either side, plains of scorched stubble stretched away into a vague penumbra of heat and dust. Crouched beneath sweltering hills, Stanton and Broadway played dead. The temperature lurched into the high nineties.

Luke and I found we were good at heat and hills. By the time we'd climbed to the weird, Italianate fantasy that is Broadway Tower, we knew we must be close on the heels of the leaders.

As we crossed the finish line, there was the merest smattering of applause. At first we were crestfallen: then we realised that *there was nobody there to applaud*. Almost everyone else was behind us.

This was a new concept to us: the less applause, the better your position. Excellent.

'This', whispered Cunliffe, 'is like Dumb and Dumber reaching the finals of *Mastermind*.'

I agreed to run the MOB for two reasons: 1) Coleman 2) I'd run up the Himalayas, across the Sahara, through the rainforests of Guiana. But my knowledge of England was largely restricted to what I'd glimpsed from the window of a speeding car on the M1.

I figured I should try to catch at least a flavour of the landscapes that had inspired such giants as Elgar, Vaughan Williams and The Chuckle Brothers.

I wasn't disappointed. We descended upon Stratford-upon-Avon. There we saw the swans that Cyril, as the highly-unlikely mayor of that famous town, had once tried to protect. (His efforts brought down upon him the wrath of the fishing fraternity. They placed a mischievous advertisement in the *Angling Times* which resulted in his receiving around ten thousand unsolicited telephone calls. 'So I gave up politics. Now I'm just a folk singer. And every year, me an' the missus go to Lapland to help Santa.')

We wound through Leicestershire — a county of extraordinary beauty (and vicious hills) that I would have underestimated to the grave, if not for the MOB.

We were about 35 miles into the Long Day and it was unbelievably hot and I was having trouble keeping up with Cunliffe, Anker (former MSD winner) and the amazing Andy Rivett.

We reached the summit, capped by an ancient tower and affording fantastic, panoramic views of the surrounding country.

The leaders, though, didn't pause for a moment. They just peered at their maps, poking and grumbling.

'Look!' I barked (they tell me). 'I'm all for competition. But this is beautiful! If you don't look at it, what's the fucking point? We might as well be on a fucking treadmill!'

They stared at me like a schizophrenic who had neglected to take his medication — then they were off down the hill with me flailing uselessly along behind them.

Anyway, five of us crossed the line that night, fourteen hours and 56 miles after setting out, and I've never run so well nor felt so fulfilled.

The next morning's ten, beautifully flat miles up the River Soar to the gates of Nottingham Castle were almost a formality.

The MOB does what all great races do. It binds a band of people together in a huge, pointless, epic enterprise that each of them will always count among the defining experiences of their lives.

Aloo! Aloo!
I make a meal of the Mumbai Marathon

TAKE MY advice — don't go to Bombay for the weekend. It's not good for you. Especially if, after a night spent folded in half at the back end of an aeroplane, then another failing to adjust to the time difference, you start a full marathon at an hour your body insists is 01:30, in 28 degrees of heat and humidity you could wring out of the air with your bare hands.

Like all such great ideas, this one was Seaton's. In retrospect, I realise it was my punishment for having omitted to start, let alone finish, December's Nairobi race.

But despite all the stress and discomfort (and what turned out to be my worst ever marathon time) I wouldn't have missed it for anything.

If you lived every day as intensely as I did those three, you would cram ten lifetimes into one. That's not quite immortality, but it's getting there.

The Mumbai Marathon is really two races. Sponsored by Standard Chartered, it represents part of the Bank's mission to encourage marathon running in regions where it enjoys no historical tradition.

I arrived at my hotel at 4am on a Saturday morning and the race Welcome Desk was still open. My goody bag was like a wardrobe — tracksuit, T-shirt, headband with cooling crystals, water bottle, treadmill. OK, not the treadmill — but enough kit to render redundant most of the contents of my suitcase.

The hotel was the Oberoi which to jet-lagged ears sounded like a Buddy Holly number, but was actually much quieter. There was just the sigh of the air conditioning and the discreet purr of limitless wealth.

My suite (sic) was on the 21st floor of the atrium, an architectural rainforest of aerial walkways and hanging gardens.

The panoramic view from my bedroom embraced the majestic sweep of Marine Drive. Dubbed the Queen's Necklace in colonial times, it is still the jewel in Mumbai's crown — Cannes' Croisette meets *Blade Runner*.

Elegant lamp standards march in a cutlass curve past towers of glass and steel. Between these glittering monuments to the new India, the stucco facades of Victorian residences slowly rot like bad teeth.

The heat and the damp have humiliated these pompous relics of the Empire, crumbling their decorations like cake icing and smearing their faces with a green-black patina of mould.

On Sunday, feeling like a Victorian relic myself, I would hobble past them during the final, ghastly miles of the marathon.

But when I wake on Saturday, the natural electricity of this fantastic city, the fourth biggest in the world, is focused on tomorrow and the race that is, to its population, evidence that the giant has yawned and stretched and is set to take on the West in the real and deadly-serious 'greatest race on Earth'.

The *Bombay Times* that has arrived at my suite in a linen

bag apparently without human intervention, is clearly excited by the race.

'Wheelchair competitor Ankara Raman says, "If I can travel on the uneven roads of Tamil Nadu, then Mumbai will be a cake-walk for me."'

Last year, disabled groups boycotted the marathon because no special provision was made for them. This year, they have their own race.

'I am running the 7k Dream Run,' explains actress Tara Sharna, 'because such festivals help to put the city on the international map.'

The Dream Run is attracting huge popular attention because many Bollywood stars are participating for charity. This was to turn the final miles of the race into something between a movie premiere and the Pamplona Bull Run.

After lunch, I stroll down the Drive — ten-man teams are digging holes in the tarmac and planting rough-lopped branches as pedestrian barriers. In a country of a billion people, 'labour intensive' is not a meaningful notion.

The roads have been specially cleaned. There is even a rumour that traffic has been banned for 12 hours to reduce pollution, but there's little evidence of this — snakes of battered Ambassador cabs grind along at a glacial pace, exchanging pointless horn blasts beneath curtains of vines and the aerial roots of the great hardwoods that line the streets and create a premature twilight.

Out on the promenade, crowds of beautiful young people are enjoying the afternoon sun. A deep golden haze hangs over the bay, lending an ephemeral quality to the skyscrapers of the business district across the water. The effect is Turner-esque although the haze is probably caused by the unromantic adulteration of diesel fuel with paraffin.

There's a lot of sitting going on, I notice — sitting and squatting and contemplating nothing very much. It's almost a national pastime, and it seems strangely at odds with the frenzy and frustration just a few feet away in the roadway.

I return to the Oberoi for a briefing by the Race Director, *RW*'s own Huw Jones and the Elite Field Coordinator Ian Ladbroke.

For administrative purposes only (believe me) I'm Elite. I sit among the whippets, elves and gazelles for whom 2:20 would be a bitter disappointment — Kim Suck-Soo of South Korea, Mika Kiembo of Kenya, Niaz Farooqi of Pakistan (for whom running in India must have a special resonance) and I feel like a walrus.

'Throughout the race,' Huw announces, 'managers and coaches can enjoy refreshments in the Hospitality Tent.' I wonder how feasible it would be to pose as my own manager.

I chat to Sameer Najib. He's 19, he's from Kabul and until yesterday, he'd never left Afghanistan. 'When I was about seven, I began running with my dad. I kept it up, not to race, just to stay healthy.'

It occurs to me that running fast is probably a necessary condition of staying healthy in Kabul.

At the Oberoi restaurant I opt for a light, early dinner of chicken salad. (Buddhists won't eat meat, Hindus beef, Jews and Mohammedans pork. I wonder, is Christianity the only omnivorous religion?)

Unhappily, the salad includes a green chilli which I chew very thoroughly indeed before it begins to destroy my tongue and oesophagus.

Here's a tip: 'hot' spices are alkaline, not acid, so the best remedy is marmalade — or failing that, fresh orange juice. Still, I could feel the chilli barrelling past my duodenum like an Exocet with a time delay, *en route* for my lower intestine. There would be trouble ahead, I gloomily acknowledged. Or rather, behind.

I slept like a baby that night: I woke every hour and cried. I finally fell into a deep slumber at 5:20, my watch went off at 5:30, the front desk called me at 5:35 and I was in the shower at 5:38. By 6:30, I was on Elite Coach B, rumbling through the dissipating gloom of a stirring city.

Around every tree and lamp post along the way, someone had thrown up a tenuous dwelling of planks, plastic sheeting and rotten tarpaulin.

Outside these fragile lean-tos, people were brushing their teeth, cooking vats of soup on LPG rings, setting out arrays of jewellery, carvings, even fans of glossy business magazines. There was no sense of desperation — this was business as usual for a large portion of Mumbai's 23 million inhabitants.

In front of the impressive Air India building was a huge poster advertising the airline's commitment to the comfort of elderly passengers. And in front of the poster an old man was asleep on the pavement, a dog licking an open sore on his forearm.

In the Elite Area, the athletes were warming up in a tiny, dusty square. They looked like an army of clockwork toy lunatics.

And now we were off. The streets were lined with fans, five deep, twenty-six miles long and wildly excited, like devotees at a guru's motorcade.

When I ran the San Diego, the constant repetition of 'Way t'go!' and 'Good job!' almost drove me into the arms of Al-Qaeda. Here the exhortations were much quainter: 'Keep going, sir, thank you sir!' Or straight from *Tom Brown's Schooldays*: 'I say! Buck up!'

The route presented a mad, kaleidoscopic view of contemporary India. We ran past a 500-year-old mosque on a peninsula and a Japanese Buddhist temple, past a couple of Mumbai's 17 shopping malls, past the wildly expensive Hinduja private clinic then straight into the poor Muslim quarter where goats roamed the streets and beggars, off duty for a few hours, waved their twisted limbs at the runners. One clutched a carrier bag that read, 'There is no anything that money cannot buy'.

Then it was past the charitable tenements built by the automotive tycoon, Sir Ratan Tata, across a flyover that flies over the 'fishing area' (a maze of huts on the margins of a stinking by-water), past the little park where Gandhi conceived the 'Quit India' campaign that finally ousted the British. In my pain and exhaustion, I wished momentarily that I, too, could quit India — goodness, how ungracious of me!

There were hundreds of posters with a marathon theme. One,

advertising the *Times of India*, displayed a photo of Osama bin Laden with the caption, *Now you can be on the run, too!*

Another screamed: *Forget your legs. Run with your heart!* By Mile 20, I wanted to drag the copywriter responsible for that particular gem from the bar where I'm sure he wrote it, stub out his cigar on his nose and force him to endure just one mile of my ordeal.

I hit some kind of wall at around fifteen miles. The lack of sleep, the chilli, the running on concrete after training on mud — it all caught up with me. But the sheer spectacle of this astonishing place kept me going.

Mumbai (from the Hindu goddess, Mumba Devi) contributes 35% of India's income taxes. The city was built on seven islands but the lagoons between them have been largely reclaimed. The metropolitan area includes a rainforest where tigers and cheetahs roam.

Six million people commute in daily on trains designed to carry 1,500 passengers, but which actually carry 8,000. Eight of these are killed every day, either by falling from moving trains or trying to cross the tracks.

When the survivors disembark they are swept through the city in a flash flood of 60,000 cabs, 4,000 buses and 80,000 rickshaws.

The result is a bit like a Grateful Dead album — a sort of majestic chaos, forever teetering on the brink of falling apart but held together by rough ingenuity and the magnetic energy of its population.

Over here, when we renovate a building, we remove the old parts and replace them with new. In Mumbai, they just nail the new bits over the old. So the buildings have this organic quality — painted shop signs half-overlaid with Perspex lettering in red and green, festoons of redundant wiring, rusting junction boxes, drunken lamp brackets and fire escapes more lethal than any fire.

Up above, I notice, a flock of crows is harrying a vulture. You don't get that in the Fleet Half-Marathon.

By the time I reach the home straight, we've merged with the Dream Runners. Their race is well-named. They're clearly hypnotised. When they wake, they will remember nothing. But meanwhile, they're charging along in the wake of the Bollywood film stars in an ecstatic state not witnessed in the West since the Beatles. Many of them are weeping real tears.

I'm reduced to a walk. I am overtaken by fifty people dressed as a bus. I don't care. For me, this is no longer a Marathon — it's a carnival, a massive explosion of cheerful optimism by people who just love a good time, whatever the excuse.

As I totter past a rather stressed Huw and over the line, I'm guided gently through a sea of Indian faces towards the elite enclosure. I wonder vaguely what Gandhi would have made of it all — whether he would have condemned the marathon as an attempt by the Western banking community to impose a new kind of cultural colonialism upon his beloved India.

But the day had proved one thing beyond all doubt — that modern Indians see the marathon as a symbol of India becoming... modern.

On the bus back to the Oberoi we passed a cow, tethered outside an electrical goods store. I'd always associated India with random cows, wandering aimlessly about in unlikely places, but this was the only one I'd seen since my arrival.

I suppose that's what they call progress.

Out of it in Africa.
I'm a mile high in Nairobi

THE BRIEFING for Stage One of the Greatest Race on Earth in the Mezzanine of the Nairobi Hilton. I hover, disconsolate, at the door as files of tiny, expectant Kenyans fill up the ranks of chairs. If they're whippets, I'm a St Bernard.

They're the eighty-strong elite who will lead the field in the Standard Chartered Bank's Nairobi Marathon — for the GROE is really a race within a race. These whisp-like Africans, along

212

with equally-frightening teams from Mauritius, Vietnam, Hong Kong and goodness-knows where else, will go on to compete in Mumbai (the Historic Race), Singapore (the Island Race) and Hong Kong (the Harbour Race).

And the team of four (or indeed the single runner) with the lowest aggregate time will hobble away with $1m.

For me, as the Nairobi representative of the *Runner's World* team, the occasion has a nightmarish quality. These guys have a combined weight of around 200 kilos. The size labels on their running vests are marked with an L, an M or an S — Lean, Mean or Skeletal.

Worse, far worse, I've come down with a cold. It began last night on the flight over — the tell-tale tickle at the back of the throat, then the head/balloon feeling that warns you this isn't just a temporary trick of the air conditioning.

Of course, it doesn't help that Nairobi (the Highest Race) is situated around a mile above sea level. My symptoms are compounded by mild altitude sickness, but I don't find this in the least consolatory.

I'm introduced to Mike Denoma, the brains behind the Bank's invention and sponsorship of this intercontinental event. He's in training for an iron man triathlon and as soon as he hears the 'C' word, he retreats a good six feet. 'Well, at least there isn't green slime coming out of your nose!' There is, actually, but I don't have the heart to spoil Mike's noble attempt at cheering me up.

So I sit alone, way out on the flank of the hall, a social pariah.

The Race Director, with forty international marathons under his belt, inspires the runners' confidence. 'I can assure you that you will be attacked by hardly any wild animals at all during the race.

'It won't be like my last time here, when I was chased out of the Game Park section by five buffalo. We've changed the route.

'However, you *will* have to squeeze between the legs of a giant elephant as you approach the finish.' More of which later.

Behind the official time car and a police motorcycle escort, the bus creaked and jolted around the marathon route — the circumference of the city, more or less, plus a few brief double-backs.

Had I been a mere competitor, I'd have given the tour a miss. They only serve to remind you how pestilentially long the event is, and you end up daunted and more apprehensive than ever.

Nevertheless, the trip provided me with my first, perfunctory impression of Nairobi. Nice place, all told. Big, old colonial buildings around generous, shady squares and broad boulevards. A little scruffy and faded now, but all the more homely for that — a bit like the sofas in the Groucho Club.

Tall, watercolour trees, some ablaze with red and purple blossom.

Past Hope House Babies' Home into a leafy suburb. Glimpses of rambling bungalows behind high gates, coils of razor wire and banks of security cameras.

A poster advertising margarine declares, 'Breakfast without Bento is like a marathon without Kenyans'.

Abruptly, the discreet prosperity dissolves into a shanty town, tenuous shacks of corrugated iron and disintegrating plasterboard, sacks and car body panels.

The camp is flanked by a terrace of brick dwellings, inexplicably abandoned, windows smashed and roof tiles looted.

I drove through Toxteth a week after the riots and the similarity was striking. Apart from the cows — for in a tiny garden, a dozen angular cattle are grazing. Apparently, they were herded down to Nairobi by tribesmen from the far north where the harvest has failed and thousands are starving.

We pass the elegantly understated Norfolk Hotel, currently celebrating its centenary. Overweight Americans lounge on shady terraces, unwinding no doubt after some sanitised 4WD foray into the Heart of Darkness. All that was missing was Teddy Roosevelt with a Gin Sling in one hand and a 24-bore elephant gun in the other.

At my 5am alarm call I leapt out of bed and promptly fell over. My head, I noted with interest, had been cunningly pumped full of marsh gas during the night, and my limbs ripped off and crudely stuck back on, back to front.

I even tried to attach my number to my shirt, but the infinite complexities of this operation overwhelmed me and I was forced to lie down again.

And that, folks, was my marathon. The one I'd trained for (well, a bit, eventually). The one I'd travelled 9,000 miles there and back for in BA's Dizziness Class.

At 7am I made it as far as the hotel lobby, just in time to watch the excited competitors making their final adjustments to their laces, laughing and joshing in that nervously-charged mood of pre-race camaraderie. 'Once more unto the breach, dear friends... '

I've seldom felt more miserable.

The biggest bird I've ever seen wheeled lazily over the finish line as the tannoy announced the approach of the leaders.

The square was heaving with tired, happy runners from the half-marathon and 10k races. I was close to heaving, too, but I figured I should at least witness the denouement of this epic African drama.

Kenya has two rainy seasons and we were smack in the middle of the shorter one. The lawns at the Finish area were reduced to a ruddy swamp.

A huge cheer went up as Benjamin Kipchumba Kemboi crossed the line. It had rained steadily throughout the race. Given the weather and the hills — several, short and sharp — his winning time of 2:11:50 was remarkable.

Nairobi stands a mile above sea level, and I doubt his achievement could have been equalled by anyone who wasn't born and raised at that sort of altitude.

As I staggered back to the hotel in a state bordering on delirium, I was hijacked by a polite gentleman with an umbrella who insisted I tell him all I knew about 'your famous veterinary surgeon, James Herriot'. I was too ill to resist, and somehow the interview involved me giving him £20.

I then narrowly avoided arrest by a Kenyan secret policeman with a far more impressive umbrella for "aiding and abetting" a terrorist. But that's another story.

In which I kit up for the only ultra marathon that anybody's ever heard of

THE MARATHON des Sables has the same initials as the Marquis de Sade. This is no coincidence. Its 145 miles are run over six one-day stages of 25, 33, 39, 76, 42 and 18 kilometres respectively. And this with a 10-kilo pack in temperatures reaching 120 degrees.

Everything you need, you carry on the back. No, that's not true. I needed a nurse and possibly a camel.

Water is strictly rationed and doled out at compulsory checkpoints in 1.5-litre instalments. Only the French would ration water in the Sahara.

The organisers specify a minimum equipment list: compass, knife, venom pump (*venom pump?*), burns treatment, et cetera.

During Day Three of the race, I passed the time fantasising that I was Sebastian Strange — a darkly enigmatic poet to whom the official kit inspection was a personal statement, an ironic commentary on the human condition in all its poignant complexity.

While the Japanese produced their crepe bandages, their multi-vitamins, their industrial catering packs of Immodium, I would solemnly arrange upon the sand the random selection of *objets* that would sustain me in the wilderness. A cello. A stuffed gannet. A pair of aubergines. A portrait of Pope Innocent XI. The dust bag from a Goblin vacuum cleaner. A tin of Swarfega. The sheet music for the Shostakovitch piano concerto. A ouija board. A sample of iron pyrites. And (brilliantly) a bag of sand.

The French check your rucksack at the start so you can't cheat. Even your water bottles bear your race number — ditch anything in the desert and you lose points. And what do points mean? Nobody ever told us.

Weight is all. Your rucksack becomes progressively lighter as the days go by (so do you) but you soon become obsessed with minimising your load. Food packs and valuable items of kit are offered around the camp to an uninterested market, then surreptitiously dumped.

In the Sahara, I became an expert fast. If only I could have nipped back to Black's, I'd have traded in half my stuff for something far... smaller. And lighter. And yes, I know, probably useless. But frankly, after a day in the desert, I didn't give a toss. I'd have carried a Tommee Tippee Junior Venom Pump (including realistic polypropylene 'scorpion') if I could've got away with it.

But now you can benefit from my mistakes. Next spring, when you set out on that fateful five-hour bus ride from Ouzazate to nowhere, at least your kit will represent the optimum trade-off between weight, bulk and function.

RUCKSACK

Most competitors had trained with their rucksacks for months. Nevertheless, after two days, their backs looked like explosions in an abattoir.

The first time I wore mine, on the other hand, was on my way to the airport. Yet by the end of the race, my skin would have impressed Claudia Schiffer.

The Lowe Alpine Contour Runner 30 is a technological miracle to compare with the ring accelerator and laser eye surgery.

SHOES

Nike Triax. Expensive, superb. My only mistake was to buy my usual size, forgetting that my feet would swell in the heat. My toenails fell off. A minor inconvenience compared to my chum Weatherby's experience. He took out a mortgage to buy the top of the range Nikes and punctured an air bag on Day One. He spent the whole race listing dangerously to starboard.

SLEEPING BAG

The Sahara is very much like Lesley Bullard, the go-go dancer and county hockey player I dated when I was seventeen. Unbearably hot during the day, but depressingly cold at 3am.

Your only clothes are the ones you run in, so you need a bag that keeps you warm when you're more or less naked. Like all your kit, it must be light and small. Go to Black's and ask for their lightest and smallest one.

GROUND MAT
 Most competitors found it hard to sleep on the little pointy stones that the desert's made of. Not me. I slept like a baby. Although only two-thirds of my length, my mat is a miniature lilo. When you unleash it, it automatically sucks air into its honeycomb structure and inflates. Brilliant — unless you have your lips around the inflation tube at the time, in which case it sucks all the air from your body until you implode, a wizened, lifeless husk.
 Next month, I'll tell you some of the little things you can do to make the Marathon des Sables a little easier to endure.
 Like going to a beach club in Barbados instead.

Like Webster's Dictionary, I'm Morocco Bound

A TIP from a gnarled old runner: when you're at a critical stage in your training programme and the race of your life is just a month away, do resist the urge to ram high-powered motorcycles into stationary BMWs.
 It really is to no one's advantage.
 The poor, overworked souls in the A&E Department, especially, may resent having to reassemble your skeleton for the second time in three weeks.
 This advice isn't founded entirely in the realms of hypothesis — i.e. I have a couple of cracked ribs, I can't run and the Marathon des Sables is now just a few pant-wetting weeks away.
 However, in a curious sort of way, I'm rather pleased. How dull it would have been if I'd merely had to complete 145 miles in the Sahara desert with a full pack, heatstroke and third-degree sunburn.
 Despite a medical textbook's worth of unspeakable injuries, I dragged myself into Black's, the Outdoor People.
 I believe in the direct approach. 'I'm going outdoors. Very outdoors. I need... stuff.'

The assistant regarded me with that mixture of compassion and slight nervousness that I seem to evoke nowadays. 'Why of course, sir. Exactly what kind of... stuff... did you have in mind?'

'You know,' I barked, 'the usual. Snake venom pump. Burns treatment. Scorpion repellent.'

'F-fine. Are you sure you're all right, sir? You seem to be clutching your side.'

'Eh? Oh, it's nothing. Just a smashed ribcage.'

I left Black's 9.8 kilograms heavier and almost three hundred pounds lighter.

It was all I could do to stuff the items on my 'essentials' list into my new 30-litre Lowe rucksack. It was more than I could do to lug it the two hundred yards to my car — let alone run with it for 145 miles across the most inhospitable landscape on the planet, 5,000 enervating feet above sea level in 120 merciless degrees of searing heat.

It wasn't that any one thing weighed a lot (excepting the miniature cast-iron Aga cooker and the solar powered respirator). It was just the sheer number of widgets deemed necessary by the race organisers for one's survival.

Take the Swiss Army penknife, for instance. Now the American GI carries an M16 semi-automatic weapon and a week's ammunition. It'll flatten a house at half-a-mile and it still weighs less than your Swiss Army penknife. No wonder the Swiss never took Okinawa.

Anyway, I staggered into the Fitzroy Tavern where Dylan Thomas used to fall off his barstool with such monotonous regularity and George Orwell found the inspiration for *Animal Farm*. 'Give me the strongest can of lager in the house,' I demanded. 'The kind of thing that gets stuck between your teeth and makes you swear at the sky in Glaswegian. I need to forget.'

'Of course, sir. That'll be the Special. Are you all right, sir? You seem to be clutching your side.'

It was now three days before I left for Morocco and nearly five weeks since I'd run. I poked my ribs experimentally.

The effect was like having a white-hot poker inserted into your aorta via your pancreas — a definite improvement. I donned my stiff, bright new Nike Triax and wiggled the lead encouragingly at the dog. He stared at me morosely, farted and went back to sleep.

'Come on, you pathetic canine slob,' I hissed between clenched teeth. 'It's not your ribs that are broken. Yet. Your grandad was champion working dog at Crufts. Let's go work.'

Eight miles later, my pulse was faltering dangerously around the 190 mark and my quads felt as if they'd been tenderised with a plumber's lump hammer.

The dog was fine. Positively smug, in fact. For the first time in his life, he'd caught a squirrel. It had taken me two hours of threatening, pleading, pursuing, feinting, retreating and cajoling to wrest the little grey corpse from his slavering jaws.

To my horror, but not really to my surprise, the squirrel was wearing a tiny rucksack, crammed with a wren-down sleeping bag and half an ounce of dried nuts.

No wonder the poor little bugger couldn't run.

The Marathon des Sables.
Oh, look! There's Infinity

WEATHERBY RAISED his glass and stared through it speculatively at the pretty Moroccan waitress who had just brought us our fourth beers of the evening.

'Take a good look, Blackford. That's the last woman you'll see for a week who couldn't beat you at arm wrestling.'

'After four beers, I'm not sure *she* couldn't beat me. Remind me why we're drinking the night before the world's toughest footrace. Everybody else is on water.'

'Everybody else has trained,' he replied. 'They have something to preserve. We haven't.'

He was right, of course. But the idea filled me with a dark sense of foreboding.

And yet a week later, we were back in England — tired but basically alive, and trying to answer the same, unanswerable question for the tenth time in an hour.

'You're back, then. What was it like?'

They might as well ask for a six-word definition of Life, or a quick precis of the General Theory of Relativity.

For the Marathon des Sables is, above all, enormous. The sheer scale of the endeavour and the epic proportions of the landscape against which it is set, almost defy description.

For instance: it was three hours since we'd passed the second checkpoint on Day 4 — the 76k so-called 'killer stage'. The temperature, as ever, hovered around 125 degrees. We ploughed across the flank of a vast dune, our shoes breaking through the corrugated crust into the sucking morass beneath. Two feet forward, one foot back, fingers raking the sand as we dragged ourselves to the crest of yet another petrified wave.

And there before us lay a lake of blinding light, stretching away into an infinity of rippling, liquid heat between walls and towers of the blackest basalt. The lake, of course, was dry — had been since some unknown cataclysm ruined this land in a time before history. Its crazed surface was salt-white and flung back the onslaught of the sun, making it impossible to look at, even through polarised sunglasses.

'Control Point 3,' Weatherby read from the race guide, 'is situated on a small hillock on the plain.'

Sure enough, a windscreen glinted at the top of a little mound in the immediate foreground. And yet logic and the evidence of our own eyes placed the point at a distance of at least three miles.

So the basalt bank of the lake must be, what, fifteen miles away? And the thin blue line of mountains straight ahead, swimming in the heat, eighty? A hundred?

'A photo opportunity, methinks,' remarked Weatherby, and he scanned the immense panorama through the eye of his tiny Kodak. He quickly clicked it shut, though. No camera could capture the grandeur of that alien spectacle, any more than words could adequately describe it.

A fragile line of runner ants struggled out into the desert. Wearily we clumped down the dune onto the bitter salt pans and joined them.

'The sun'll be down in an hour,' Weatherby pointed out. 'We'd better dig out our headlamps.'

We spent a couple of hours at the checkpoint on the hillock. Once the medics had lanced and dressed the worst of my blisters and I'd swallowed a couple of industrial grade anti-inflammatories for the tendonitis in my shin, I settled myself against the wheel of a Land Rover. I dropped two blocks of hexi-fuel into my miniature tin Aga and boiled up a few centilitres of my last, precious water ration.

Weatherby peered at an array of packets. 'And what do you recommend this evening, Alfredo?' he demanded of the imaginary major-domo who had accompanied him throughout this escapade. 'The coq au vin and custard or the porridge with asparagus tips?'

I stared glumly at my own, 'wholesome and nutritious' freeze-dried alternatives. Vegetable stroganoff or sweet and sour chicken?

I had not yet discovered the secret of dehydrated rations: namely, never compare them to the real dish they purport to be. If you set out in the expectation that you will experience something remotely resembling chicken, let alone something that is sweet, or sour, or (heavens to Betsy) both, then you will be at best disappointed and at worst, sick.

But start from an expectation base of zero and at least you will be intrigued by the strange new sensations that assault your taste buds and confound your digestive juices.

Or you could simply do as Weatherby did — go to Tesco and buy packet foods at a tenth of the cost of my paramilitary ration packs and eat like a bloody king (relatively speaking).

As a musician, I have played to smaller audiences than the one that watched me force down my disgusting risotto. A crowd of doe-eyed children had spontaneously created itself out of the desert dust, seemingly. They stared at me mutely, not even demanding the compulsory 'stylo'. They reminded me uncomfortably of the Midwich Cuckoos.

It was almost dark as we straightened our pain-riven limbs and struck out again onto the endless plain.

I unwound my Bedouin headdress and pushed my shades up onto my forehead. A cool breeze played about my temples as I broke into a modest trot, and my spirits soared.

The spotlight from my headlamp danced on the ground before me, but I turned it off once the moon had suffused the land with its cold enchantment.

Staring up, I recalled a long-ago night in an Oxford meadow when, enthralled by mescalin, I'd felt I could reach out and pluck the stars from the sky. But nothing could compare with the glorious, glittering tapestry that hung above us now.

There are ten thousand million stars in our galaxy and ten thousand million galaxies in our universe and I swear I could see them all. Carving a fantastic silver swathe from horizon to horizon was a comet, a beautiful, lonely runner in an astral desert.

The cathedral silence was broken only by the intake of our breath and the soft, slow fall of our feet.

There were other times, of course, that were distinctly less inspirational.

Hobbling across a field of sharp stones in a gale straight from the gates of Hell, a 25lb backpack pile-driving your heels into the ground with every step.

Trying to wash down a snatched chunk of super-dense power bar on the move with a mouthful of hot, sulphurous water.

Shivering at 4am in a rough shelter of jute sacks, open to the freezing, sand-laden wind, with only the clothes you run in for a pillow.

Hanging around pointlessly for two hours as the Sahara stokes up the furnace for the day and the race director (a person of megalithic self-importance) addresses the multi-national field in French.

These are a few of my favourite things.

The medical tent was fun, too — somewhere between Dante's *Inferno* and the set of *Reservoir Dogs*.

An evening didn't go by when some poor sod wasn't stretched out, pale and cold as a snowdrift, with a drip in his arm. And by the end of Day 2, the general condition of our feet would have impressed a Crimean field surgeon.

Amongst the worst victims was Diana Godfrey-Fausset, who won our growing admiration as she soldiered uncomplainingly through each day on soles the colour and consistency of raw mince.

Our tent was home to a bizarre assortment of individuals:

- a distant relative of the Queen and her stockbroker husband who wore his business suit all the way out to Ouzazate
- a freelance war correspondent who'd witnessed cannibalism in Liberia
- the man who is currently redecorating David Hockney's London studio
- a retired headmistress (who subsequently took the trophy for second woman home)
- a dead ringer for McMurphy in *One Flew Over The Cuckoo's Nest*
- an old Etonian who'd spent his last holiday on a dog-sled in Greenland
- a Bohemian lady called Veronica who might've been there to sketch the wildflowers
- me.

Amazingly, we all got on rather well. When I returned to London and a bleak, retarded April, I found I missed them.

Flicking through the little notebook I allowed myself on the run, I came across an exchange that had made me laugh in spite of all the pain and stress and apprehension. It instantly recalled the brave, funny individuals with whom I'd shared the indignities and victories of 'the world's toughest foot race'.

S I keep breathing sand. We need those things rugby players stick on their noses.

C What — other men's bottoms?

My friends ask me whether I'd do it again. I wouldn't, even if I could. Such intense experiences should be remembered, respected and never repeated.

Which is not to say I'd reject any other madcap scheme Seaton might wish to suggest — always providing, of course, that it is sufficiently stupid and inherently unfeasible.

I'd never buy a Paula Radcliffe CD.
So why did I run the Rock 'n' Roll Marathon?

IN THE Old Days, you crossed the marathon finish line and you got a kiss from the type of girl who spent her weekdays handing out perfume samples in airports. It didn't exactly trigger an involuntary orgasm, but it was better than a poke in the eye with a sharp stick.

In today's USA, of course, sex is virtually forbidden. Congress is currently debating a Bill which will segregate the genders geographically. The women will get California, Florida, New England, the Carolinas and the nice bits of Louisiana. The men will be herded onto a reservation in New Mexico and force-fed psychotropic drugs.

Such is the prevalence of PC-induced paranoia that the best you can hope for at the end of a race is a painful blow on the back from a grizzly old war veteran in slacks and a Fred Perry shirt.

Indeed, the scene at the end of San Diego's debut Rock 'n' Roll Marathon™ resembled nothing more than Hanoi, ten minutes before the VC turned up.

Runners wandered aimlessly in the streets, exhausted and bewildered, while helicopters roared above, rendering all communication impossible and reinforcing the forlorn isolation of the shocked survivors. Nobody seemed to know where the drinks were, nor the space blankets, nor the complimentary Hershey bars, nor the gleaming UPS trucks with the kit bags in, nor the hotel courtesy coaches, nor even the rest of San Diego.

The sun was so hot and dry, you could feel your skin shrinking over your bones. I stopped a cop on a mountain bike. He wore a black and white cycling helmet and a .38 nestled against his police regulation Lycra™ shorts. Whatever it was that I asked him, he didn't know the answer.

Primitive, post-race logic told me that since this had been the Rock 'n' Roll Marathon, and I wanted to leave, I should walk away from the rock 'n' roll. Before long, I had left the Historic Gaslight District™ behind me. I spotted a Yellow Cab™ idling at the lights — but my heart sank as I saw another runner hobbling furiously towards it, waving and bleating.

Of the 21,000 poor sods it might have been, it turned out to be Seaton, your editor. Too exhausted to be amazed, we tumbled into the cab's air-conditioned cocoon, and allowed the complaints of the deeply depressed cabbie to wash over us like embrocation. 'Can you believe it? They closed every major route into town for the goddam marathon. You can't even get to the goddam airport! An' then they go an' fix the goddam race for the same weekend as the goddam X Games!' (For X Games™, read Extreme Sports — a suicidal but highly televisual circus of lunatic pastimes in which the participants bungee jump, wrestle rhinos and juggle with plutonium.)

Back at the Best Western™ hotel, the quality of life improved rapidly. My girlfriend led me like a conquering hero to the open-air jacuzzi and I sprawled in its boiling cauldron, feeling my muscles revive like tomato plants in a cloudburst.

A few feet away, M and T, our Hollywood movie star friends, cavorted in the pool with our shrieking three-year-old daughter. Soon, I promised myself, I would be able to manage a small beer. Or two. And a lightly-roasted horse. But not just now. Just now, I was in the company of friends and family, soaking up the sun in the most amiable climate on the planet, enjoying the sensuous caresses of mankind's finest invention, and most important of all, *not running*.

I had really thought the nightmare would never end. For

the last six miles, I'd felt as if I were running towards the point where parallel lines meet — a cruelly hypothetical one that recedes at precisely the speed at which you run. Dehydrated, exhausted, hallucinating, I jogged feebly on the spot under the merciless sun while a double conveyor belt of hysterical, suntanned *Baywatch* extras slipped slowly by, waving and braying the drab mantra of the American running fraternity: 'G'd JA-A-A-ARB! Way-t'-GO!'

I wasn't doing a G'd Jarb. I was doing a Crap Jarb. In fact, I was running the slowest marathon of my long and undistinguished career. Even the four-hour mark was rapidly receding into the realms of fantasy.

Beside me, the sparkling wavelets of the Pacific Ocean danced a joyous mazurka. In the distance, through the exemplary, smog-free air, the polished towers of the downtown district flashed out 'G'D JARB!' in semaphore. San Diego was so clean, it hurt my eyes. No matter where I looked, I could see nothing older than the last episode of *Friends*.

Some 55% of the runners, I learned later, were women — bronzed, lissom, long-haired, clean-limbed women of marriageable age, straight out of a Beach Boys lyric — and now they were skipping lightly past me in an endless, galling commercial for the American Way.

I felt so Old World, somehow, amidst all this bright and effervescent youth. I creaked along, a crumbling anachronism, like a barquentine in a powerboat race.

Then I spotted the sign for Mexico.

I could so easily have missed it — faded paint on sun-bleached pine, hanging drunkenly from a blasted thorn tree. I edged across the freeway and onto the dusty track indicated by the sign. Nobody seemed to notice as I slipped away into the dusty hinterland, where the monotony of the juniper scrub was broken only by the occasional, battered cactus.

I crossed the Rio Grande on a wild pinto I'd managed to hog-tie in the dead-end of a dry gulch. By nightfall, we'd hit Tijuana — a badlands border town if ever there was one. The streets resounded to the crackle of small arms fire. Half the population seemed to live in cartons at the roadside. The other half were prostitutes and drug dealers. I was robbed three times in as many minutes.

I might as well have stayed in London.

When I regained consciousness, I was back in San Diego, just a hundred metres from the finish line. Like a somnambulist Moses, I parted a Red Sea of bright-eyed, hysterical Californians, screaming 'G'D JA-A-A-ARB!' at the tops of their rosy-pink lungs.

If I could have got my hands on a chainsaw, I would have shown them what a bloody *g'd jarb* was. Instead, I tottered over the line and, with a surge of relief that was almost sexual, left the whole, ghastly fiasco behind me.

Why had it been such an ordeal? A number of reasons. Firstly, the San Diego authorities had gaily invited 21,000 runners to shuffle through their city streets — and had only set about clearing the thoroughfare of parked cars on the morning of the race. Result: a small town's worth of athletes, all of them filled to the gills with mineral water, stuck, quietly broiling, at the Start for the best part of an hour.

As Seaton and I watched, whole chunks of the crowd would split off and sprint into the park to relieve themselves. It wouldn't have surprised me to learn that down at the foot of the hill, whole neighbourhoods had been washed away by flash floods of urine.

I idled away the time by imagining how the London mob would have reacted to a 50-minute delay. It hardly bore thinking about. The race would have started with or without official permission, and the crucified bodies of the organisers would have lined the route in a macabre pastiche of the final scene in *Spartacus*.

As it turns out, the only parked car we encountered in 26 miles and 385 yards was a police patrol cruiser.

More critical to the success of the race was the absence of drinking water. By the time the second half of the field reached the first four feed stations, they were dry. But in a touching attempt to furnish us with at least the *idea* of water, the roadside staff had lined up rows of empty cups.

Still, the route was flat, the runners almost irritatingly cheerful, and the rock bands that performed along the way were so good, they sent shivers down your spine.

And once you give up trying to run through it, San Diego is an agreeable, almost picturesque, city. There's the World Famous Zoo™ where the animals are afforded so much freedom, you get the uncomfortable feeling they're there to see *you*.

And once you've tired of meeting animals, you can eat them on an undreamed-of scale at Morton's steak house. At this American institution, even a child's meal is bigger than most European cars.

Would I run it again? No. But then, I wouldn't run any race again. This is because I'm driven by the belief that the next event can't possibly be as awful as the last.

Which is not to say that you shouldn't try it for yourself. So they leave you standing in the sun for an hour with a full bladder. So they starve you of liquid intake for the first four, critical miles.

But, hey — that's rock 'n' roll!

In which I am racked and I am pinioned. And then the real torture started...

EXPERIENCE IS the great consolation of age.

It's not true, of course, but when you're as old as I am you cling to any straw, however rotten.

Nevertheless, my experience of last weekend did teach me one thing: never play *Snap!* with a seven-year-old in the back seat of a Golf while his mother negotiates mountain passes in the Swiss Alps. You will be sick.

In some ways, the extreme nausea and disorientation I felt in the back of Peter Fordham's hire car was the high spot of the weekend. It was certainly far less distressing than the 28th Sierre-Zinal mountain race — the reason I was in Switzerland.

Twenty miles doesn't sound far, does it? Little more than your long weekly training run. The pleasant bit of a marathon. But Everest is only five miles high and there are satellites orbiting not much more than twenty miles above the Earth's surface.

The point being that distances are misleading when they're vertical.

I'd decided to run this classic Alpine race at very short notice — egged on by Fordham's inexplicable enthusiasm for debilitating mountain events.

I was quite cavalier about the whole affair — I even drank a half-bottle of wine as the train sighed along the Lake Geneva riviera. The evening sun caught the sails of a thousand bobbing yachts. Behind them the eternal snows of Mont Blanc glowed with an inner, rosy fire. And by the time I'd downed the last glass of Chilean Merlot, so did I.

The train was almost empty — despite the warnings of the clerk who'd persuaded me to buy a first class ticket to ensure that I got a seat. There was one other passenger in my compartment. He worked in Geneva during the week and returned home to Sierre on Fridays. He looked incredulous when I told him I was running the Sierre-Nival. His eyes travelled from my greying locks to the empty wine bottle to the homely belly, swelling comfortably beneath my fleece.

'I am admiring you!' he pronounced finally. 'Look! There is the mountain up which there will be the racing!' He pointed out to a lowering, black mass that was rapidly devouring the sky.

The vertiginous southern wall of the valley, stunted pines clung desperately to its flanks. To see the top, I had to lie on my back on the seat with the crown of my head pressed against the window. As running terrain, it might as well have been the north face of the Eiger.

I shrugged and mustered my most rugged, devil-may-care grin, but I could tell he wasn't convinced. Neither was I.

After a frenetic week at the front line of toothpaste advertising, I'd intended to laze the next day away by the hotel pool. But I'd hardly finished breakfast when Fordham arrived with his wife and kids and abducted me. They bundled me into the back of their car. 'You're going to Zermatt,' I was informed. 'It's the best view in the world and you're bloody well going to see it.'

We parked up in the valley, took the shuttle train up to Zermatt and switched to a little rack and pinion railway.

The sky was a cloudless azure, the sun was hot, the air cool and fragrant with the scent of pine and heather.

We'd baulked at the cost of our tickets — around £35 each — but as the train clambered out of Zermatt and up a track that wormed in and out of the rock, arched across dizzy ravines and skirted breath-taking precipices, we realised that the journey would have been cheap at twice the price.

We rounded a bulging bluff on the mountainside. Far below, the town was spread out like an illuminated manuscript. And then, with an eye-searing blaze of white, the Matterhorn reared up from the trees and exploded in the blue heavens.

Words nor photographs can convey the sheer power of this peak: a crooked pencil of ice-encrusted basalt, it is the magical mountain of some myth or fairy tale.

As the train climbed above the tree line, it loomed ever closer. And then we were at our destination — a curious hybrid of Mount Palomar Observatory and the Restaurant at the End of the Universe. Even the prices were astronomical. 'I wonder if they sell Hubble gum?' Fordham mused.

The air was now so thin that I found it quite taxing to climb the last few yards to the viewing point. This didn't bode at all well for tomorrow's race. But nothing could dampen the sheer exhilaration of being in this amazing place, encircled by a dazzling army of majestic peaks and glaciers.

The Fordhams dropped me at my hotel in time for dinner and an early night. I'd tried to order a cab to the start, which lay a little way out of town. But the hotelier assured me that a special bus would pick me up a couple of hundred yards from the hotel.

The hotelier was clearly related to the nice woman at the race registration desk who'd told us we had to start at 5am. There was no bus and I ended up walking.

I chucked my spare T-shirt and knickers into the back of a lorry. There was no labelling system, nor anything on the truck to connect it to the race. As Fordham pointed out, they could have been a bunch of cowboys with a market stall in Geneva, flogging cut-price running kit.

And then we were off. The road rose gracefully out of the valley, hugging the side of the mountain. It wasn't so steep that you couldn't manage a sedate trot. I was cheered by the way I was able to weave my way through the Swiss and the French in their so-stylish gear. This was going to be a thoroughly uplifting three hours, I concluded.

Then abruptly we left the metalled road and lurched up a narrow, muddy path, treacherous with loose stones and half-exposed pine roots.

All conversation ceased. The path grew progressively steeper. Everyone walked — most, like me, bent double with palms pressed down hard upon knees.

Time after time, we crossed steep, rocky tracks — until it dawned on me that they were the same track. We were merely cutting off the hairpin bends that made it navigable.

An hour later and I had run for no more than 400 metres. This was impossible. There simply wasn't this much Up in the entire world.

A further thirty minutes and I staggered out of the trees into a heavenly Alpine meadow, all wildflowers and butterflies and stunning vistas of snowy peaks and sweeping, emerald forests.

The air was wonderful, but at 9,000 feet there was precious little of it. Even a modest jog had me panting. The combination of the altitude and the lunatic climb — 2,500 metres in ten kilometres — made my legs weak and my head light.

The route traced the side of a deep valley. The general direction was Up, which suited me fine. You can trust Up. It's when you go Down that you know you'll eventually be made to pay with some dreadful new Up.

Sure enough, we dropped down into a postcard village with its flower-bedecked chalets, neatly tended gardens and quaintly in-bred, rabidly-Right Wing villagers. And then it was Up again to the Weisshorn Hotel, winding up a heartbreaking track that was all too clearly visible for miles ahead.

Now we were in wild, craggy terrain, with soldiers stationed at the most precipitous traverses. Slither off one of these babies, I reflected gloomily, and a Swiss Army penknife wasn't going to help much.

Then the trail began subtly to change elevation. There could be no doubt — we were beginning to edge downwards. I passed a crude sign that read, '9k (crossed out) 7k to go!' Down in the shadowy depths of the valley I could just make out a patchwork of roofs and streets that must be Zinal.

By Jimminy, I was almost home! At this rate, I'd finish in 4:30 — quite a respectable time, all things considered.

However, as it turned out, the sign writer was the incestuous issue of the hotelier and the woman on the registration desk. It was at least 10 kilometres to the finish, and I ended up slithering and cursing my way down a sheer drop into the teeth-grindingly perfect village of Zinal in 5 hours 9 minutes.

There was no water at the finish unless you paid for it — and I'd given all my money to the Zermatt railway tycoons. The baggage reclaim area had been thoughtfully located halfway back up the sodding mountain.

As I dozed fitfully on the bus back to Sierre (five francs, payable in advance, borrowable from Fordham) I reflected that I'd done all right, really.

I hadn't acclimatised to the altitude and most of the runners spent their lives charging up and down alps. I had acquitted myself honourably.

How I wish I hadn't overheard the two blokes in the seat behind me (who, bizarrely, were from my home town of Middlesbrough).

'That little bloody Mexican won it. Chest like a barrel and legs like seasoned walnut.'

'Yeah, you've got to hand it to 'im. Two hours thirty is a good time in anybody's book… '

I couldn't do 2:30 for twenty miles on the flat with a following wind.

The medal on my chest shrivelled visibly. It was high time I went home.

In which I learn to appreciate the joys of high-altitude projectile vomiting

THE JOG to the start of the 78k Swiss Alpine PostMarathon was really quite enjoyable. Even if it was a 30k jog.

From the start in the stadium at Davos to the outrageously pretty village of Bergun where the climbing begins in earnest, the route was essentially downhill.

Our tour leader and guru, Mike Gratton, spent a week trying to impress us with the necessity of taking it easy. 'If you try to race the first section, they'll have to airlift you off the mountain in a helicopter.' And helicopter mercy dashes, he pointed out, weren't covered by the group insurance policy.

Not that I needed any encouragement to saunter the course. As we dropped out of a forest of dark and solemn pines and wound between the flower-bedecked chalets of Filisur, I had to stop every fifty paces to take a photograph. Filisur, apparently, is the only village in the world to be constructed entirely from the tops of chocolate boxes.

Soon we were plunging into a sinuous canyon. Precipitous cliffs soared above, festooned with vines and dripping ropes of moss. Far below, a virile stream clattered between boulders. A litter of tree trunks in the river bed testified to the fury of the spring meltwaters. The light dwindled as the sky was cropped down to a narrow, dazzling band and it seemed as if the very air were green.

As we emerged from a tunnel hewn through a rocky buttress, an eerie shriek reverberated along the gorge. For sheer daring and engineering brilliance, the Swiss railway system surpasses the Apollo space programme. It doesn't matter how high you run, how serpentine and treacherous the path, a little red train will always beat you to it and greet you laconically with a whistle — a proper *whistle*, mind, not the flat, two-tone blare of a British diesel.

We ran next to the tracks for a mile or so, even joining the train upon a slender viaduct arching hundreds of feet above the ravine. Our footsteps rattled the ancient planks and the sound echoed nervously around the mountains.

Then we burst out onto a sunny hillside and a road that coiled down into Bergun. My legs and lungs had hardly noticed the first twenty miles, I reflected with satisfaction, and I permitted myself a daydream in which I stormed across the finish line, chipper and grinning, in just under the eight hours.

Hah.

Not even the long climb from Bergun to Chants, much of it on metalled roads, could dispel the fantasy. Everyone except the odd relay runner was walking but by means of the 'scout's pace' I had perfected in the Himalayan 100, I managed to cut through the field very effectively. A gnarled old Swede with the legs of a troll adopted my strategy and we ground up the hill together like a human caterpillar.

Meanwhile, the snowy peaks gathered ever closer: the incline steepened and the road gave way first to a rough track, then to a heartbreaking path which tore each burning breath from the lungs. There really was no running up this. You leaned forward, clamped your hands to your knees and muttered Gothic curses as you dragged your screaming body ever higher into the thin, cold sky.

I remember I passed a small man crouched at the wayside. His eyes were blank, his face the colour of dirty parchment. A strand of saliva joined his chin to the ground. 'Thank heaven I don't feel like he does,' I thought. Half an hour later, I felt like he did. As I swayed up the path like a drunk, all that kept me from fainting was the need to throw up.

All the suckers I'd overtaken on the road to Chants came storming past me now — among them Val, a rock-hard Mancunian who plans to spend Millennium Night in a bivouac in the Sahara and whose sole concession to camping comfort is a sleeping mat cut out of bubblewrap. 'Come on, Andy!' she chivvied. 'Just follow my arse!' Yet even this alluring prospect was not enough to drag me any faster up that cruel hill.

By the time I reached the Keschhutte, a traveller's rest perched high above the tree line in a landscape of glaciers and naked granite, I was utterly shagged.

While I'd made a point of swallowing three cups of water at every drink station, I still had a raging thirst. My heart was pounding, I was dizzy and disorientated. This is how you must feel, I remember noting, shortly before you die. I sat down heavily, head in hands, hands on table. If the bloke next to me had come down with anthrax, I couldn't have moved.

By the time the medical team reached me, I was busy staging a spectacular display of projectile vomiting for the rest of the field. Whoosh! Thirty miles' worth of Rivella Marathon Drink and God's good water, all gone in a single, horizontal convulsion.

At that altitude, I'm surprised it didn't instantly evaporate, form dark clouds and destroy Zurich with two-inch hailstones of sick.

As he sunk the hypodermic into my arm, the doctor explained that my stomach had gone into spasm and was preventing any liquid from entering my system. Quite a common complaint in endurance events, apparently. The injection relaxed my muscles, I drank a litre of water and felt immediately, miraculously well. This was definitely my kind of medicine:

How do you feel?

Terrible. I'm dying.

Here, have this injection.

Thanks, I feel fine now. If you'll excuse me, I'll just run another twenty-five miles.

I snatched up my lucky marathon hat and half a banana

and wobbled off down the track towards the Scaletta Pass, forty minutes later than I should have.

Of the rest of the race, I remember little. To take my mind off the pain of muscles parched to the consistency of old garden string, I set myself a series of complex intellectual problems — like trying to remember whether it was Algy or Bingo who lost the kite in *Rupert and the Imps Of Spring*.

We sliced along the flank of a mighty valley, I seem to recall, while the wimpy 42k runners filed like multi-coloured ants five hundred feet below us.

We slithered over snow fields, picked our way through glacial streams, occasionally skipped through gracious meadows of orchid, gentian, harebell and wild azalea until we reached the other side of the mountain and the rip-roaring tumble down to Durboden and the Dischma Valley.

The trouble is with ultra-marathons, the Downs don't even begin to compensate for the Ups. If anything, running downhill is even tougher on strained muscles and battered joints than the awful slog to the top.

There was now a very real danger of falling, as exhausted minds and dulled senses wrestled with split-second decisions on a steep path strewn with rocks and laced with icy slush.

The silence of these majestic uplands was broken only by the muffled imprecations of the runners and the chatter of the helicopter as it shuttled victim after victim to the Davos Compound Fracture Clinic.

Every runner, as you know, has a fairy godmother. Mine is five foot six with a Yorkshire accent and a Rotary Club T-shirt. I'd run with Whitby Jimmy two years ago in Northern India, and I'd been pleased when he'd turned up unheralded in Switzerland. Not half as pleased as I was, though, when I saw his stocky, dogged form ahead of me on the path down to Durboden. Without his quiet good nature, I might have packed it in and hitched a lift off the chopper. But he stuck with me, even sacrificing the chance to improve on his PB for the event.

And then we were down among fields and churches and

clean, sad-eyed cows and that comforting feeling of normality the Swiss are so good at.

I actually had a dream that Switzerland was invented as the control in an experiment designed to measure the effects on the rest of Europe of two world wars. The result: a society in which the buses run like clockwork, the clocks run like buswork, nobody asks to see your ticket, litter is an endangered species and everyone looks like your grandparents did in 1955. Switzerland is like comfort food. It's the national equivalent of the foetal position. There's no doubt it would drive you mental in the long term, but for a damaged and exhausted runner, it's bloody wonderful.

The last few miles were a delirious blur. I managed a sort of hobbling gait, half run, half walk, and eventually I found myself in the stadium, hammering the last few hundred metres in an attempt to get under the ten hours.

Most of our group had wisely opted for the 30 and 42k events. A couple had even made the medals — and those who didn't achieved private triumphs. Sally broke her hand early in the week, while walking in the high peaks. But with her arm rigged up by Heath Robinson, she managed a decent time in the 30k.

But it wasn't just the big day that made the Swiss trip so special. The race was the culmination of a week-long programme of races, training runs and glorious hikes in the mountains (some rather longer than intended, thanks to the unconventional approach to navigation adopted by Lord Gratton, an ex-geography teacher).

The hotel was comfortably eccentric, the food was fine and we all seemed to get on like old friends from Day One — mostly, I suspect, because of the Gratton influence. You felt that he was there less as travel agent than as ardent runner and walker with a keen interest in people.

Providing I can unbend my arms and regain the use of my legs, I'll see you there next year.

The Three Pekes Race. How do they manage it with those stumpy little legs?

'I'M TELLING you,' Seaton assured me with that penetrating, 'trust-me-I'm-being-perfectly-sincere-here' expression which never fails to beguile me, 'The Three Peaks is a breeze for someone of your experience. The toughest bit's the driving.'

Seven days later, I had to sleep on the sofa in the living room because I couldn't climb the stairs to bed.

Actually, given a couple of hours, I could have reached the first floor landing — but I'd have been stuck up there for three days until my quads recovered enough strength to prevent my knee joints working in reverse and my legs from bending backwards.

There were four in our team. I'd only met one of them before — once. I was called in to replace some bloke who'd read an account of the race, then cut off a toe to get out of running.

The team leader was Dan, about whom the Deserter had warned me, 'Don't let him spend too much time consulting his compass and admiring the view. He's prone to that.'

Then there was Max, the Derbyshire to Dan's Jennings. They'd been friends since school, but whereas Dan had become a lawyer and worked steadily up the ranks of a multi-national corporation, Max had made a career of further education and getting dumped by beautiful women. His academic studies were punctuated by long spells of tree surgery and rough labouring on building sites in Essex.

Now he was an Environmental Architect, 'designing inner-city oases for heroin addicts to shoot up in'.

He was an engaging character — a fount of tales about woodsmen cutting their own throats with chainsaws that alleviated the twelve-hour drive from central London to Fort William. But his amiability disguised a will of iron. 'You can stick to any decision, however tough,' he explained, 'once you've had your mother sectioned under the Mental Health Act.'

As we began our ascent of Ben Nevis (4,450ft) it quickly

became clear that an iron will was worth its weight in, er, iron.

Within 500 metres of the start, I was gasping.

As usual, I'd adopted the Blackford Lightweight Economy Training Package — a brief regime of three-mile jogs around the flatlands of Cambridgeshire.

I shouldn't have bothered with running at all. Half-an-hour a day on a Stairmaster would have been more to the point. You can't run up Ben Nevis — it's a bloody mountain, for God's sake. You just bend double, grit your teeth, glue your hands to your knees, do your best to keep breathing and to ignore the pain that rapidly suffuses every particle of your being.

Traffic on the mountain was heavy — we'd picked the day of the National Fire Service Three Peaks Challenge, in which twenty teams of ten runners compete annually.

Whereas we were racing against one team only, under the leadership of another lawyer, John, who was legendary for being indestructible despite his own best efforts in that direction.

They stormed off to an early lead, which they largely squandered by taking a series of 'short cuts' up vertical escarpments and across bottomless bogs.

We made the top in just under two hours. It was desolate spot: freezing fog whipped up over the edge of a 2,000-foot precipice, as we waded though a snow field to the gloomy cairn that marks the summit. I was grateful for the company of the firefighters. Without them, I think I may have slit my wrists.

As is invariably the case with mountains, going down is even more exquisitely unpleasant than going up. The others charged off like goats while I teetered and minced after them like a female impersonator in stilettos.

Still, only three hours after setting out, we were back in the van and heading for the Lakes.

In which I learn that every peak is a trough

THE HEAT of the Burmese jungle poured down like molten brass on the corrugated-iron roof of The Oven. My hip joints, rudely jammed into an agonisingly unnatural position for the long days and nights of my confinement, screamed their indignation.

My tongue was soldered to the roof of my mouth and every breath seared my throat.

Then a rough hand shook my shoulder. 'Oi! Oi! Wake up!' It must be Kito, the brutal corporal. My punishment was over! I had prevailed. Those of my men suffering from beriberi would no longer be forced to work on the bridge...

In fact, it wasn't the brutal corporal — it was Dan, the brutal captain of our Three Peaks Challenge team. I wasn't in a prison camp on the banks of the River Kwai. I was in a predicament crueller by far, suffocating in a cramped metal box devised to inflict inhuman levels of pain and distress upon its occupants. A Vauxhall Zafira.

'Come on! Get your fucking legs on, we've got a mountain to run up.'

Since our breakneck descent of Ben Nevis just six hours earlier, I'd dozed fitfully while Dan propelled us at warp speed through the Celtic fringes of Britain. My torn muscles had glued themselves to their sheaths and my blood had broken down into gloomy puddles of custard and lactic acid.

Now we were parked up in a lay-by in Wasdale as the first glimmer of dawn stroked the summit of Scafell Pike, the next in this Behemoth of obstacle courses.

I unfolded my poor, tragic frame as one might a rusty Z-Bed and chewed on a lump of curdled energy drink. It tasted like a child's drawing of a strawberry.

Since we'd left Fort William at the start of the race, I'd only eaten random objects from the chiller cabinets of filling stations. Filling being the operative word. I'd managed to force down a small pork pie into which the manufacturers had somehow contrived to stuff an entire pig. It was so dense, it bent light. Now it was lodged in my duodenum for all eternity.

And we were off. I didn't so much run as scuttle, stiff and hunched over, in a gait suggestive of an old, frost-bitten hamster.

To the dismay of my calves, the track launched rudely into a steady incline, from which it wouldn't relent for at least 3,000 feet.

Still, I reflected, at least it wasn't wet under foot. Then the path ceased abruptly at the shore of a sizeable torrent that leapt, singing, between slippery, unstable boulders. I soon came to understand the downside of waterproof trail shoes: that they keep water in, as well as out.

As Dan and the others bounded up the track like demented gazelles I paused to catch my breath. The night mist parted to reveal vivid, sun-soaked meadows on the braes above. Larks were beginning their incessant warble, to an English ear the very overture to a summer's day in the high lands, and the air was damp and rich with the smell of peat and rock and bracken. My heart swelled and the blood coursed, reviving and restoring, into my legs.

Twenty miles away, irradiating the Irish Sea in the time-honoured tradition, sprawled the concrete maze of Sellafield.

And along the ribbon of road below crept twenty identical white vans in a surreal procession. They contained the cream of the nation's firefighters, each team intent on victory in their annual Three Peaks Challenge.

Heaven help Britain, I thought, if its cat gets stuck up a tree today.

In which I discover that mountains are like amphetamines: the hardest part is coming down

SNOWDON IS a conundrum. It's the Janus of mountains.

One face is a slow, steep, arduous slog — a far longer run than Ben Nevis or Scafell.

The other, in stark contrast, is deadly dull and served by a train. Which means that the summit is infested with nuns and engulfed by the cellulite tsunami that is submerging the British Isles.

For a Three Peaks competitor, it makes the final ascent far more psychologically challenging than the others.

It's one thing to run up a mountain knowing that however slow your time, the lardarse at No. 43 couldn't even have reached Base Camp. But once you know that old Buffalo Buttocks is there at the top, waiting for you with a smug smile and a paper plate piled high with reconstituted pig prostate, then it rather saps your achievement of any element of glory.

The mood thus induced is exacerbated by one's diminished physical condition at this stage of the event. During the past 16 hours, you've run up two mountains, eaten food with a lower nutritional value than its packaging, and shared a so-called 'recreational vehicle' with three men who smell like the goat enclosure at a city farm.

Incidentally, I've been up an Alp or two in my time and when there has been food to be had at the top, sure, it's been bank-breakingly expensive. You sort of expect that — some poor sod has to hoik it up there. But it's always erred on the side of the edible.

Not so in Wales. The pricey bit still holds, but once you're more than six feet above sea level, the cuisine would induce a prison riot in the Black Hole of Calcutta.

It sounds curmudgeonly, I know, but if somebody doesn't say something, there'll be people dying of scurvy on the mountain railway.

Anyway, at 10:30am of Day Two of the Three Peaks Race, our valiant, malodorous team struck out from the car park like four penguins in post-operative therapy following double hip replacements.

The others, being relatively fit and optimistic and with a combined age that was considerably smaller than my own, soon shuffled ahead. I was left to my gloomy reflections.

The trouble is with on-off-on races like the Three Peaks, the old post-race depression catches up with you halfway through. Any elation, any sense of triumph, quickly evaporates in the foetid claustrophobia of the mobile goat pen.

So I hauled myself up Snowdon like an escapee from a long-term mental institution. The romantic associations of rock and peat and heather deserted me. Instead, I was pervaded by a powerful sense of the innate hostility of inanimate objects. Rock was there to further bruise my battered feet, heather to trip me up, peat to suck me down into the bowels of the hill.

As the summit grudgingly revealed itself, I felt a wave of despair. There was the third peak in the Three Peaks Race. As the cream of the nation's fire service stormed past me without the aid of breathing equipment or extending ladders, I knew that the rules only required us to *ascend* it.

However, the Goatmobile was down at the bottom — so while the firefighters would hit the summit in a sickening orgy of mutual backslapping before descending by train with the nuns and the obese, we would have to subject our screaming quads to the agony of the long run down.

Four hours later, we hobbled across our hotel lounge to the bar. A couple of firemen sniggered behind their hands. The only words I caught were, 'Douglas Bader' and 'impersonators' convention'.

THE RUN THAT
GOT AWAY

If the Marathon des Sables is 'The World's Toughest Foot Race', it's only because the competitors in the Trans 333 usually cross the line on their hands and knees.
To be absolutely accurate, they usually don't cross the line at all. Nearly everyone drops out or drops dead.
Even at today's exchange rate, 333 kilometres is an awfully long way to run.
Why I ever imagined I could run it is a mystery. The words Artois and Stella suggest themselves.
Whatever. This little flurry of articles charts my steep trajectory from steely determination to copping out.

So I said to her, 'Let's get one thing straight. I don't care what you do to me. We won the Ashes.'

'WHEN CAN I run again?' I asked my chiropractor. She just shrugged in that informal, Aussie, Shane Warne sort of way that we Brits privately agree is rather insolent but would never let the Aussies know that's how we felt because they would only laugh in that informal way of theirs that makes us feel pale and physically inferior and generally uncomfortable.

'Not till I tell you,' she replied in her cheery, sunny way. 'I need to work on you on Monday, Wednesday and Friday of next week. That should sort out your first pelvic misalignment. Then we'll start on the second. In the meantime, walk briskly.'

I can already hear you thinking, 'He's doing the groundwork so he can wriggle out of the Trans 333 in November.'

You're absolutely right, of course. I could hardly get all the way to the October issue and suddenly announce, 'Oh, and by the way, I know I was swaggering about, bullshitting about how

I was going to waltz through the mother of all non-stop desert races, but actually I've got a bit of a dicky back so I'm taking the family to Pontins instead.'

However, I swear I'm still determined, at this point in time, given the severe physical handicap with which I'm presently afflicted, to attempt the 333.

I'm so serious about this, I've persuaded Seaton to pay my Harley Street chiropractor's bills. I suppose in the end, it's cheaper for him than swallowing the loss of my entry fee.

I've always suspected that the sole advantage in going to Harley Street is that the property prices in the back issues of *Country Life* are in decimal currency.

I couldn't have been more wrong.

Your normal, above-average back person will pull and prod at you for half an hour, crack a few joints to justify the bill, then tell you it's going to be a long, slow job.

Christina, by contrast, whisked me straight into an X-ray booth, rattled off three shots of my lower back, printed them, stuck them up on a light box and set about them, muttering, with a slide rule and a pencil.

'Your pelvis is six millimetres out of kilter… here… and another three… here. Two separate planes. This one's the most serious, so we'll address it first. Now take off your clothes and stand on one leg with your butt facing me, like a sad old stork.'

She didn't actually say the last bit, but it's how I felt. Nevertheless, when I hobbled the half-mile back to my office, I think I looked noticeably less like Douglas Bader than I had for weeks.

She'd wrenched my skeleton back into line in much the same way that an automotive engineer repairs a buckled chassis. She told me my pelvis had probably been skew-whiff since a riding accident two years ago, so correcting it would cause me all sorts of grief as neglected muscles were suddenly jerked back into play.

She was right about that.

But I have to say that 'walking briskly' has been a revelation.

I've discovered a race of burrowing bees who throw up miniature molehills in soft soil. I've identified the flocks of little bobbing birds in the pea fields as linnets. (Or, truth to tell, just possibly corn buntings.) I've watched a brace of buzzards soaring over the Clunch Pit and I've taken the trouble to find out what clunch is.

I've also found out that most of the footpaths around our way are made of chippings from a local asbestos factory, now thankfully shut.

So a dicky back may turn out to be the least of my worries.

In which I calculate that 333 is exactly one half of the number of the Beast. (Is that all?)

IN MY heart of hearts, of course, I know that Seaton wants me dead.

I'm not a fool. It hasn't escaped me that he's gradually turning the screw – bullying and cajoling me, waving his filthy lucre in my face until like a donkey pursuing a carrot it will never catch, I am reduced to the ruin who scratches out these sorry lines for you tonight.

Was it only twenty years ago that, fresh of face and fleet of foot, I carved out my daily mile around the South Circular, from Clapham Common to Streatham Hill?

Behold me now – old before my time — the heartless glare of the Sahara indelibly etched into the wadis of my brow. And all because of Saton and his diabolical journal. Sorry: Seaton. Freudian slip.

You'll know how he's had me scramble up the Himalayan precipice and founder in the trackless dunes of deserts so wild that no man has subdued them with a name.

These abominations I have endured without complaint.

But last Sunday was the last bloody straw.

It all began with a simple email: How's the training going for the Trans 333?

For the uninitiated, the 333 is the last word in idiocy. Three hundred and thirty-three kilometres across the featureless vacuum that is Niger.

Apparently I'm running it. This December. Along with a handful of battle-hardened mercenaries, self-mutilating psychopaths and failed suicide bombers.

Seaton, in his usual, gentlemanly, public bloody school way, was implying that I wasn't putting in the proper training. And he was absolutely right.

My friend Eadie ran the Trans 333 last year. Now, I've run with Eadie and he's like Robocop. He eats shale and shits granite. He can sprint across continents without food. He once fashioned his own Camelback by strapping a dead dromedary across his shoulders.

And he dropped out of the 333.

So this is a very, very grown-up race. And so I'm utterly paralysed by the prospect, drinking heavily and just occasionally managing a feeble set of ten reverse crunches in the gym.

And so Seaton's email was like God clearing his throat. 'Game's up – do the work or your bleached bones will sink forever beneath the timeless sands of Niger'.

It was with a cruel hangover that I stumbled last Sunday from The Old Slaughterhouse with the World's Fittest Dog. My legs seemed to operate independently of my torso, like those of Barbie's friend, Ken. I'd subdued my stomach with four Rennies, but I knew it was a temporary measure at best.

A tune resonated stupidly around my head on an endless loop. A mild case of alcoholic poisoning will often produce Bryan Hyland's *Sealed With A Kiss*. But this was serious: the first movement of Elgar's *Cello Concerto*, from the classic recording by Jacqueline Du Pré.

I let the dog off the lead – forgetting in my befuddled state that his quarterly anti-shagging shot was overdue. He stared at me with comic incredulity: Are you mad? Before I could reply, he raced off to indulge in a canine orgy of deviant sexuality that made the last days of Sodom seem like a damp weekend in Harrogate.

For my part, I tripped on a root and jarred my neck. Then I was sick behind a bush. Where I was spotted by Tim, ex-treasurer of the Willesden Wankers who spent the next three, excruciating miles telling me how he got lost on the Rhubarb Patch 10k in 1983.

The sun was like a great, bronze gong, ringing in my ears. Tim's voice ceased to make sense: the sound became a monstrous confluence of sound and smell, like bile dripping on red-hot corrugated iron.

The dog grinned lecherously at me as it rogered a patient old Labrador.

I collapsed, delirious, into the nettles by the Gents on the Heath Extension. When I came to my pedometer was pressed to my face. It read 3.33 kilometres.

God help me.

In which I introduce a wholly new concept in survival equipment

AS THE Trans 333 looms ever closer, a frisson of pure terror is rippling through our little band of British 'disties' — we who are either too old, too fat, too lame or generally too congenitally useless to run anything under 100 miles in a time that wouldn't invite the derision of our friends and relations.

The Fear was fuelled by a meeting in the Yorkshire Grey at which James Henderson, a veteran of last year's event in Mauritania, described his experiences with a chilling matter-of-factness.

Some members of his audience pretended to make notes. In fact, they were trying to write their own epitaphs.

Almost all of the attendees of this singularly depressing meeting were on soft drinks. Which seemed to me a terrific waste, since the Yorkshire Grey serves three varieties of lager.

The first is the sort favoured by adventurous spinsters between visits to National Trust gardens in the home counties and invariably served in halves with a lemonade top.

The second is a decent brew, chemically speaking, containing a dollop of the synthetic testosterone that differentiates a good fighting lager from the flat and impotence-inducing gruel so beloved of pale, round-shouldered geography teachers.

The third is a truly serious proposition — a weapons grade tipple that separates the men from the boys and aligns them with the hyenas. Knock over a pint and, if you're quick, you can pick it up without spilling a drop.

So alarming was Henderson's account of his desert tribulations that I felt myself drawn to the bar and then, inexorably, to the Type 3 Lager.

The first pint went down like oxygen to a drowning man. The second levelled me out, bringing a kind of equilibrium to the headlong rush of wild, irresponsible elation engendered by the first.

I felt rejuvenated, incandescent with a spring-like optimism that propelled me back to the meeting.

The conversation had moved on to Equipment — always a major consideration in endurance events.

'…and so,' concluded Henderson, 'I would strongly advise that you peruse the list of mandatory kit and choose your options very, very carefully.'

Suddenly, to everyone's surprise including my own, I was on my feet. 'He's so right!' I exclaimed. 'Your choice of gear will be crucial!'

I went on to elaborate at great length upon my own folly when preparing for the Marathon des Sables — my first ever endurance race.

'The French organisers being French, of course, they stubbornly refused to translate any of their notes into English.

'And my French being what it was, I had to translate the equipment list as best I could. With the result that my rucksack contained the following: a stuffed Spider Monkey; a speculum; a plaster effigy of the Greek–Armenian mystic, Gurdjieff; the horn of a black rhinoceros; Risk!, the game of international diplomacy by Waddingtons; an unusual study of Princess Michael of Kent; a detailed plan of the sewerage system of Coventry and its environs, dated 1948 — and a hula hoop.'

There had been some mention, I recalled, of the need to pack some small, edible luxury — something that might restore one's sagging morale when beleaguered by the sheer enormity of the ordeal. And so I had chosen a modest hamper from Fortnum & Mason.

My inventory was greeted with a long, almost palpable silence, so that I felt obliged to continue.

'But that was nothing! Partridge [the human glue that binds together our fragile alliance of British endurance runners] took along a sousaphone.'

This induced a gasp of astonishment from the assembled.

'Have you any idea?' I demanded, 'what a Saharan sandstorm can do to the valve mechanism of a sophisticated brass instrument?'

Judging by the reaction of my audience, apparently not.

The End

THIS WEEK, I pulled out of the Trans 333 — the desert race I've been banging on about for months.

Why? It's a long story.

At the last minute, the race venue was switched from Niger to Mauritania. And I won't run in Mauritania. Well, not so much 'won't' as can't.

Back in the 1950s, my mother caused a scandal when she ran away with a sausage salesman from Penge. They met at a ballroom dancing class and rumba'd round the world for a year before settling in Mauritania. By this time, she was expecting her first child — me.

My father introduced the largely nomadic population to sausages. They took off in a big way and to this day, Black Pudding is the national dish of Mauritania. However, he soon became the victim of his own success, which had attracted the attention of rival chieftains. There followed the brutal Salami Wars. The world looked on in horror as brother rose against brother, armed with industrial catering packs of saveloy.

My father sold military materiel to both sides and quickly became rich. But greed got the better of him and an entire shipment of weapons grade chipolatas proved to be faulty. The result was a massacre in which the Mahutsi tribesmen, brandishing their fearsome chorizos, made mincemeat of the defenceless Dong.

My father was captured and after a brief show trial, sentenced to death. Without going into too many details, his remains were returned to Cumberland over the course of a year, in a form he would have recognised only too well.

Ever since, the name of Blackford has been synonymous in Mauritania with colonial exploitation of the worst — or more accurately, the wurst — kind. To attempt to enter the country would be suicide.

Actually, you may be surprised to learn that none of the above is true. I made it up to conceal the real reason why I pulled out of the Trans 333. But the time has come to reveal my strange secret.

It is no accident that 'secret' was the 333rd word in this article. As a student of the occult, I am acutely aware of the magic that lurks in numbers.

It was between August 23rd and August 30th that I decided to run across Britain in preparation for Mauritania. It occurred to me as I jogged from Whitehaven to Whitby that this was the 33rd week of the year. This was ominous enough in itself — but imagine my amazement when, as I dropped down from the North Yorkshire Moors, my pedometer read 300 kilometres — and I calculated that Whitby was just 33 kilometres away.

However, my calculations proved to be wrong. It was actually 36 kilometres to Whitby. But three kilometres from my goal, at 3pm, I slipped and twisted my ankle. Not wishing to exacerbate my injury, I decided to catch a bus into town.

The number 33 bus arrived at 3:33pm precisely.

Recovering at home, I knew that only by resting my foot completely would I be fit enough for the big race. The next time I ran would be in Mauritania.

While I recuperated, I reflected upon the series of 'coincidences' that had so affected my training. And it occurred to me that since I had already run 333 kilometres, upon completing the Trans 333 itself, I would have completed 666 kilometres. And 666 is the most dreaded number of all — the Sign of the Beast.

The realisation filled me with a dark sense of foreboding. And I knew with a profound certainty that I must on no account run the race.

Actually, the real reason I pulled out was because I was so busy at work that to bugger off to Africa for ten days would have been professional suicide.

But why let the truth spoil a good story?

Other books from SportsBooks

All-Time Greats of British Athletics
Mel Watman
Profiles of the greatest British athletes from Walter George to Paula Radcliffe.
Paperback ISBN 1899807 44 6 £15.00

Growing up with Subbuteo
My Dad invented the world's greatest football game
Mark Adolph
The story of Subbuteo from the son of the inventor.
Paperback ISBN 1899807 40 3 £15.00

Accrington Stanley - the club that wouldn't die
Phil Whalley
Accrington Stanley returned to the Football League this year after resigning in 1962. This tells the story of the years of struggle and eventual triumph.
Hardback. ISBN 1899807 47 0 £16.99

Fitba Gallimaufry
Adam Scott
Everything you need to know about Scottish football and some things you didn't.
Hardback ISBN 1899807 45 4 £9.99

Ode to Jol
Alasdair Gold
A sideways, and very funny, look at Tottenham Hotspur's' 2005/06 season.
Paperback. ISBN 1899807 43 8 £12.99

Wembley – The Complete Record
1923–2000
Glen Isherwood
Every football match ever played at the world's most iconic football stadium is detailed in this exhaustive reference work.
Paperback. ISBN 1899807 42 X £14.99

Harry Potts – Margaret's Story
Margaret Potts and Dave Thomas
Harry Potts was Burnley's manager in the days the small-town team won the league and reached the
FA Cup final. Great photographic section.
Hardback. ISBN 1899807 41 1 £17.99

Ha'Way/Howay the Lads
Alan Candlish
A fascinating and detailed history of the rivalry
between Newcastle United and Sunderland.
Paperback. ISBN 1899807 39 X £14.99

Black Lions – a history of black players in English football
Rodney Hinds
The story of black players in English football, with
interviews with players such as Garth Crooks, John Barnes and Luther Blissett. Hardback. Rodney Hinds is the sports editor of The Voice.
Hardback. ISBN 1899807 38 1 £16.99

Rowing with my Wife
Dan Williams
A year in the adventures of a gig rower, the Cornish sport that is spreading around the world.
Paperback. ISBN 1899807 36 5 £7.99

Local Heroes
John Shawcroft
The story of the Derbyshire team which won cricket's county championship in 1936, the only time the county has finished first.
Paperback. ISBN 1899807 35 7 £14.99

Willie Irvine – Together Again
Willie Irvine with Dave Thomas
The remarkable story of the Burnley and Northern Ireland centre forward who grew up in abject poverty, rose to the heights only to fall into depression after he stopped playing. He also found out some remarkable things about his family while researching the book, chiefly that his parents had never married!
Hardback. ISBN 1899807 33 0 £17.99

Another Bloody Tangle!
Peter Bishop
The author loves fishing, sadly the sport doesn't reciprocate. Amazingly just before publication, Peter won his first competition and then when the cup was presented promptly dropped it.
The Liverpool Echo said: "echoes of the black humour of Alan Bleasdale".
Paperback. ISBN 1899807 28.4 £7.99

The Rebel – Derek Roche – Irish warrior, British champion
Nigel McDermid
The tale of boxing hero Derek Roche is a journey from an Irish council estate to becoming the first Irishman to win a Lonsdale Belt outright. It also tells of Roche's days as a doorman in Leeds as he sought to earn a living outside the ring. The Irish Post called it a "modern classic". The Guardian said: "refreshingly honest and... genuinely funny".
Paperback. ISBN 1899807 25 X £7.99

Are You a Proper Teacher, Sir?
Gary Boothroyd
Twenty-seven years of teaching at an inner city comprehensive school might sound like a life sentence to some, but as Gary Boothroyd found out there was a lot of fun to be had as well. His story encompasses the downright hilarious and the occasional stark tragedy.
The Times Educational Supplement called it "a good light-hearted read". The Yorkshire Evening Post said: "Ten out of ten".
Paperback. ISBN 1899807 26 8 £7.99